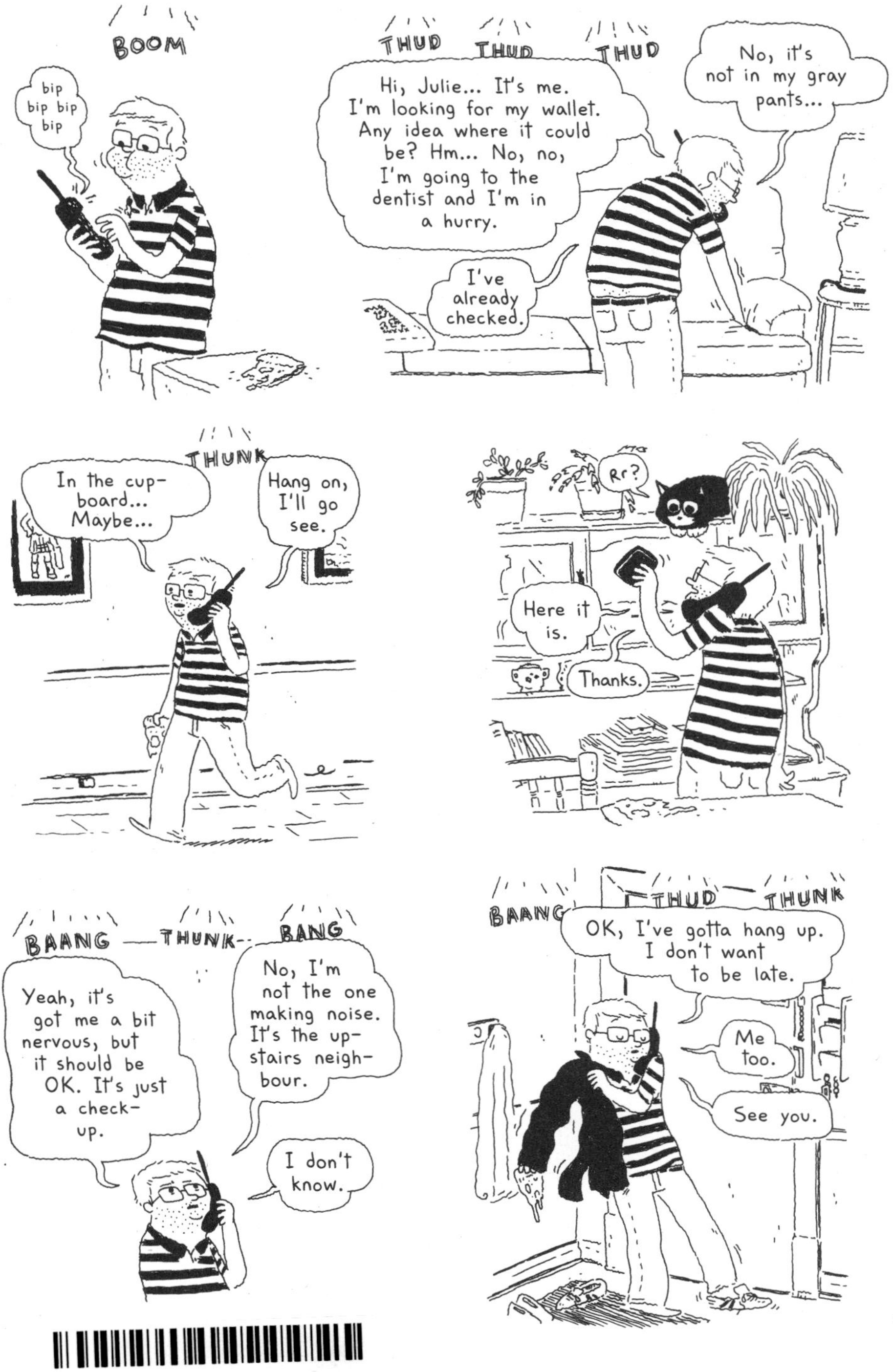
BOOM
bip bip bip bip
THUD THUD THUD
Hi, Julie... It's me. I'm looking for my wallet. Any idea where it could be? Hm... No, no, I'm going to the dentist and I'm in a hurry.
No, it's not in my gray pants...
I've already checked.
THUNK
In the cup-board... Maybe...
Hang on, I'll go see.
Rr?
Here it is.
Thanks.
BAANG THUNK BANG
Yeah, it's got me a bit nervous, but it should be OK. It's just a check-up.
No, I'm not the one making noise. It's the up-stairs neigh-bour.
I don't know.
BAANG THUD THUNK
OK, I've gotta hang up. I don't want to be late.
Me too.
See you.

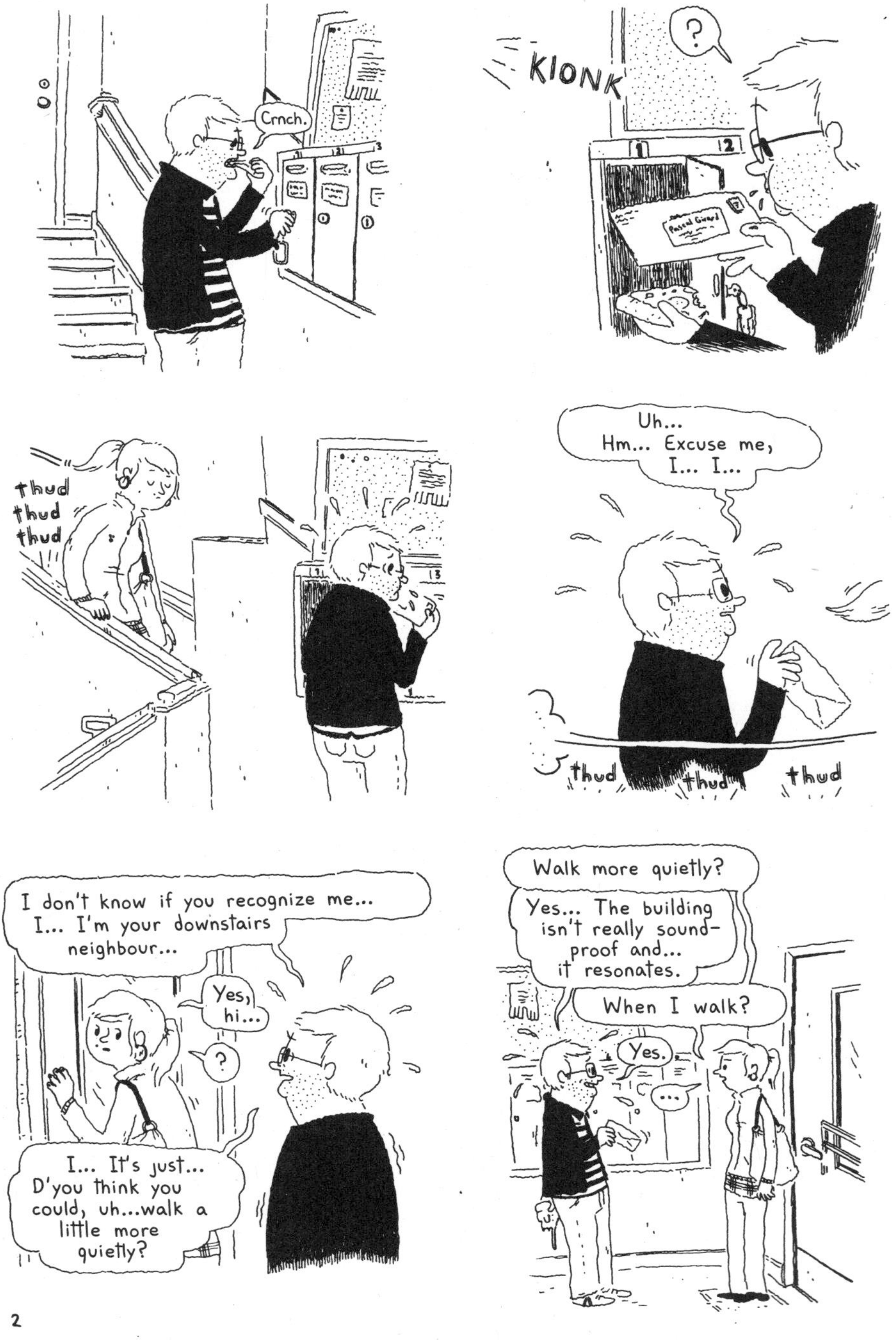

Crnch.
KIONK
?
Pascal Girard
thud
thud
thud
Uh... Hm... Excuse me, I... I...
thud
thud
thud
I don't know if you recognize me... I... I'm your downstairs neighbour...
Yes, hi...
?
I... It's just... D'you think you could, uh...walk a little more quietly?
Walk more quietly?
Yes... The building isn't really sound-proof and... it resonates.
When I walk?
Yes.
...

pascal girard

REUNiON

Translation by
Helge Dascher

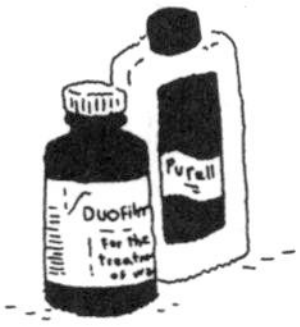
Purell

Drawn & Quarterly

Thanks to Lewis Trondheim, Rebecca Lloyd,
Drawn & Quarterly and Julie Dubé.
Translation by Helge Dascher. Cover colors by Vincent Giard.
Text font by Viktor Nübel.

Originally published in France by Shampooing, an imprint of Éditions Delcourt.

Drawn & Quarterly
Post Office Box 48056
Montreal, Quebec
Canada H2V 4S8
www.drawnandquarterly.com

First edition: April 2011
Printed in Canada

10   9   8   7   6   5   4   3   2   1

Library and Archives Canada Cataloguing in Publication
Girard, Pascal
Reunion / Pascal Girard.
ISBN 978-1-77046-037-9
I. Title.
PN6733.G57R49 2011   741.5'971   C2010-907543-9

Drawn & Quarterly acknowledges the financial support of the Government of Canada through the Canada Book Fund, the Canada Council for the Arts, and the National Translation Program for Book Publishing for our publishing activities and for support of this edition.

Distributed in the USA by:
Farrar, Straus and Giroux
18 West 18th Street
New York, NY 10011
Orders: 888.330.8477

Distributed in Canada by:
Raincoast Books
2440 Viking Way
Richmond BC
V6V 1N2
Orders: 800.663.5714

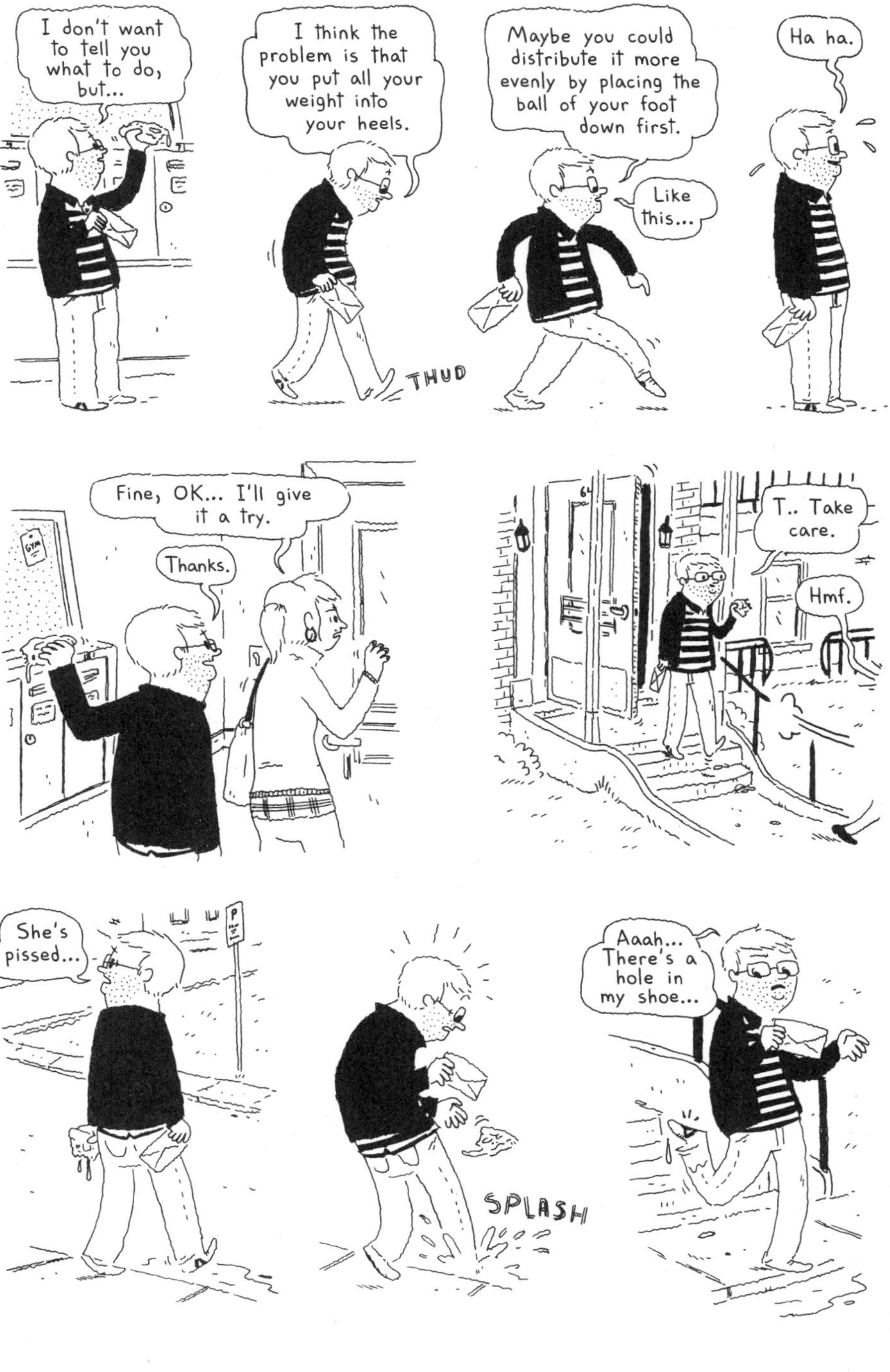
I don't want to tell you what to do, but...
I think the problem is that you put all your weight into your heels.
THUD
Maybe you could distribute it more evenly by placing the ball of your foot down first.
Like this...
Ha ha.
Fine, OK... I'll give it a try.
Thanks.
GYM
64
T.. Take care.
Hmf.
She's pissed...
P
SPLASH
Aaah... There's a hole in my shoe...

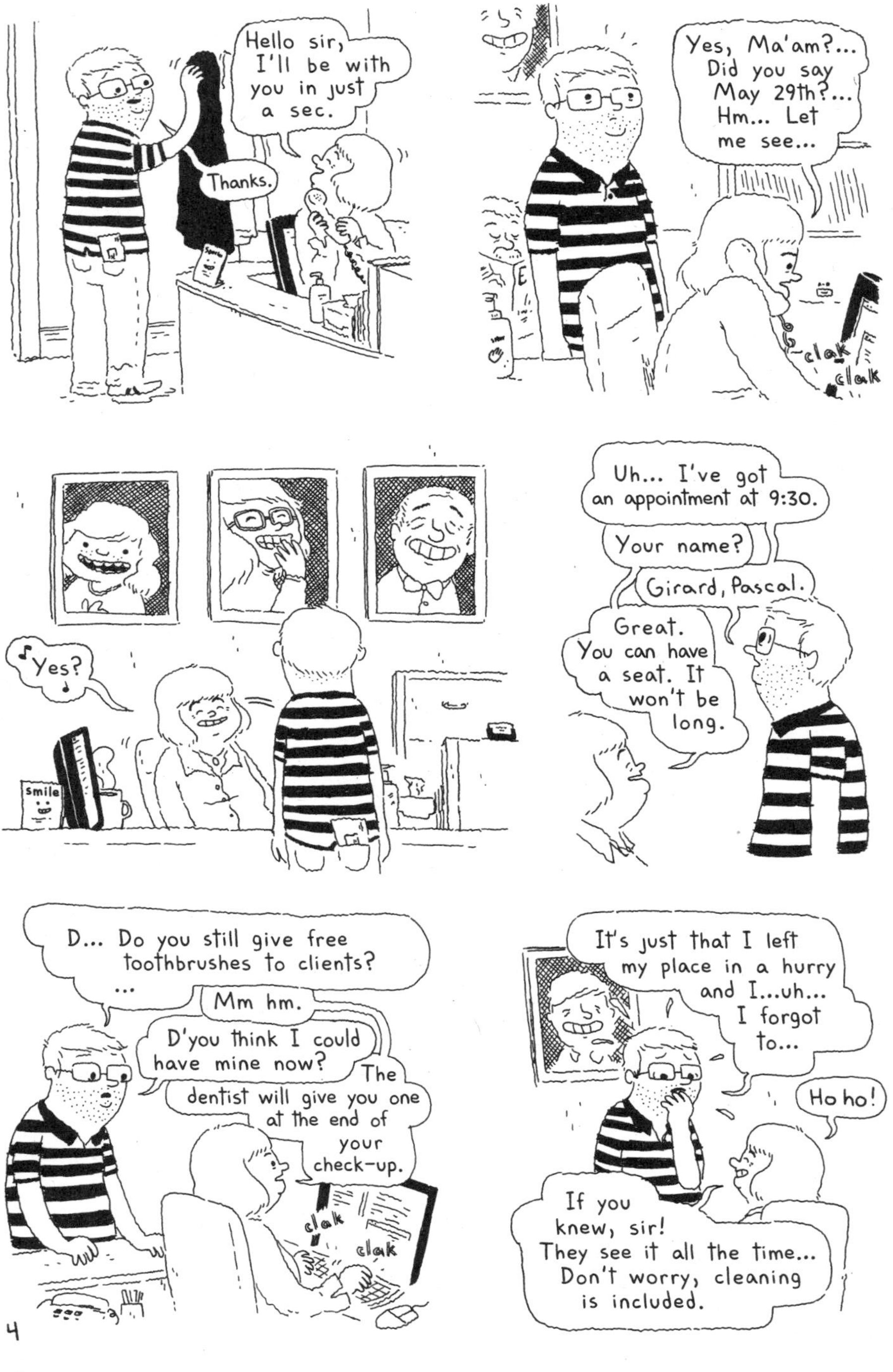
Hello sir, I'll be with you in just a sec.
Thanks.
Yes, Ma'am?... Did you say May 29th?... Hm... Let me see...
clak
clak
smile
Yes?
Uh... I've got an appointment at 9:30.
Your name?
Girard, Pascal.
Great. You can have a seat. It won't be long.
D... Do you still give free toothbrushes to clients? ...
Mm hm.
D'you think I could have mine now?
The dentist will give you one at the end of your check-up.
clak
clak
It's just that I left my place in a hurry and I...uh... I forgot to...
Ho ho!
If you knew, sir! They see it all the time... Don't worry, cleaning is included.

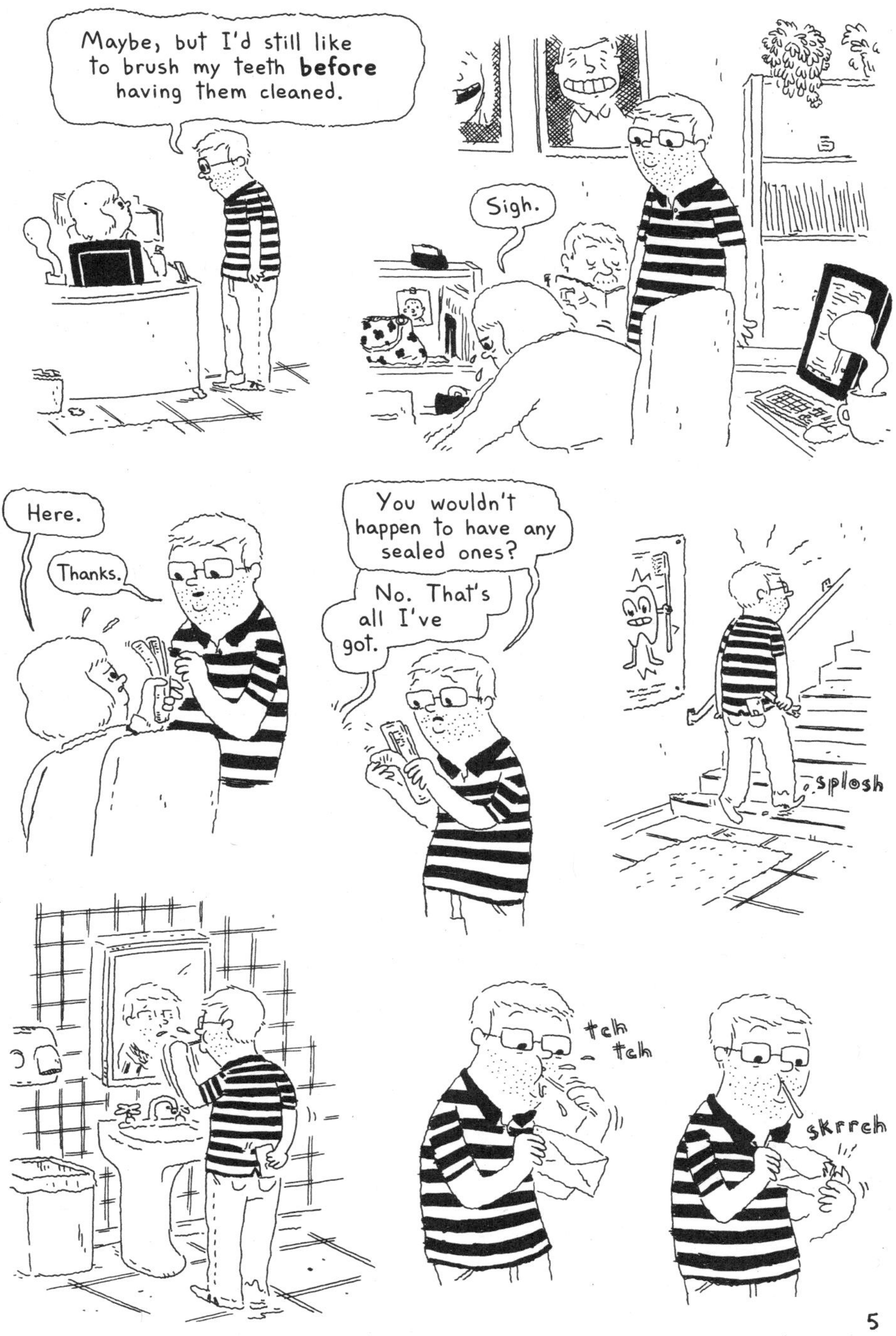
Maybe, but I'd still like to brush my teeth **before** having them cleaned.
Sigh.
Here.
Thanks.
You wouldn't happen to have any sealed ones?
No. That's all I've got.
splosh
tch tch
skrrch

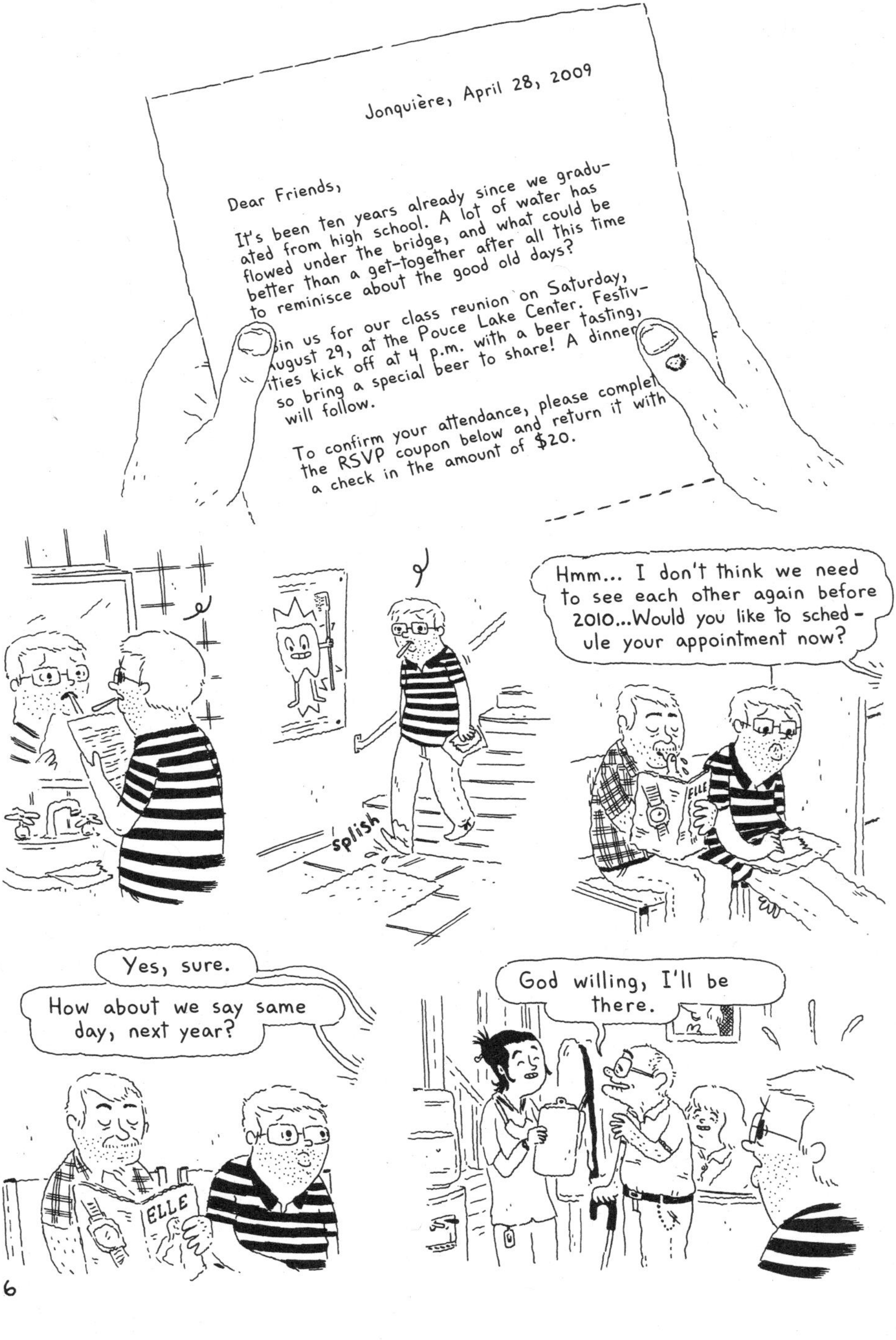
Jonquière, April 28, 2009
Dear Friends,
It's been ten years already since we graduated from high school. A lot of water has flowed under the bridge, and what could be better than a get-together after all this time to reminisce about the good old days?
in us for our class reunion on Saturday, ugust 29, at the Pouce Lake Center. Festivities kick off at 4 p.m. with a beer tasting, so bring a special beer to share! A dinne will follow.
To confirm your attendance, please complet the RSVP coupon below and return it with a check in the amount of $20.
splish
Hmm... I don't think we need to see each other again before 2010...Would you like to schedule your appointment now?
ELLE
Yes, sure.
How about we say same day, next year?
ELLE
God willing, I'll be there.

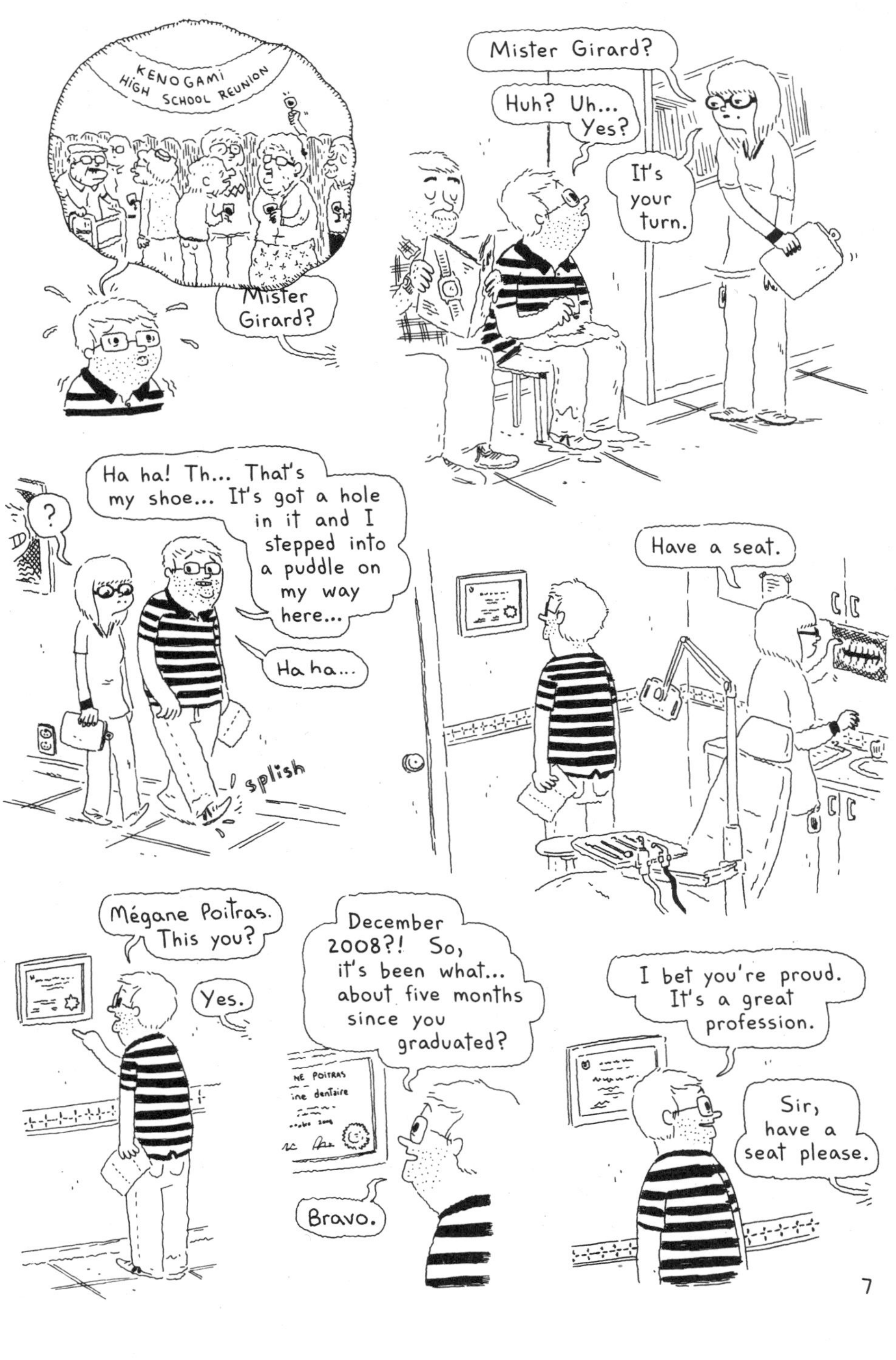
KENOGAMI HIGH SCHOOL REUNION
Mister Girard?
Mister Girard?
Huh? Uh... Yes?
It's your turn.
Ha ha! Th... That's my shoe... It's got a hole in it and I stepped into a puddle on my way here...
?
Ha ha...
splish
Have a seat.
Mégane Poitras. This you?
Yes.
December 2008?! So, it's been what... about five months since you graduated?
Bravo.
I bet you're proud. It's a great profession.
Sir, have a seat please.

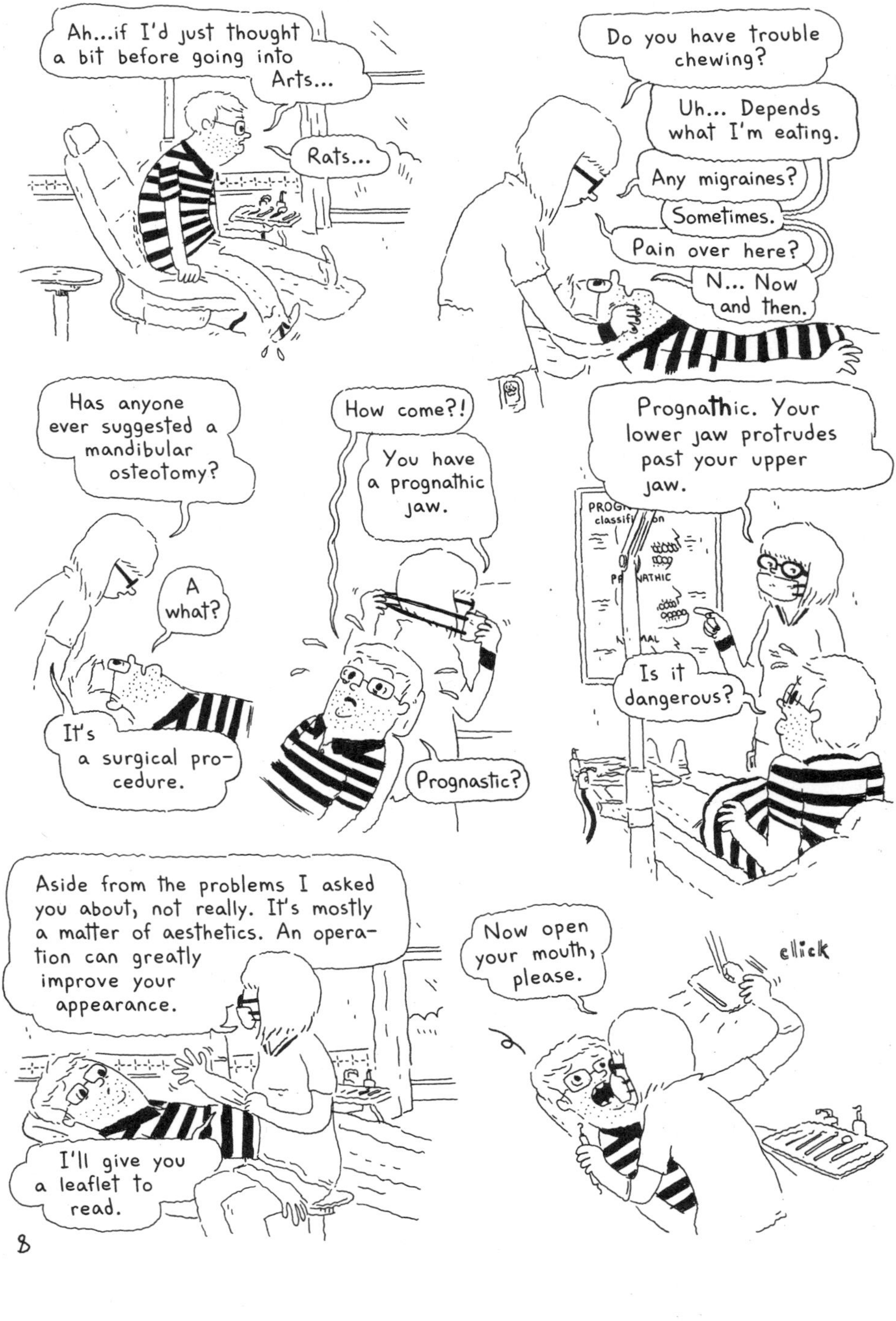
Ah...if I'd just thought a bit before going into Arts...
Rats...
Do you have trouble chewing?
Uh... Depends what I'm eating.
Any migraines?
Sometimes.
Pain over here?
N... Now and then.
Has anyone ever suggested a mandibular osteotomy?
A what?
It's a surgical procedure.
How come?!
You have a prognathic jaw.
Prognastic?
Prognathic. Your lower jaw protrudes past your upper jaw.
NATHIC
Is it dangerous?
Aside from the problems I asked you about, not really. It's mostly a matter of aesthetics. An operation can greatly improve your appearance.
I'll give you a leaflet to read.
Now open your mouth, please.
click

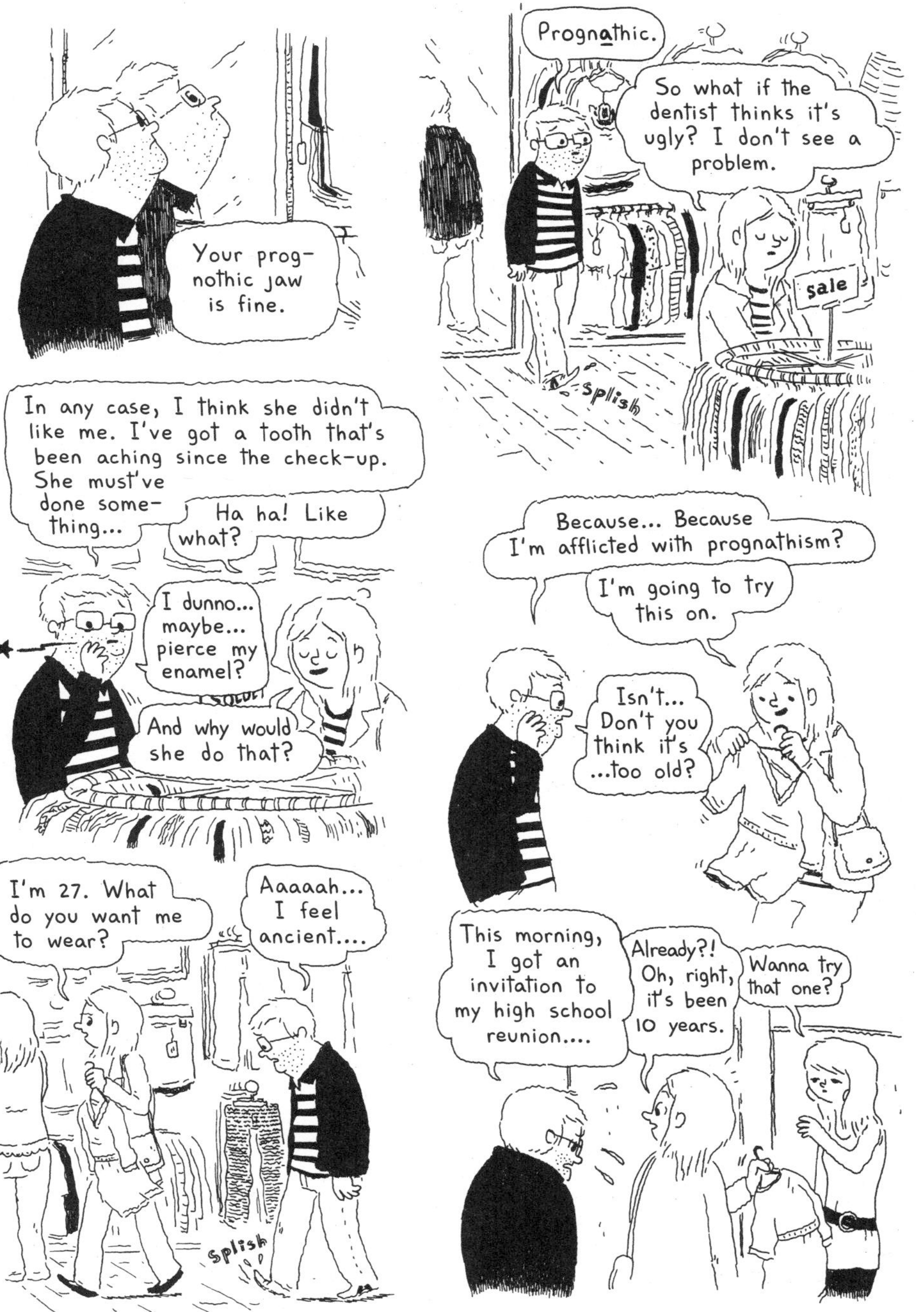
Your prog-nothic jaw is fine.
Prognathic.
So what if the dentist thinks it's ugly? I don't see a problem.
sale
splish
In any case, I think she didn't like me. I've got a tooth that's been aching since the check-up. She must've done some-thing...
Ha ha! Like what?
I dunno... maybe... pierce my enamel?
And why would she do that?
Because... Because I'm afflicted with prognathism?
I'm going to try this on.
Isn't... Don't you think it's ...too old?
I'm 27. What do you want me to wear?
Aaaaah... I feel ancient....
splish
This morning, I got an invitation to my high school reunion....
Already?! Oh, right, it's been 10 years.
Wanna try that one?

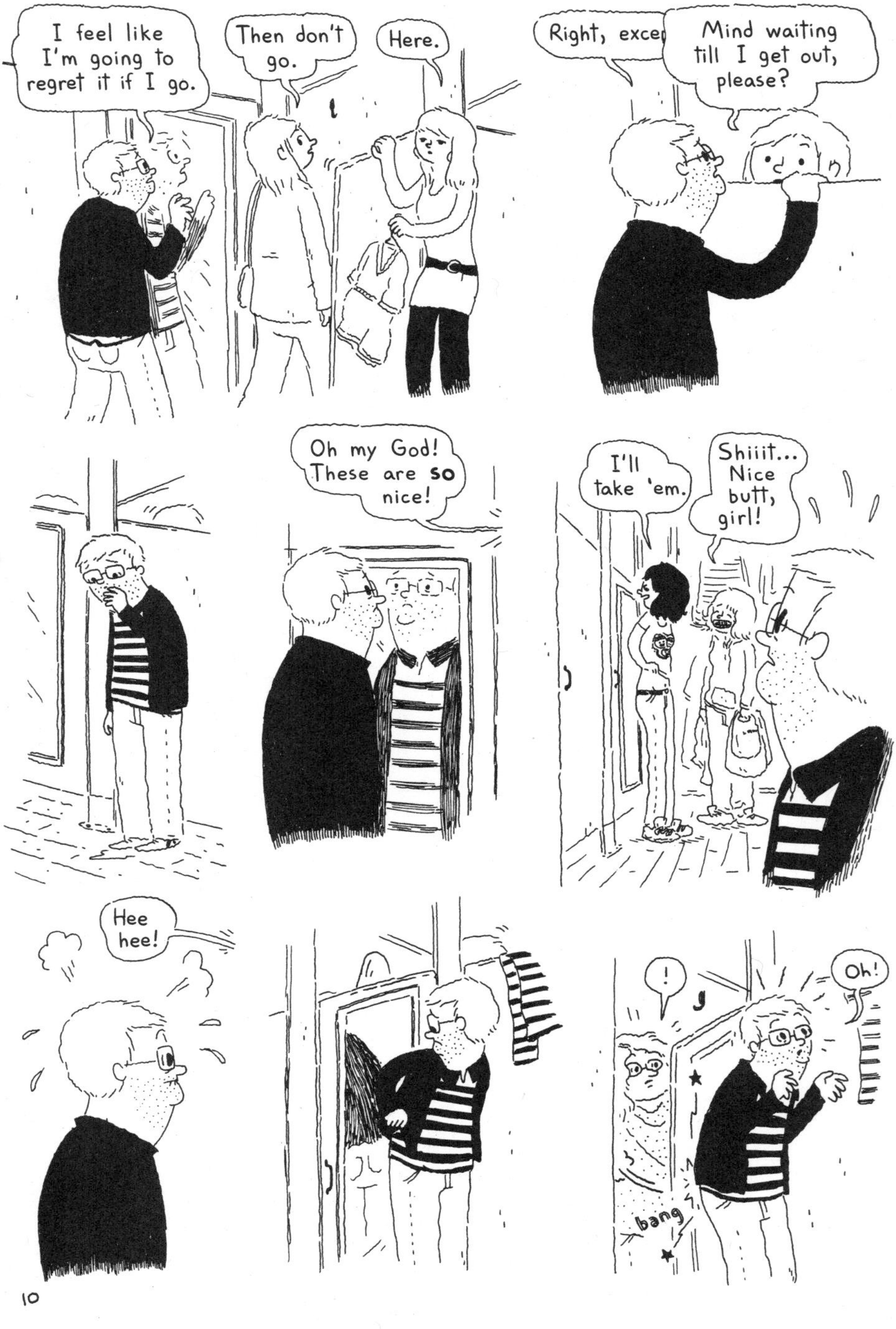

I feel like I'm going to regret it if I go.
Then don't go.
Here.
Right, excep
Mind waiting till I get out, please?
Oh my God! These are SO nice!
I'll take 'em.
Shiiit... Nice butt, girl!
Hee hee!
!
Oh!
bang

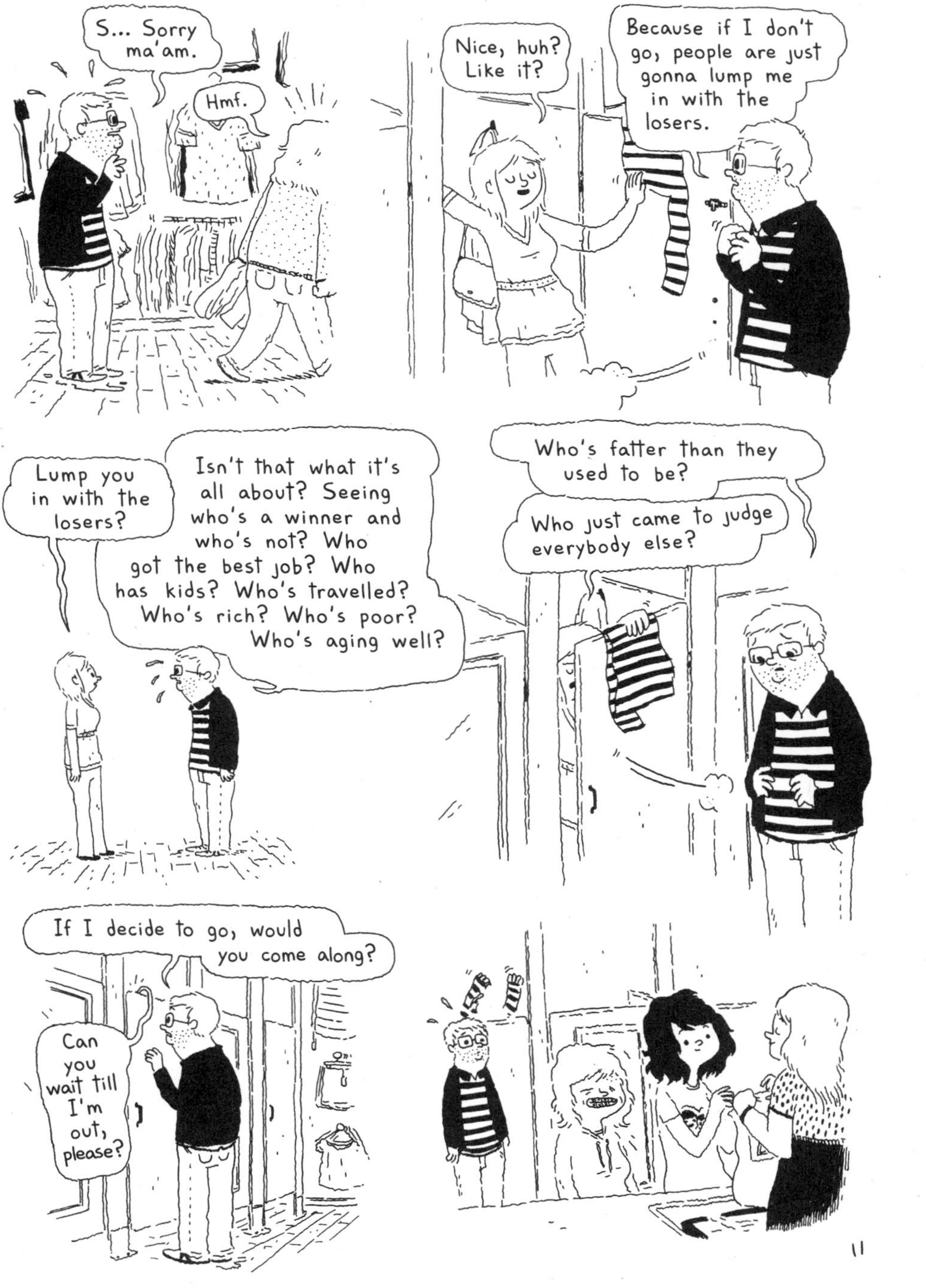
S... Sorry ma'am.
Hmf.
Nice, huh? Like it?
Because if I don't go, people are just gonna lump me in with the losers.
Lump you in with the losers?
Isn't that what it's all about? Seeing who's a winner and who's not? Who got the best job? Who has kids? Who's travelled? Who's rich? Who's poor? Who's aging well?
Who's fatter than they used to be?
Who just came to judge everybody else?
If I decide to go, would you come along?
Can you wait till I'm out, please?

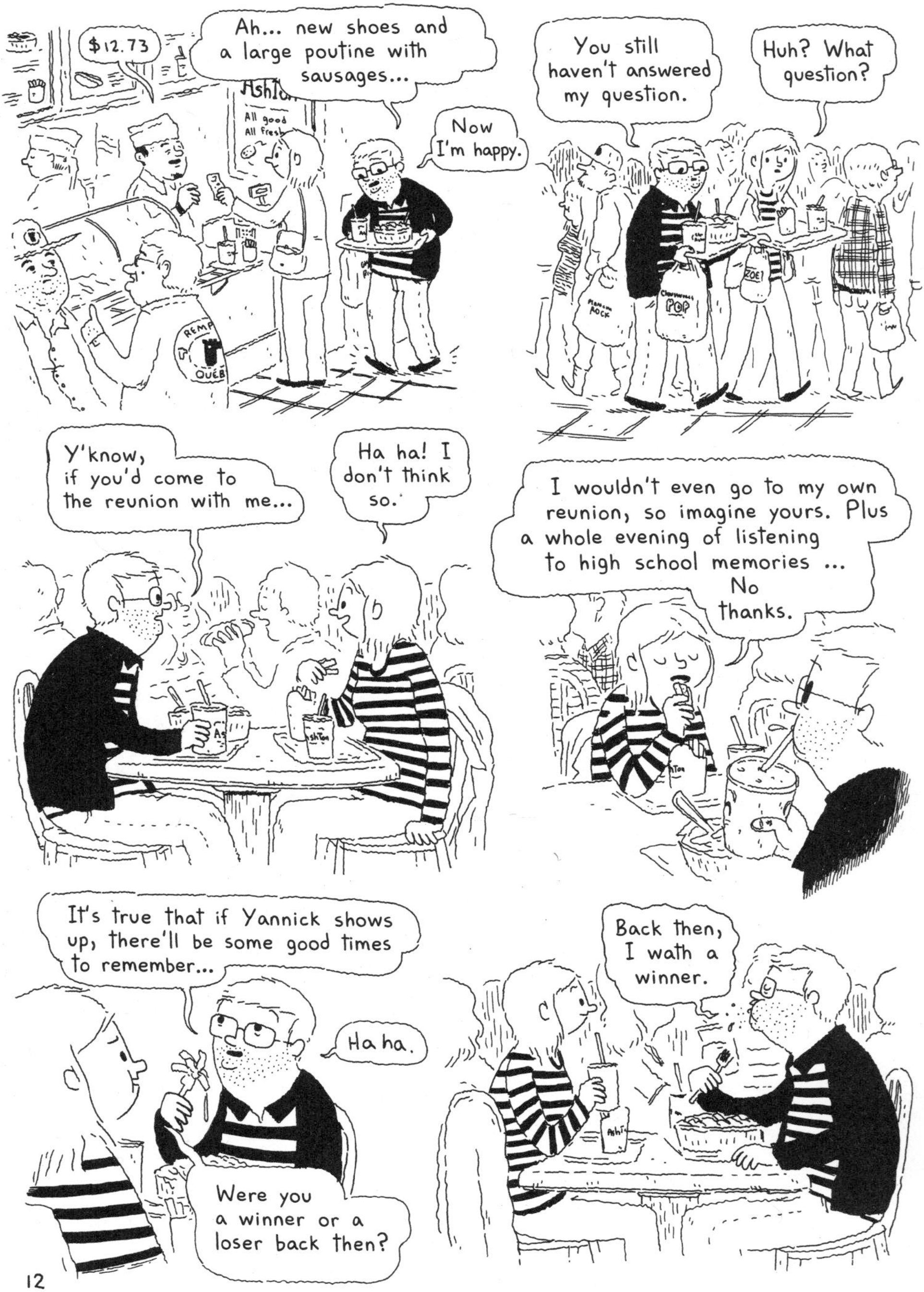
$12.73
Ah... new shoes and a large poutine with sausages...
Now I'm happy.
You still haven't answered my question.
Huh? What question?
Y'know, if you'd come to the reunion with me...
Ha ha! I don't think so.
I wouldn't even go to my own reunion, so imagine yours. Plus a whole evening of listening to high school memories ... No thanks.
It's true that if Yannick shows up, there'll be some good times to remember...
Ha ha.
Were you a winner or a loser back then?
Back then, I wath a winner.

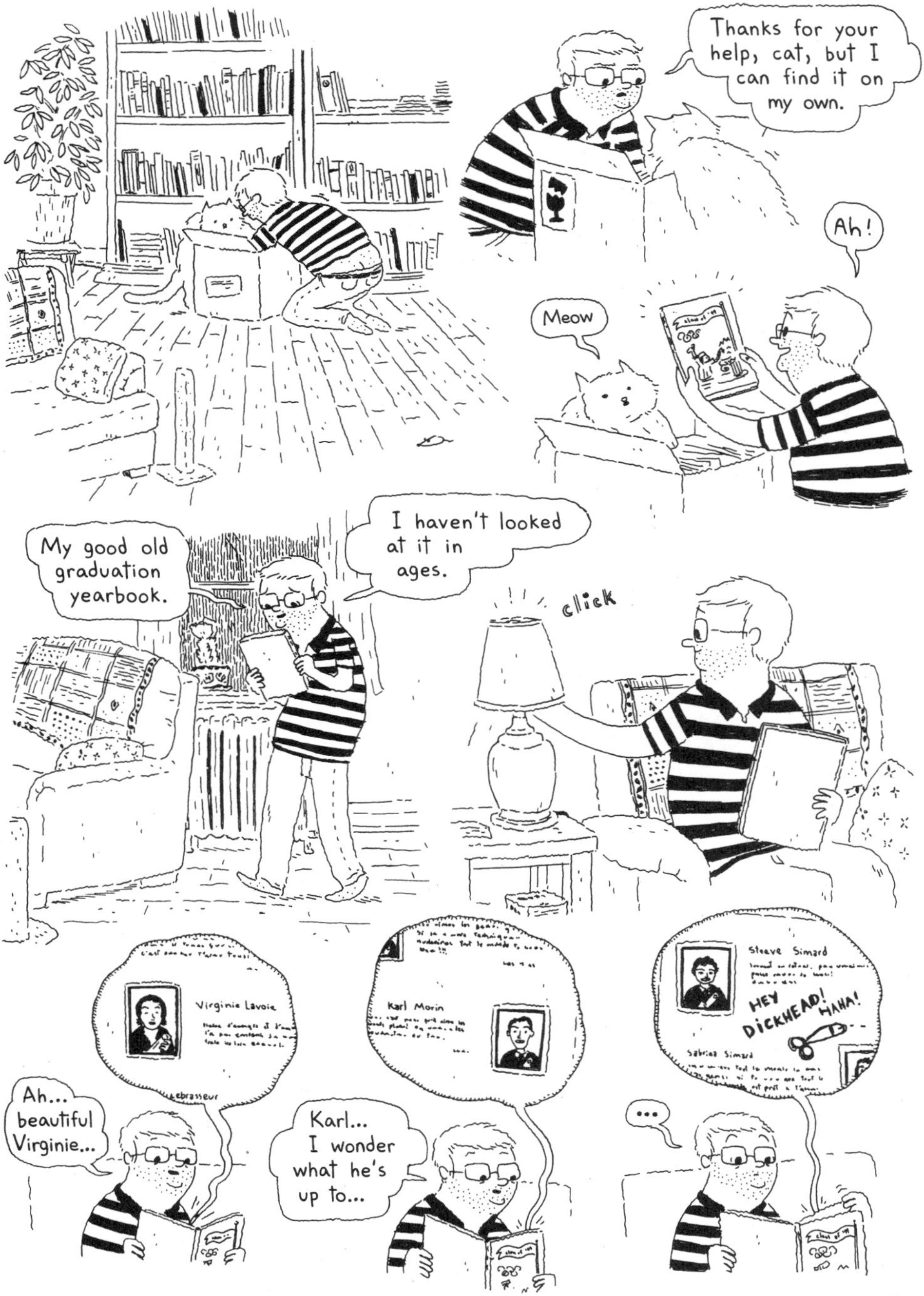
Thanks for your help, cat, but I can find it on my own.
Ah!
Meow
My good old graduation yearbook.
I haven't looked at it in ages.
click
Virginie Lavoie
Ah... beautiful Virginie...
Karl Morin
Karl... I wonder what he's up to...
Steeve Simard
HEY DICKHEAD! HAHA!
...

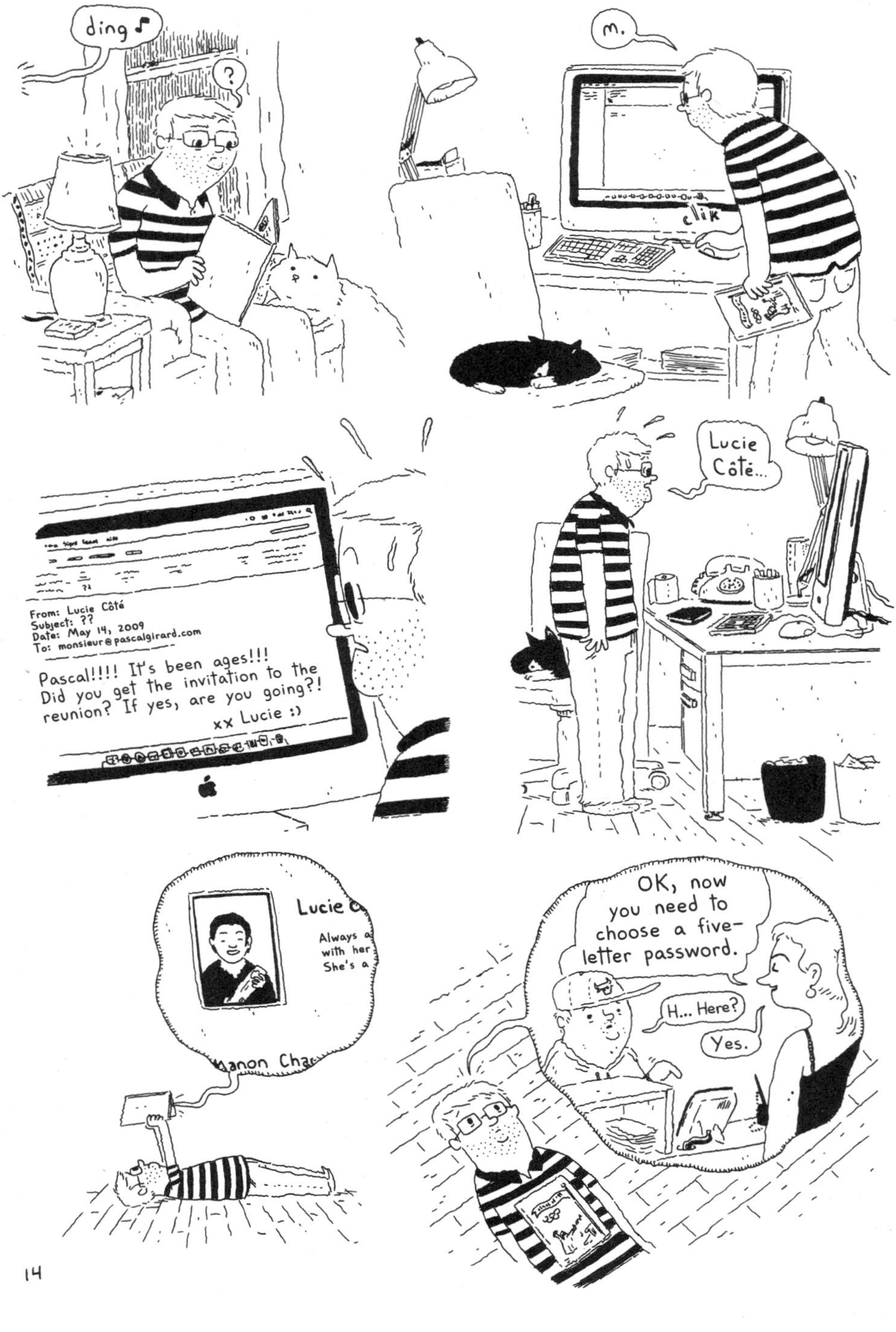
ding ♪
?
m.
clik
From: Lucie Côté
Subject: ??
Date: May 14, 2009
To: monsieur@pascalgirard.com
Pascal!!!! It's been ages!!! Did you get the invitation to the reunion? If yes, are you going?!
xx Lucie :)
Lucie Côté...
Lucie C
Always a
with her
She's a
Manon Cha
OK, now you need to choose a five-letter password.
H... Here?
Yes.

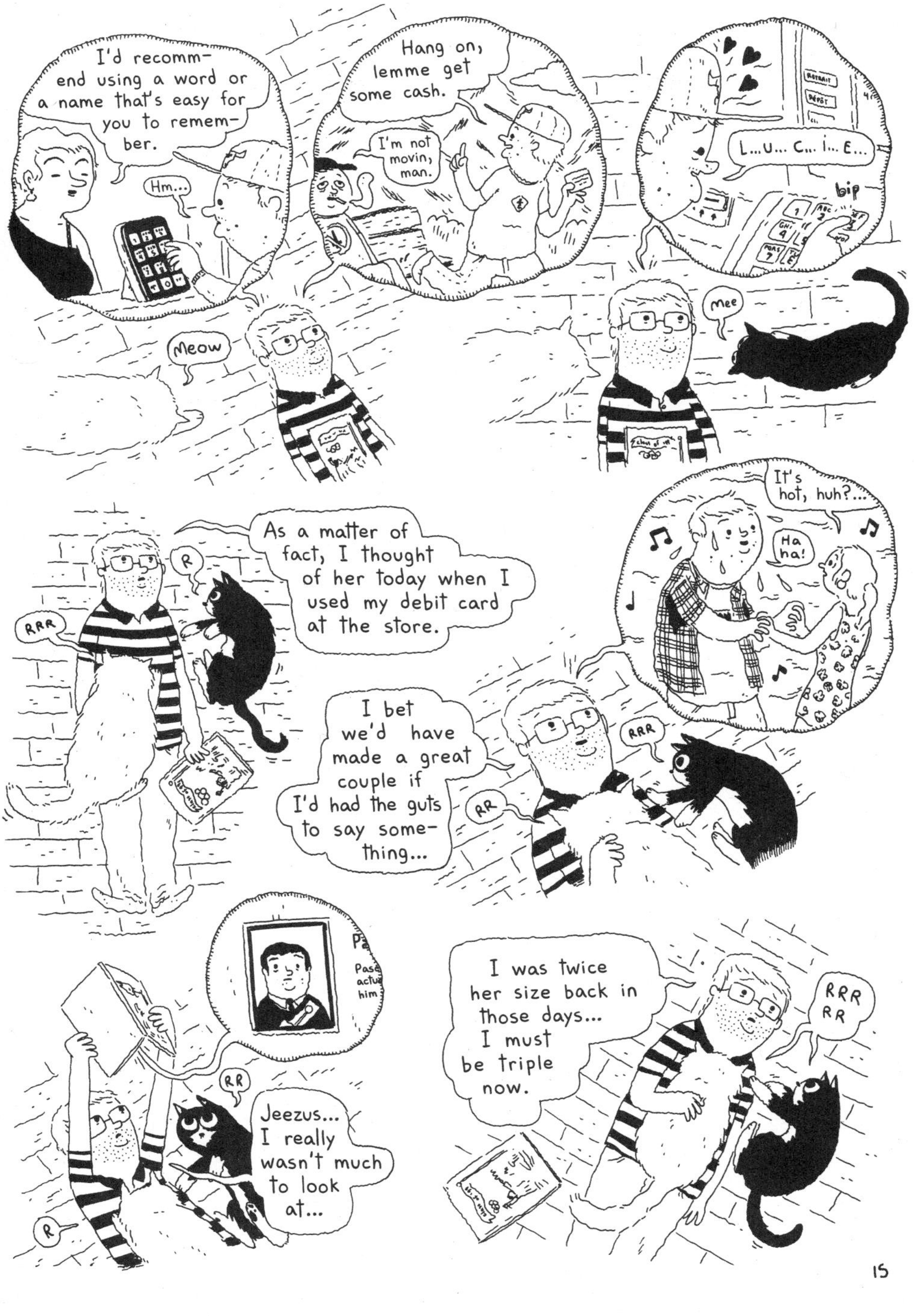

I'd recomm-end using a word or a name that's easy for you to remem-ber.
Hm...
Hang on, lemme get some cash.
I'm not movin, man.
L... U... C... I... E...
bip
Meow
Mee
As a matter of fact, I thought of her today when I used my debit card at the store.
R
RRR
It's hot, huh?...
Ha ha!
I bet we'd have made a great couple if I'd had the guts to say some-thing...
RRR
RR
RR
Jeezus... I really wasn't much to look at...
R
I was twice her size back in those days... I must be triple now.
RRR RR

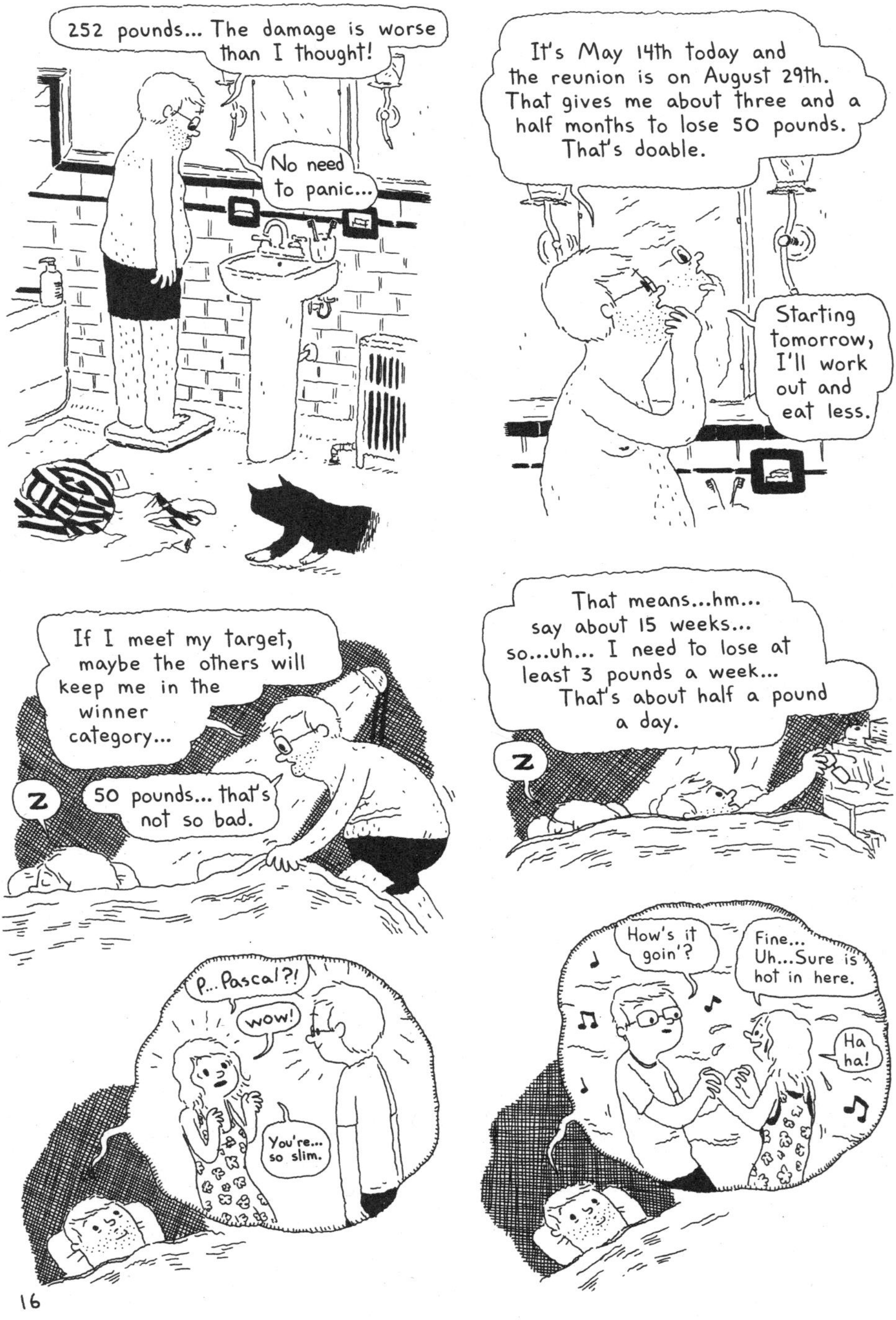
252 pounds... The damage is worse than I thought!
No need to panic...
It's May 14th today and the reunion is on August 29th. That gives me about three and a half months to lose 50 pounds. That's doable.
Starting tomorrow, I'll work out and eat less.
If I meet my target, maybe the others will keep me in the winner category...
Z
50 pounds... that's not so bad.
That means...hm... say about 15 weeks... so...uh... I need to lose at least 3 pounds a week... That's about half a pound a day.
Z
P... Pascal?!
WOW!
You're... so slim.
How's it goin'?
Fine... Uh...Sure is hot in here.
Ha ha!

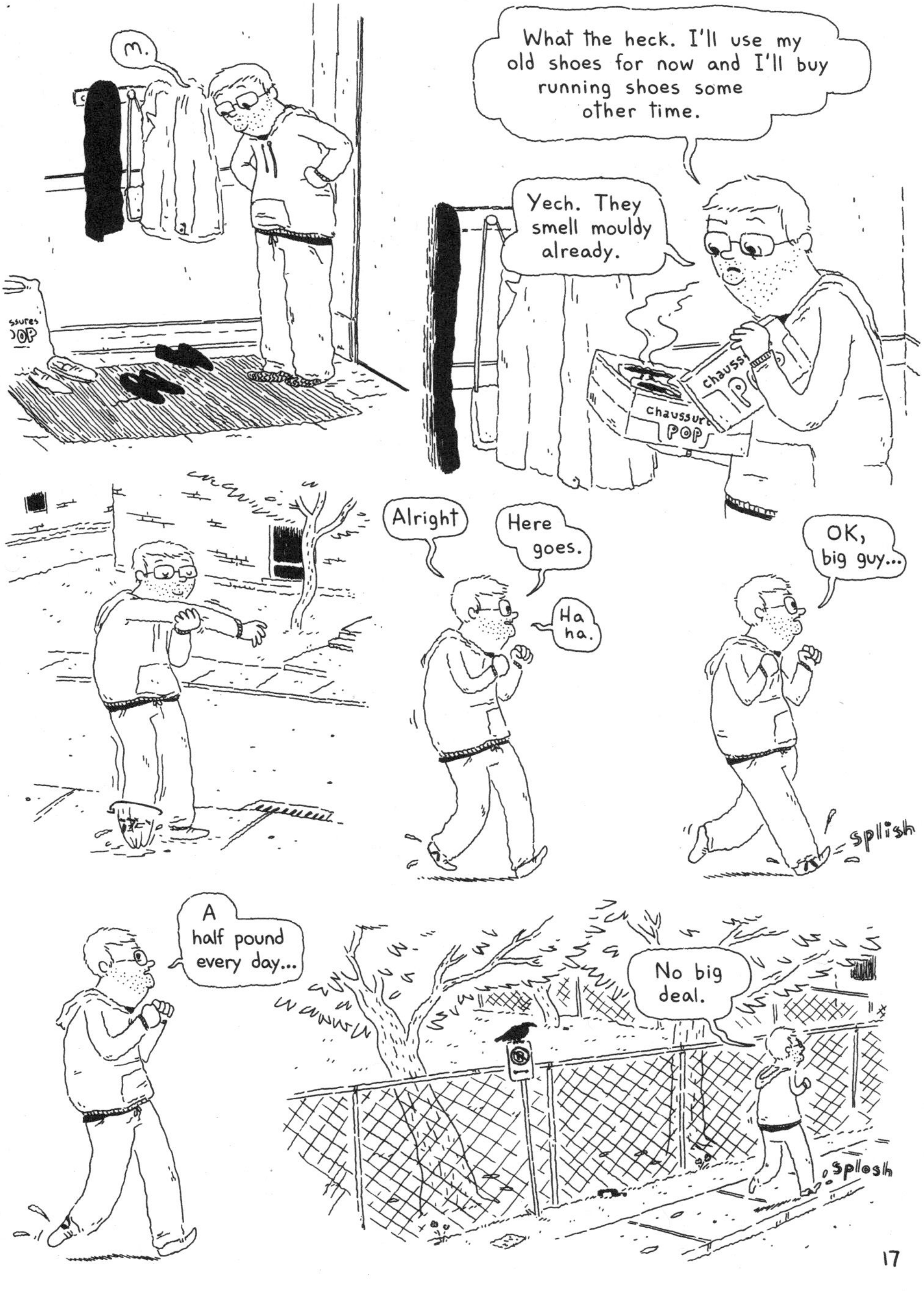
m.
ssures POP
What the heck. I'll use my old shoes for now and I'll buy running shoes some other time.
Yech. They smell mouldy already.
chauss POP
chaussure POP
Alright
Here goes.
Ha ha.
OK, big guy...
splish
A half pound every day...
No big deal.
splosh

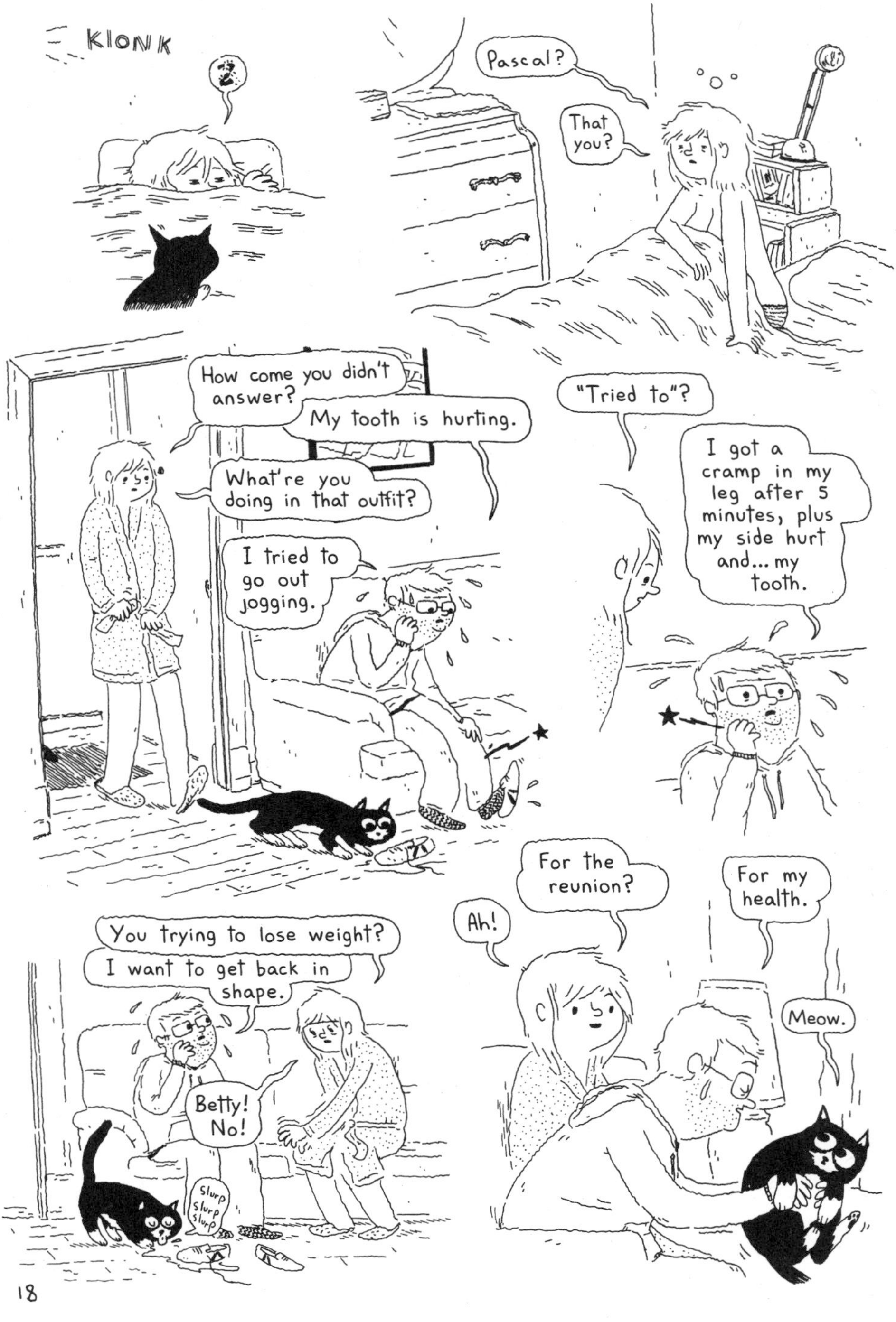
KLONK
Pascal?
That you?
How come you didn't answer?
My tooth is hurting.
What're you doing in that outfit?
I tried to go out jogging.
"Tried to"?
I got a cramp in my leg after 5 minutes, plus my side hurt and... my tooth.
You trying to lose weight?
I want to get back in shape.
Betty! No!
Slurp Slurp Slurp
Ah!
For the reunion?
For my health.
Meow.

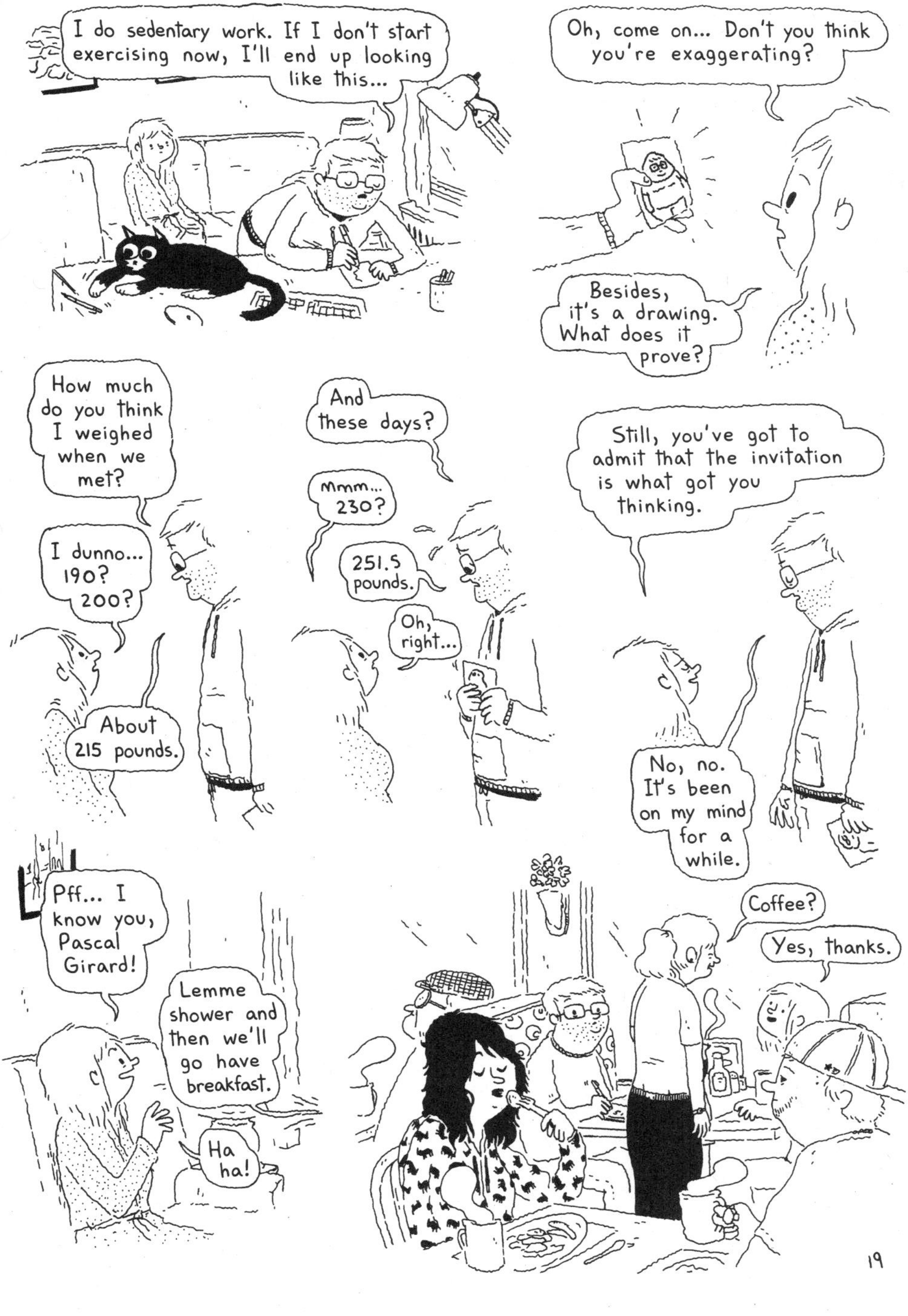

I do sedentary work. If I don't start exercising now, I'll end up looking like this...
Oh, come on... Don't you think you're exaggerating?
Besides, it's a drawing. What does it prove?
How much do you think I weighed when we met?
I dunno... 190? 200?
About 215 pounds.
And these days?
Mmm... 230?
251.5 pounds.
Oh, right...
Still, you've got to admit that the invitation is what got you thinking.
No, no. It's been on my mind for a while.
Pff... I know you, Pascal Girard!
Lemme shower and then we'll go have breakfast.
Ha ha!
Coffee?
Yes, thanks.

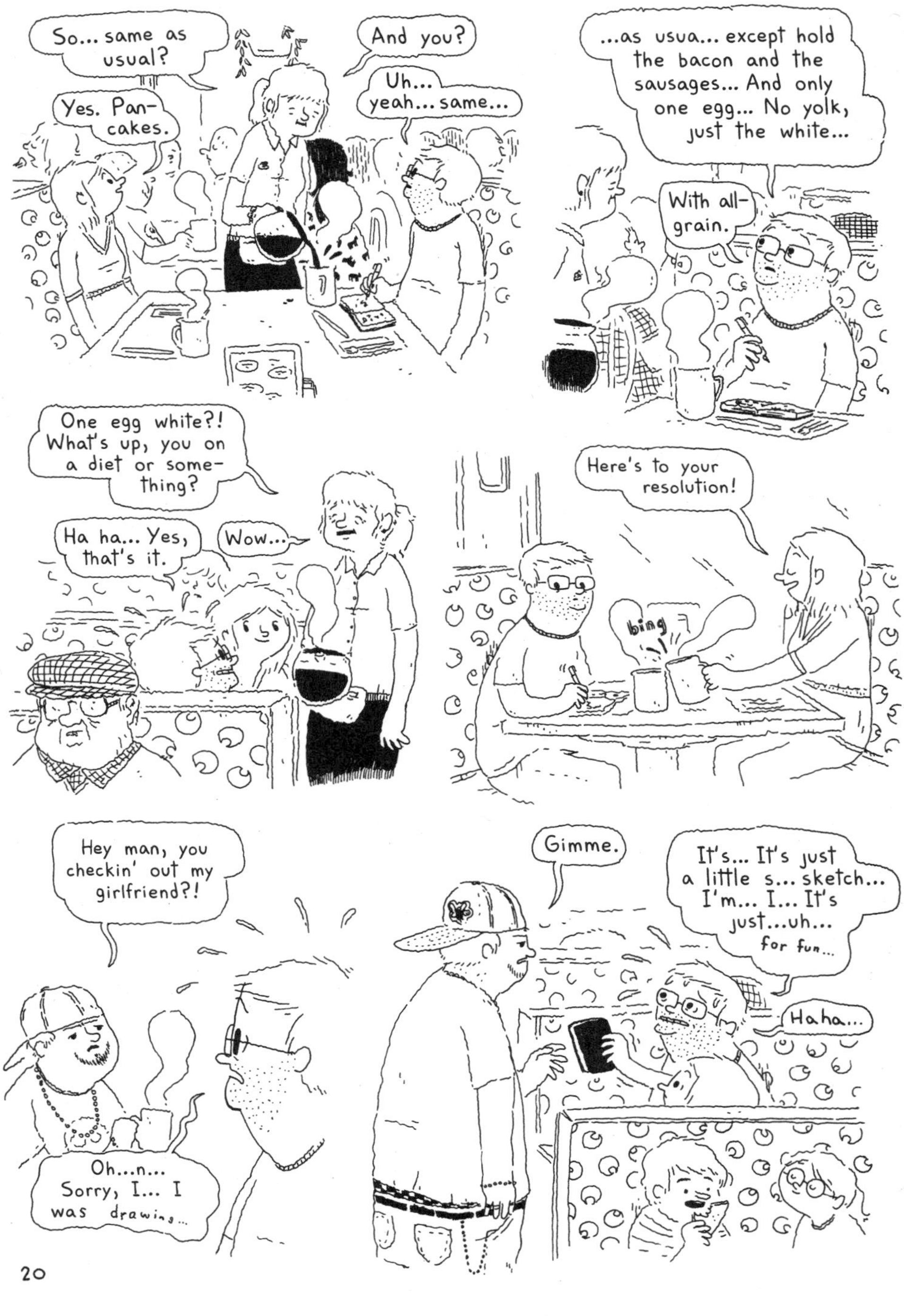
So... same as usual?
Yes. Pancakes.
And you?
Uh... yeah... same...
...as usua... except hold the bacon and the sausages... And only one egg... No yolk, just the white...
With all-grain.
One egg white?! What's up, you on a diet or something?
Ha ha... Yes, that's it.
Wow...
Here's to your resolution!
bing
Hey man, you checkin' out my girlfriend?!
Oh...n... Sorry, I... I was drawing...
Gimme.
It's... It's just a little s... sketch... I'm... I... It's just...uh... for fun...
Haha...

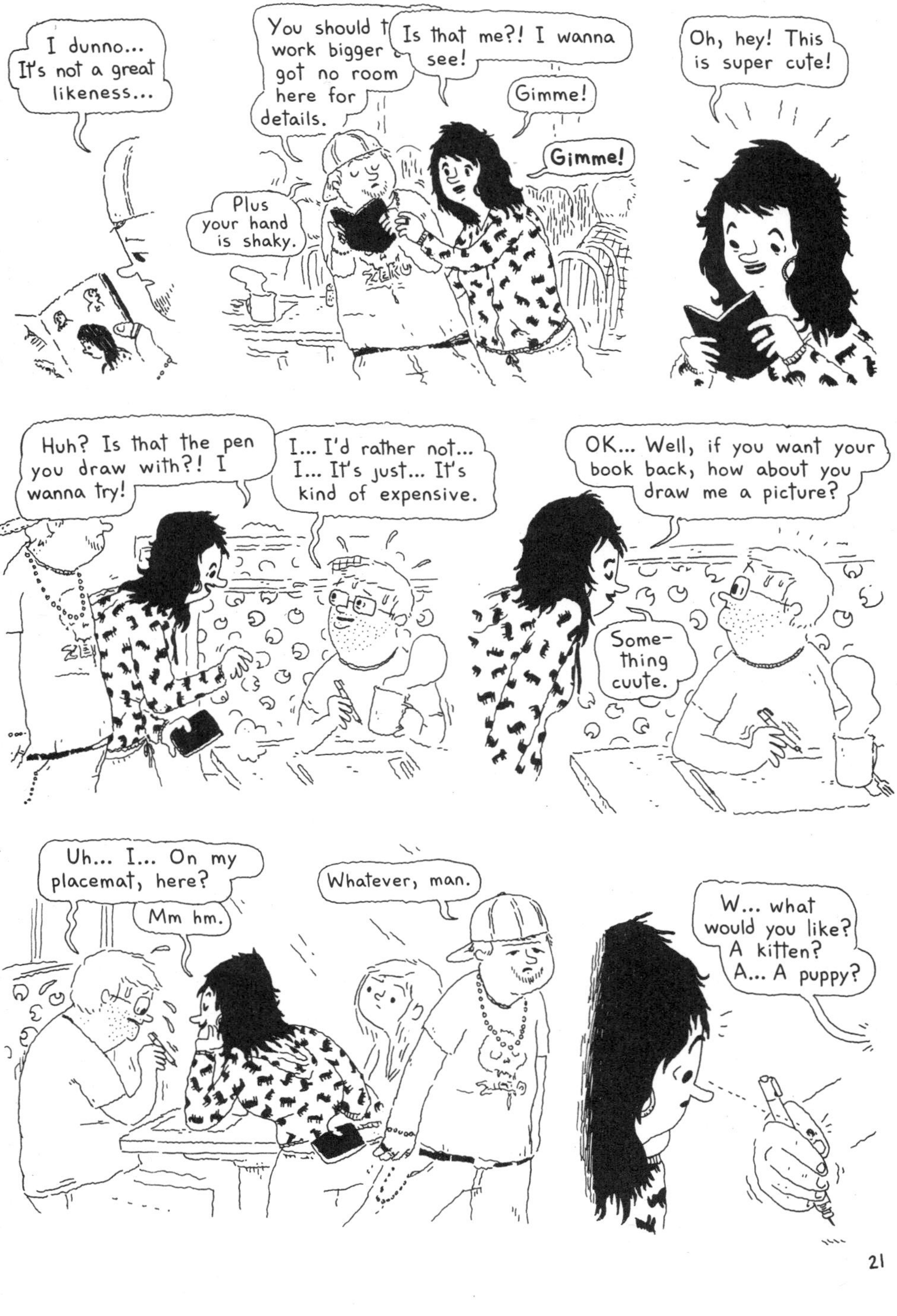
I dunno... It's not a great likeness...
You should t work bigger got no room here for details.
Is that me?! I wanna see!
Gimme!
Gimme!
Plus your hand is shaky.
Oh, hey! This is super cute!
Huh? Is that the pen you draw with?! I wanna try!
I... I'd rather not... I... It's just... It's kind of expensive.
OK... Well, if you want your book back, how about you draw me a picture?
Some-thing cuute.
Uh... I... On my placemat, here?
Mm hm.
Whatever, man.
W... what would you like? A kitten? A... A puppy?

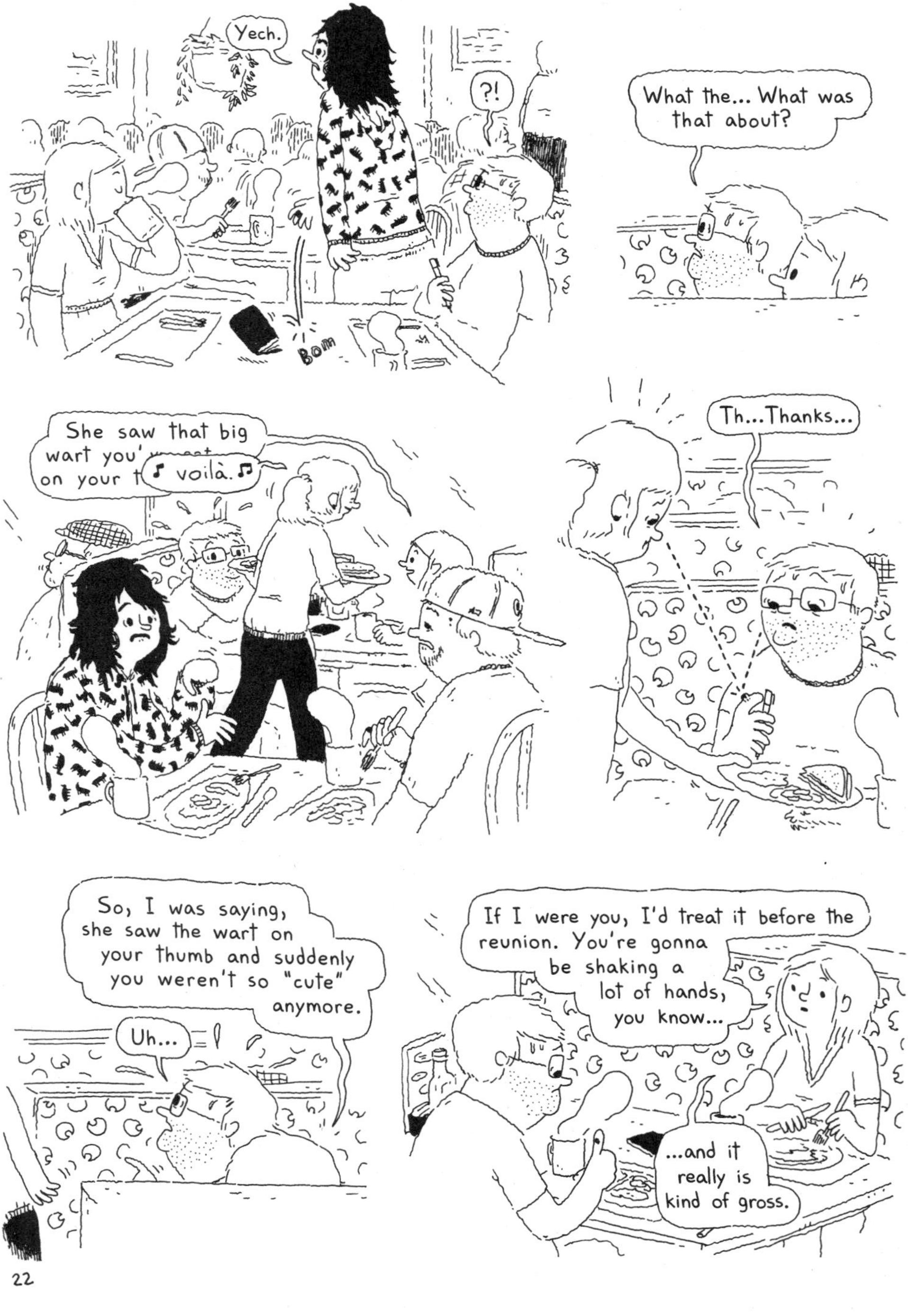
Yech.
?!
BOM
What the... What was that about?
She saw that big wart you'
on your t
♪ voilà. ♫
Th...Thanks...
So, I was saying, she saw the wart on your thumb and suddenly you weren't so "cute" anymore.
Uh...
If I were you, I'd treat it before the reunion. You're gonna be shaking a lot of hands, you know...
...and it really is kind of gross.

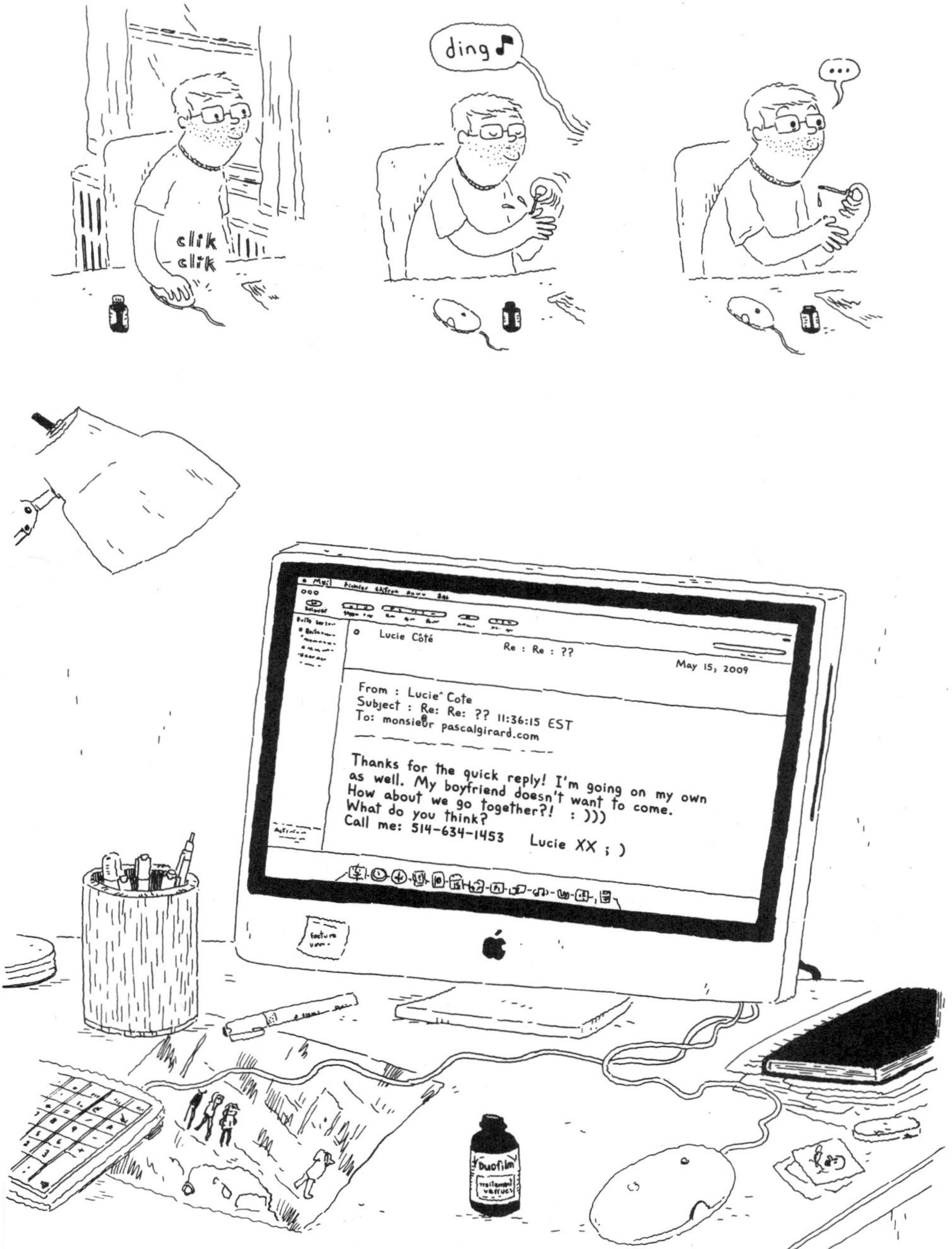
clik
clik
ding
...
Lucie Côté
Re : Re : ??
May 15, 2009
From : Lucie^ Cote
Subject : Re: Re: ?? 11:36:15 EST
To: monsieur@pascalgirard.com
Thanks for the quick reply! I'm going on my own as well. My boyfriend doesn't want to come.
How about we go together?! :)))
What do you think?
Call me: 514-634-1453 Lucie XX ;)
Duofilm

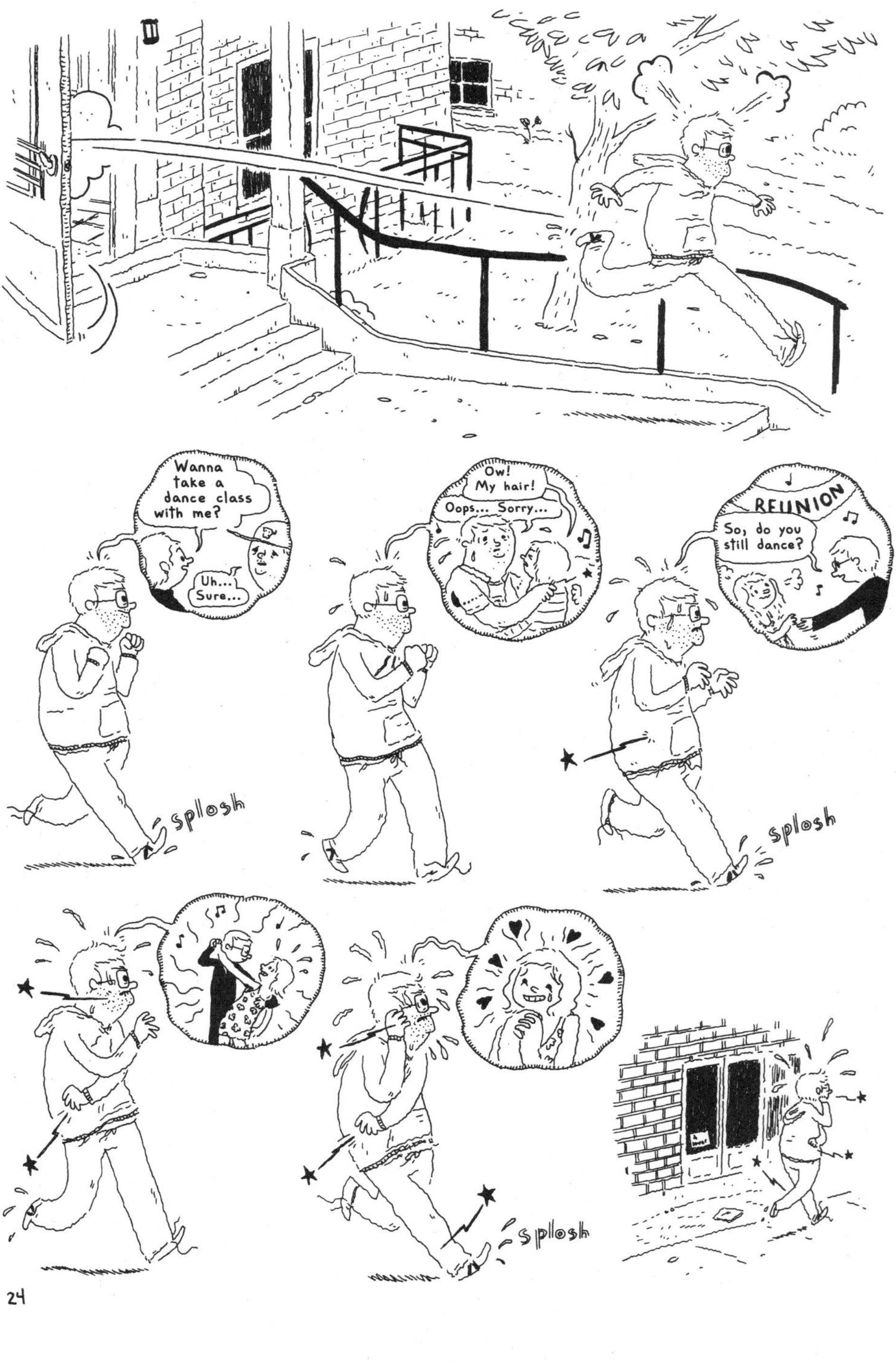
Wanna take a dance class with me?
Uh... Sure...
splosh
Ow! My hair!
Oops... Sorry...
REUNION
So, do you still dance?
splosh
splosh

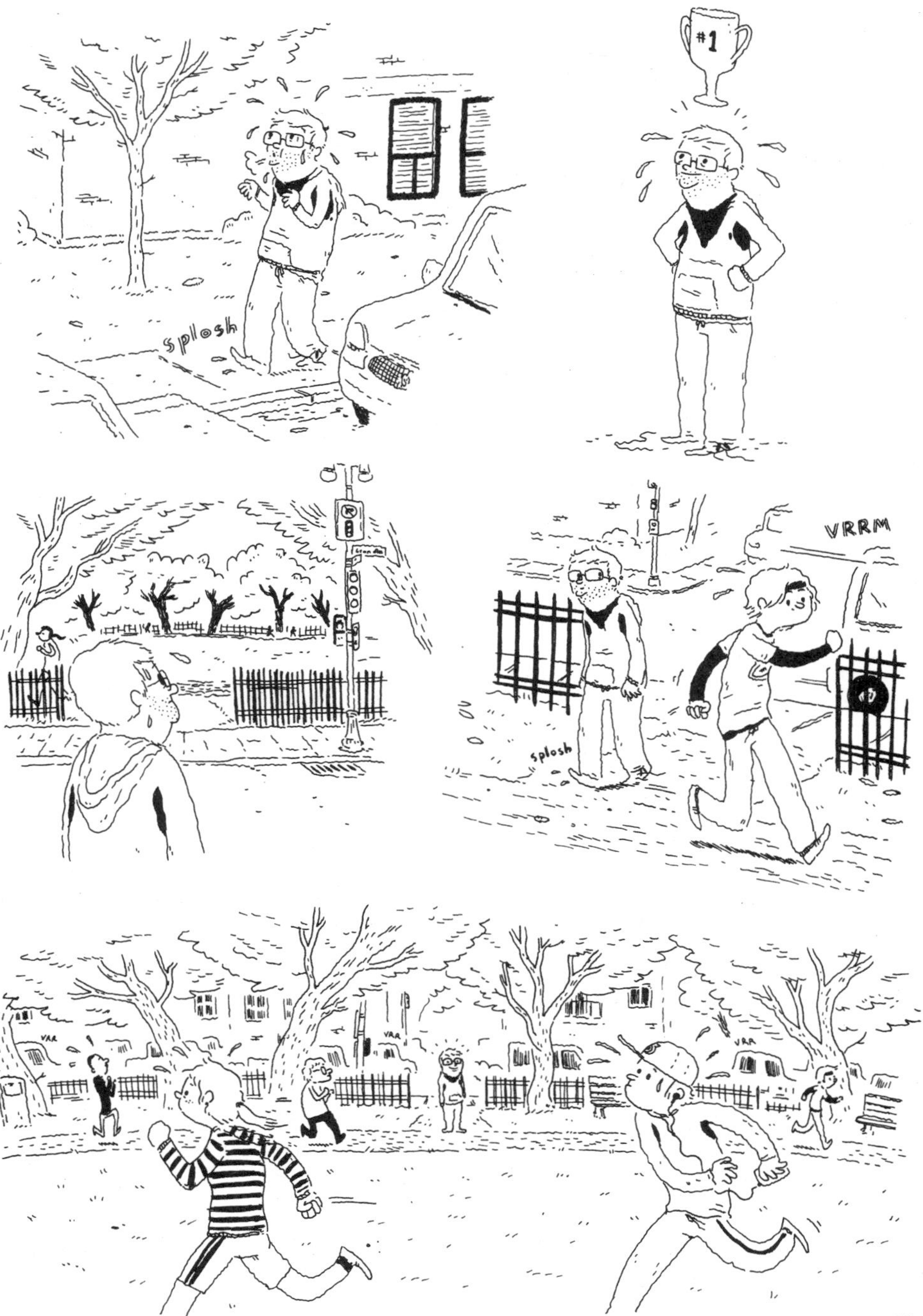

splosh
#1
VRRM
splosh

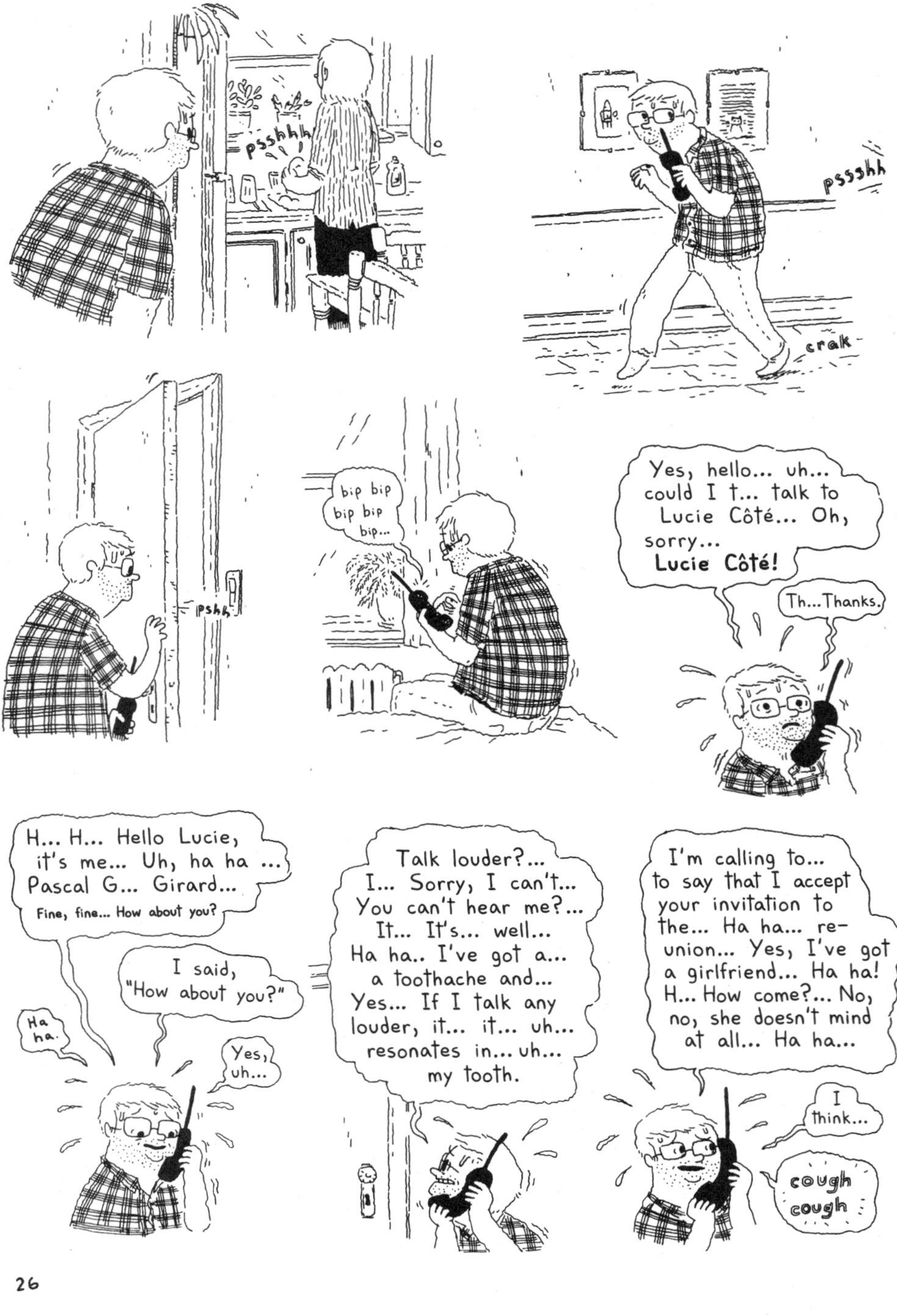
psshhh
pssshh
crak
pshh
bip bip bip bip bip...
Yes, hello... uh... could I t... talk to Lucie Côté... Oh, sorry... **Lucie Côté!**
Th...Thanks.
H... H... Hello Lucie, it's me... Uh, ha ha ... Pascal G... Girard... Fine, fine... How about you?
I said, "How about you?"
Ha ha.
Yes, uh...
Talk louder?... I... Sorry, I can't... You can't hear me?... It... It's... well... Ha ha.. I've got a... a toothache and... Yes... If I talk any louder, it... it... uh... resonates in... uh... my tooth.
I'm calling to... to say that I accept your invitation to the... Ha ha... re-union... Yes, I've got a girlfriend... Ha ha! H... How come?... No, no, she doesn't mind at all... Ha ha...
I think...
cough cough

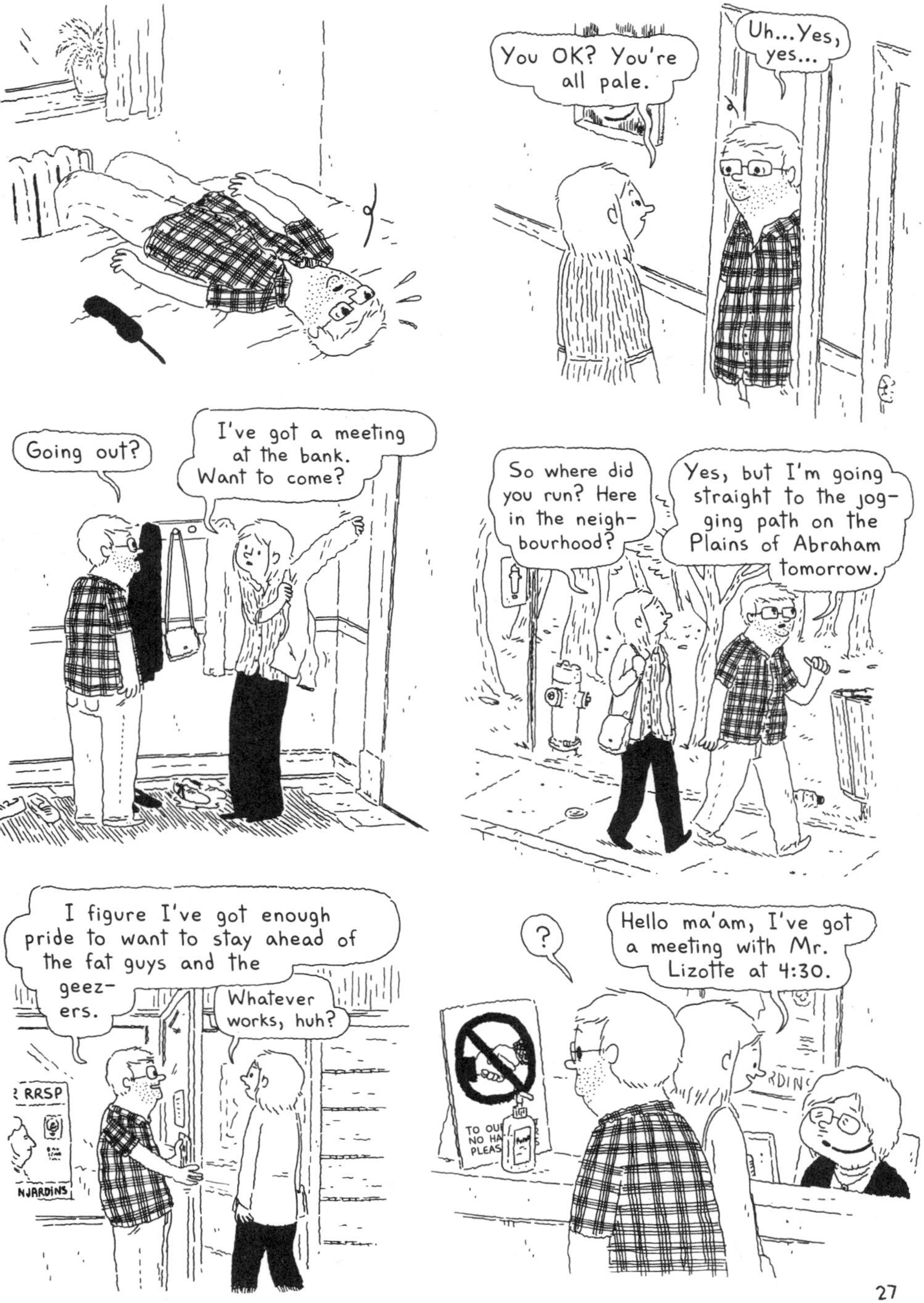
You OK? You're all pale.
Uh...Yes, yes...
Going out?
I've got a meeting at the bank. Want to come?
So where did you run? Here in the neighbourhood?
Yes, but I'm going straight to the jogging path on the Plains of Abraham tomorrow.
I figure I've got enough pride to want to stay ahead of the fat guys and the geezers.
Whatever works, huh?
RRSP
?
Hello ma'am, I've got a meeting with Mr. Lizotte at 4:30.

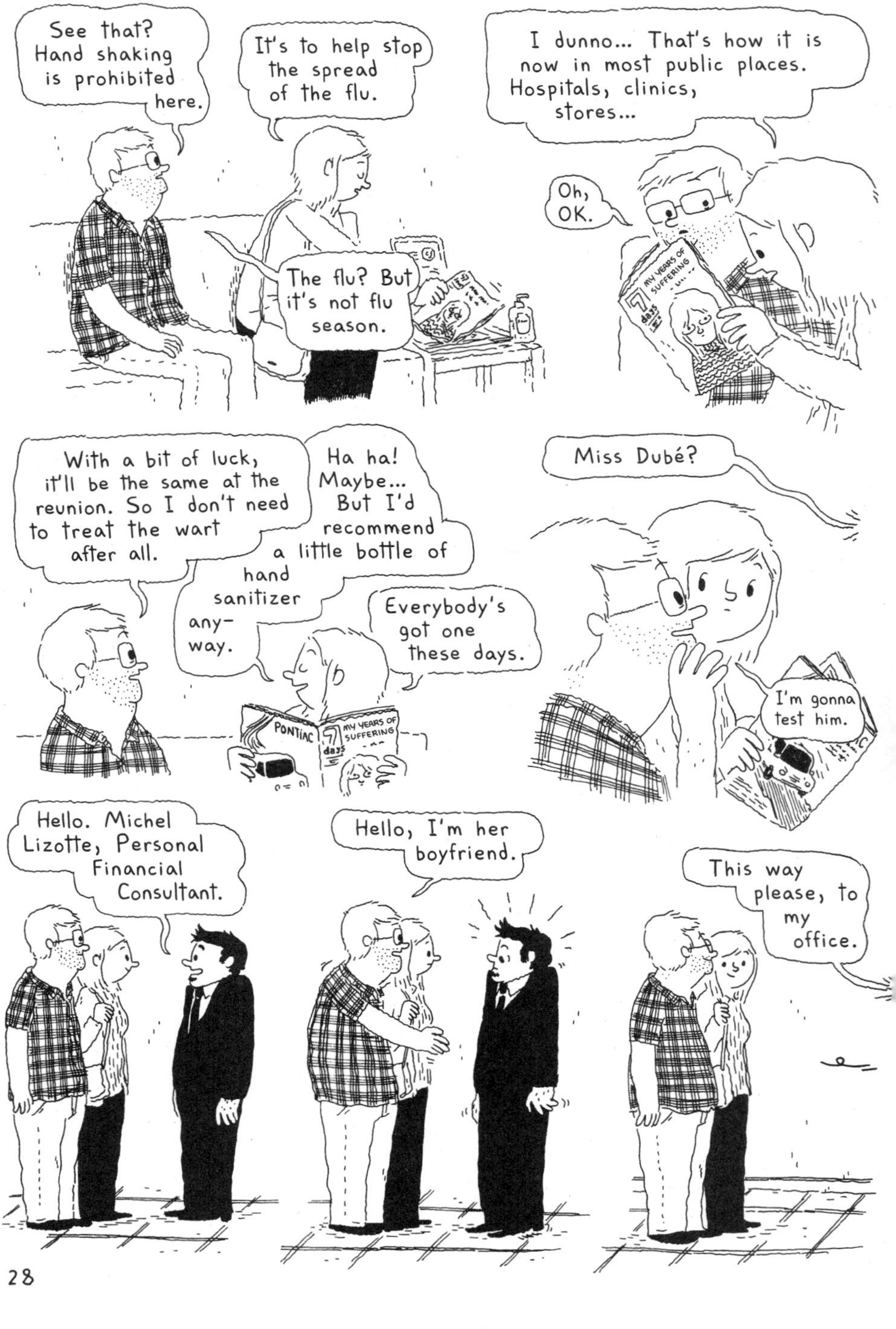

See that? Hand shaking is prohibited here.
It's to help stop the spread of the flu.
The flu? But it's not flu season.
I dunno... That's how it is now in most public places. Hospitals, clinics, stores...
Oh, OK.
7 days
MY YEARS OF SUFFERING
With a bit of luck, it'll be the same at the reunion. So I don't need to treat the wart after all.
Ha ha! Maybe... But I'd recommend a little bottle of hand sanitizer any-way.
Everybody's got one these days.
PONTIAC
7 days
MY YEARS OF SUFFERING
Miss Dubé?
I'm gonna test him.
Hello. Michel Lizotte, Personal Financial Consultant.
Hello, I'm her boyfriend.
This way please, to my office.

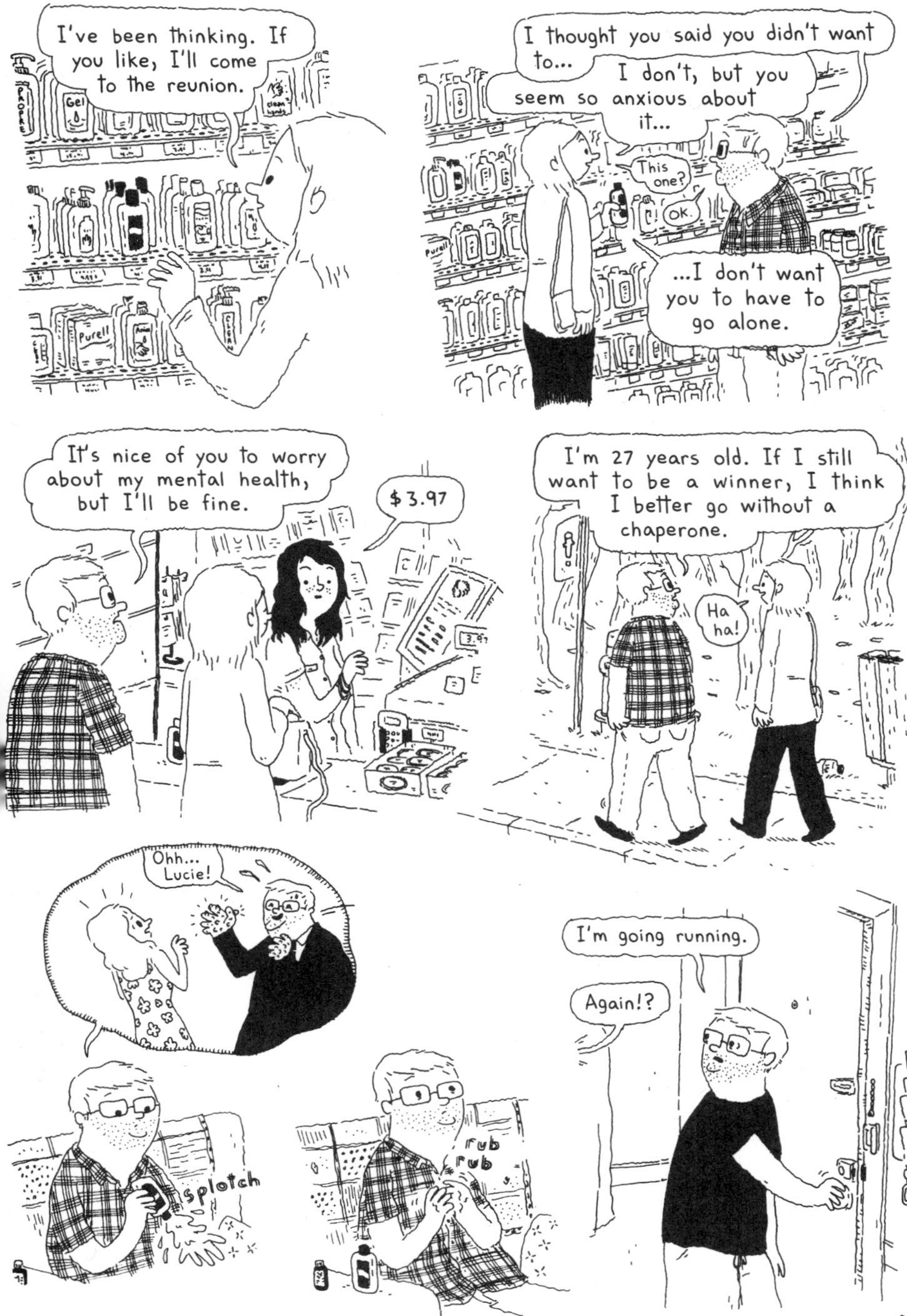
I've been thinking. If you like, I'll come to the reunion.
I thought you said you didn't want to...
I don't, but you seem so anxious about it...
This one?
OK.
...I don't want you to have to go alone.
It's nice of you to worry about my mental health, but I'll be fine.
$3.97
I'm 27 years old. If I still want to be a winner, I think I better go without a chaperone.
Ha ha!
Ohh... Lucie!
splotch
rub rub
I'm going running.
Again!?

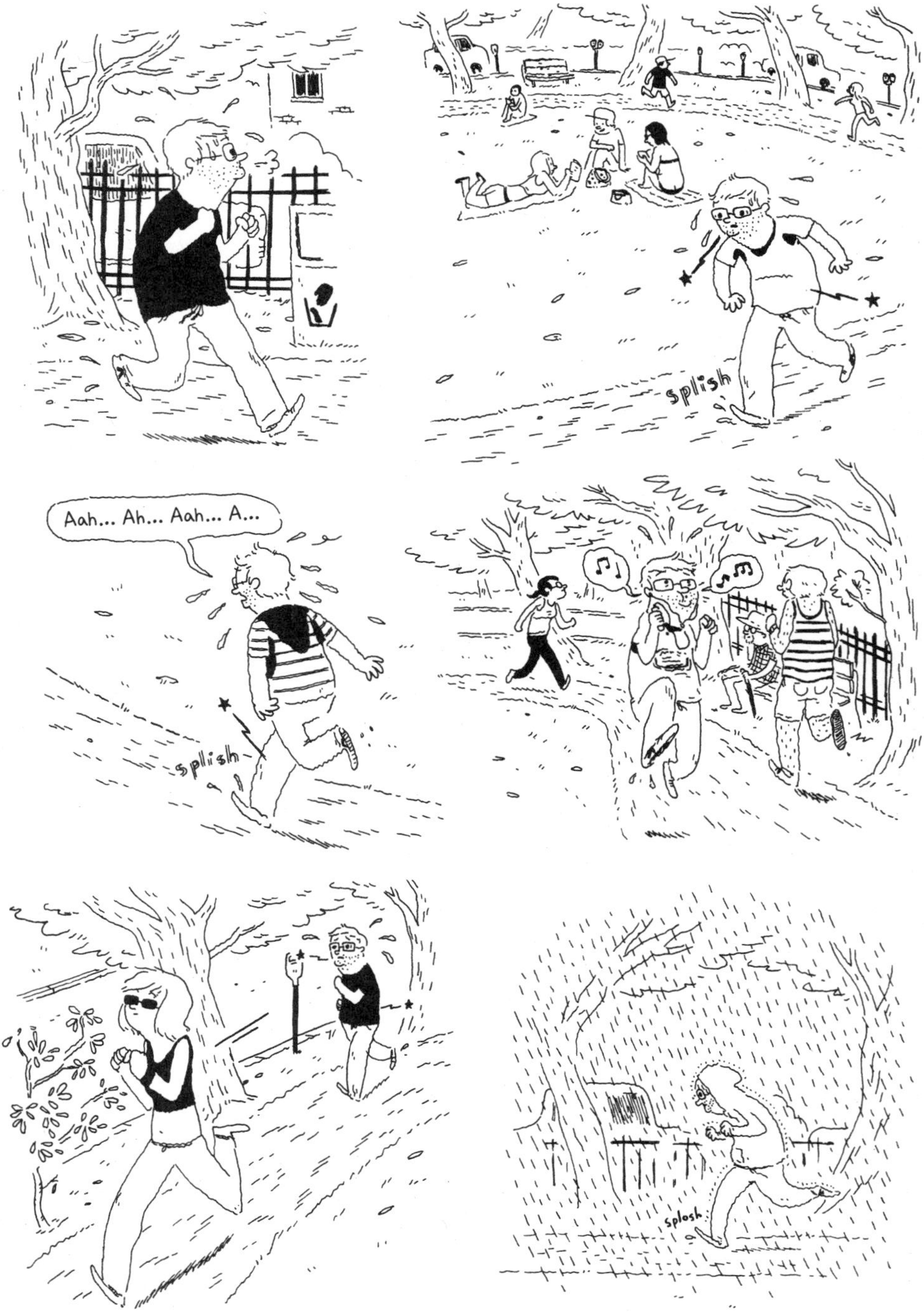
splish
Aah... Ah... Aah... A...
splish
splosh

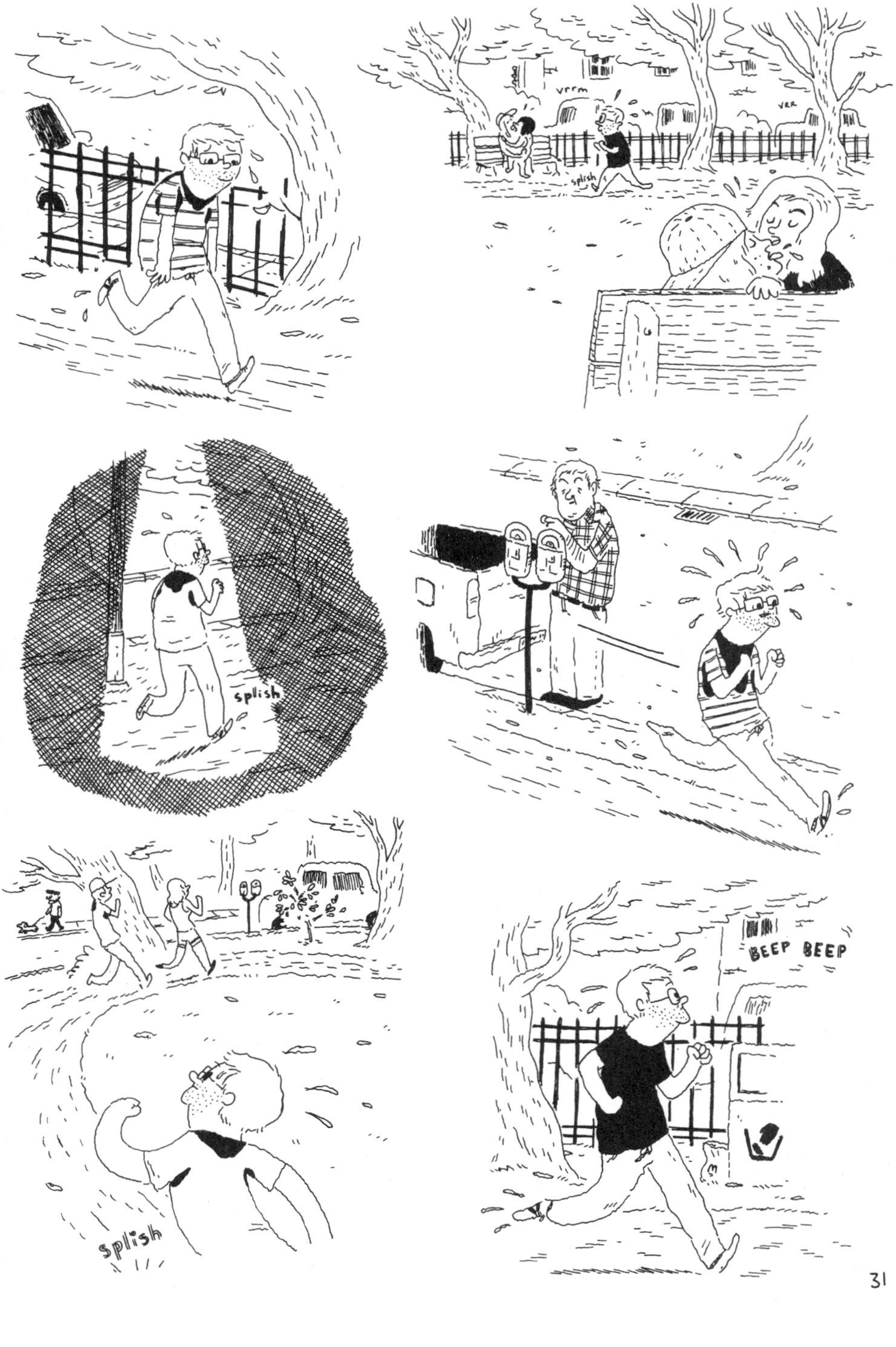
vrrm
splish
vrr
splish
splish
BEEP BEEP

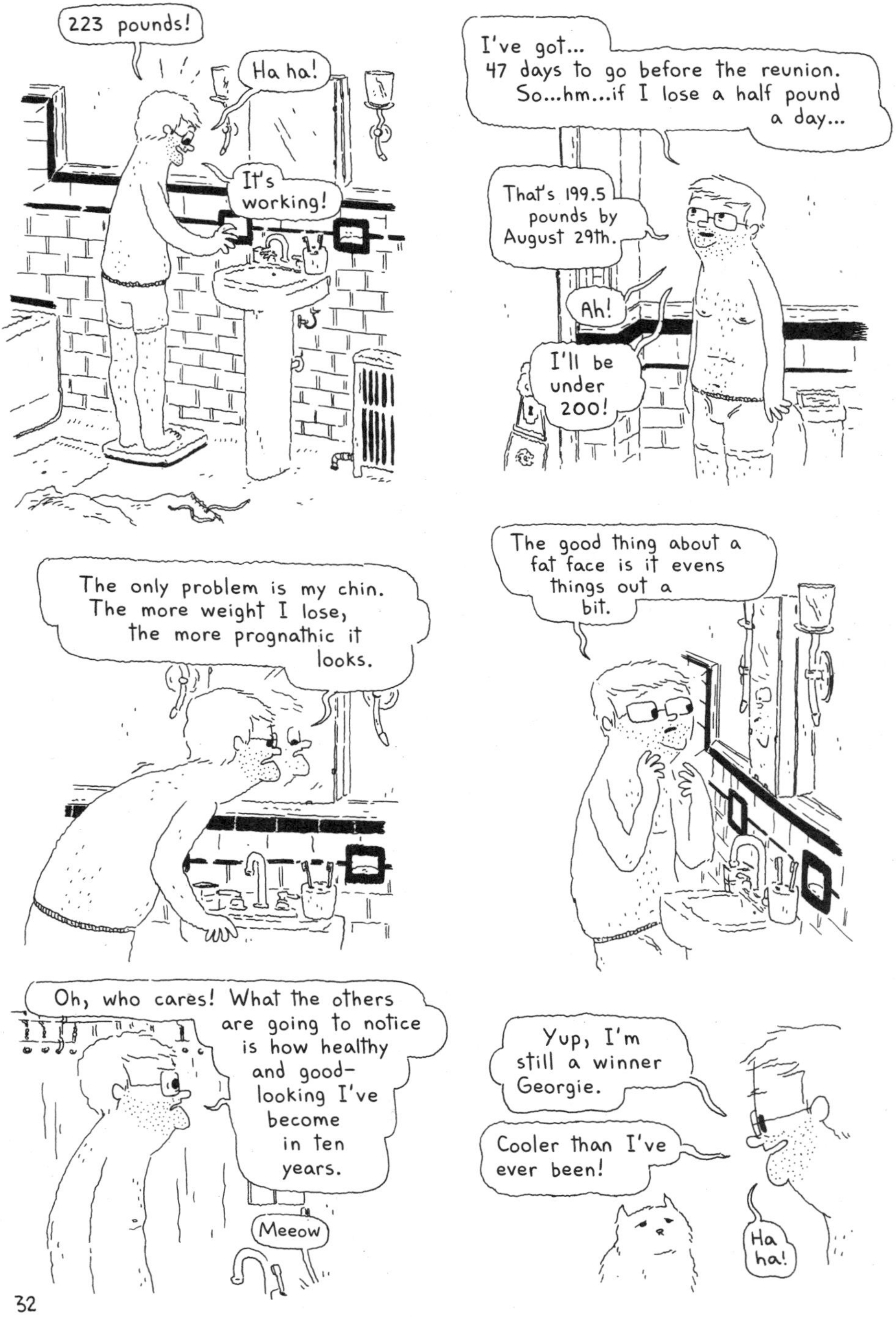
223 pounds!
Ha ha!
It's working!
I've got... 47 days to go before the reunion. So...hm...if I lose a half pound a day...
That's 199.5 pounds by August 29th.
Ah!
I'll be under 200!
The only problem is my chin. The more weight I lose, the more prognathic it looks.
The good thing about a fat face is it evens things out a bit.
Oh, who cares! What the others are going to notice is how healthy and good-looking I've become in ten years.
Meeow
Yup, I'm still a winner Georgie.
Cooler than I've ever been!
Ha ha!

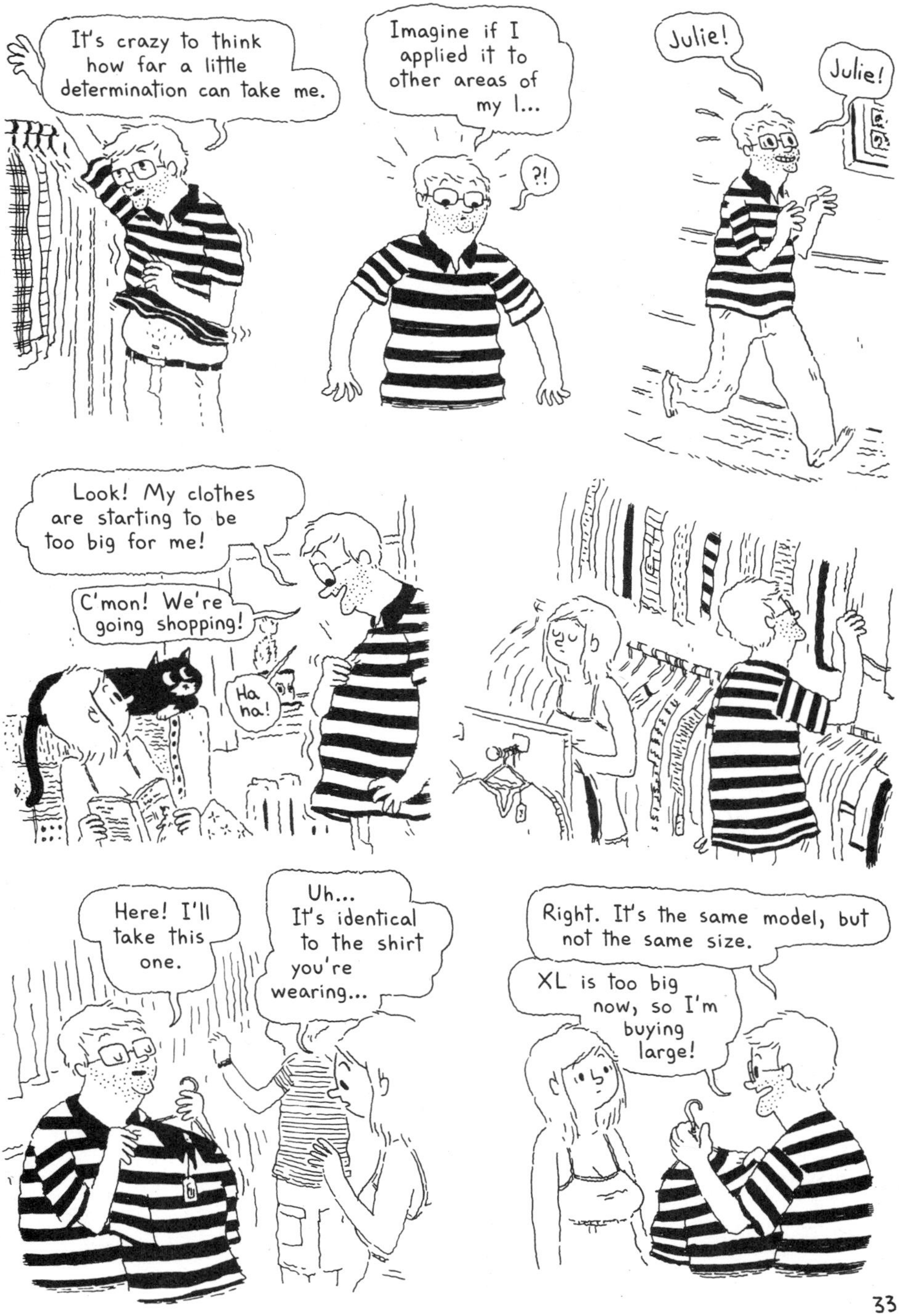

It's crazy to think how far a little determination can take me.
Imagine if I applied it to other areas of my l...
?!
Julie!
Julie!
Look! My clothes are starting to be too big for me!
C'mon! We're going shopping!
Ha ha!
Here! I'll take this one.
Uh... It's identical to the shirt you're wearing...
Right. It's the same model, but not the same size.
XL is too big now, so I'm buying large!

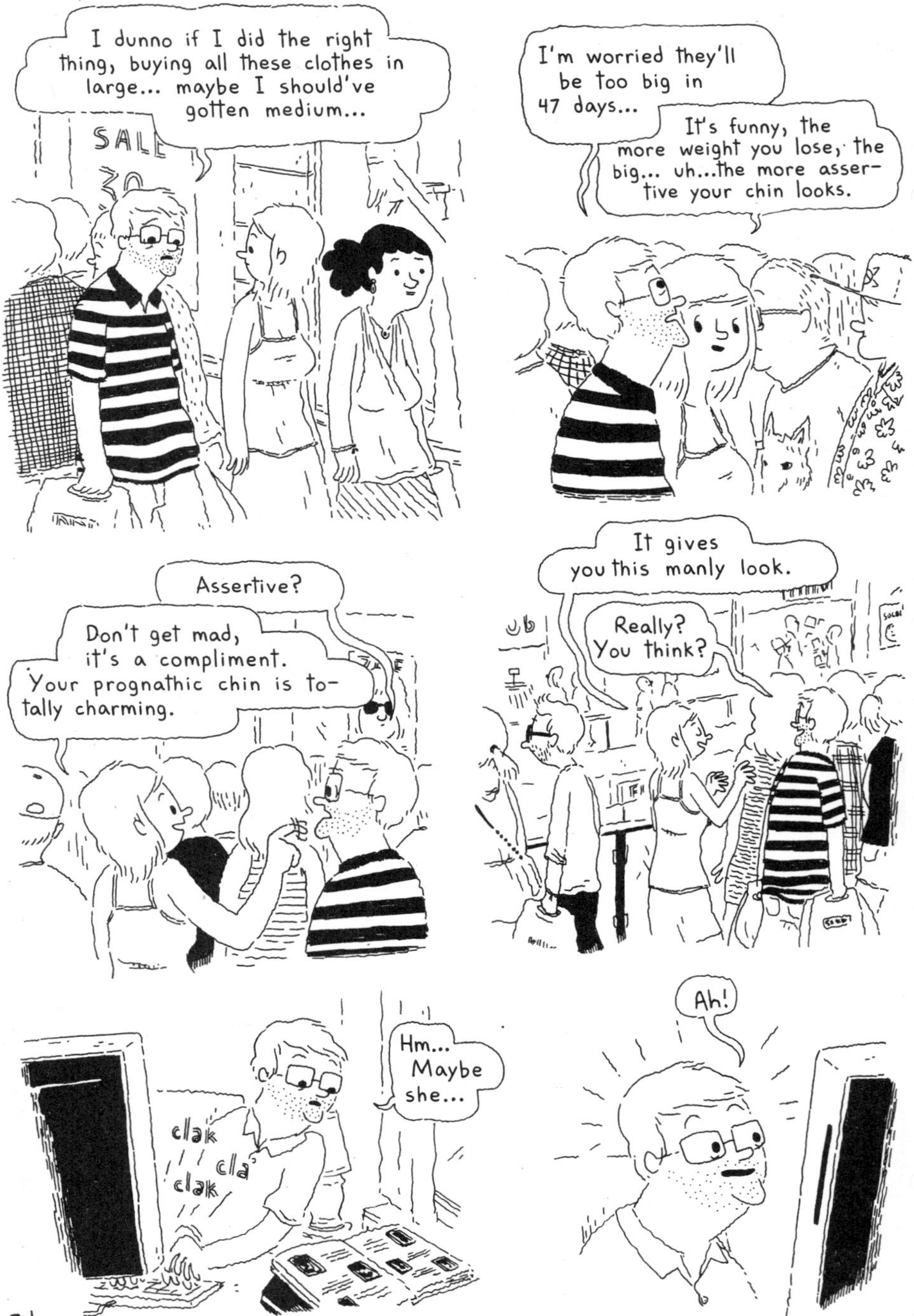
I dunno if I did the right thing, buying all these clothes in large... maybe I should've gotten medium...
SALE
I'm worried they'll be too big in 47 days...
It's funny, the more weight you lose, the big... uh...the more assertive your chin looks.
Assertive?
Don't get mad, it's a compliment. Your prognathic chin is totally charming.
It gives you this manly look.
Really? You think?
clak
cla
clak
Hm... Maybe she...
Ah!

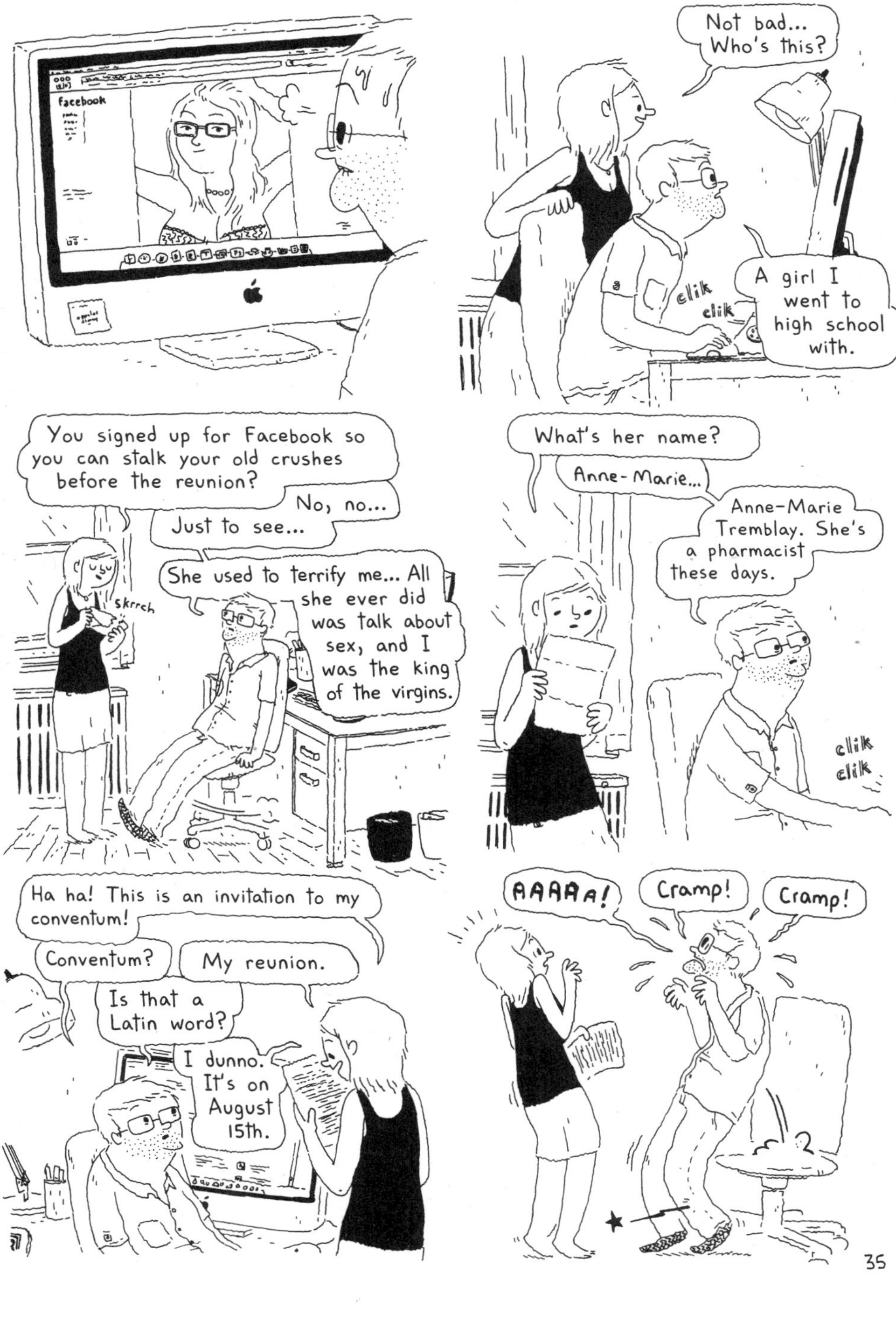
facebook
Not bad... Who's this?
clik
clik
A girl I went to high school with.
You signed up for Facebook so you can stalk your old crushes before the reunion?
No, no...
Just to see...
skrrch
She used to terrify me... All she ever did was talk about sex, and I was the king of the virgins.
What's her name?
Anne-Marie...
Anne-Marie Tremblay. She's a pharmacist these days.
clik
clik
Ha ha! This is an invitation to my conventum!
Conventum?
My reunion.
Is that a Latin word?
I dunno. It's on August 15th.
AAAAA!
Cramp!
Cramp!

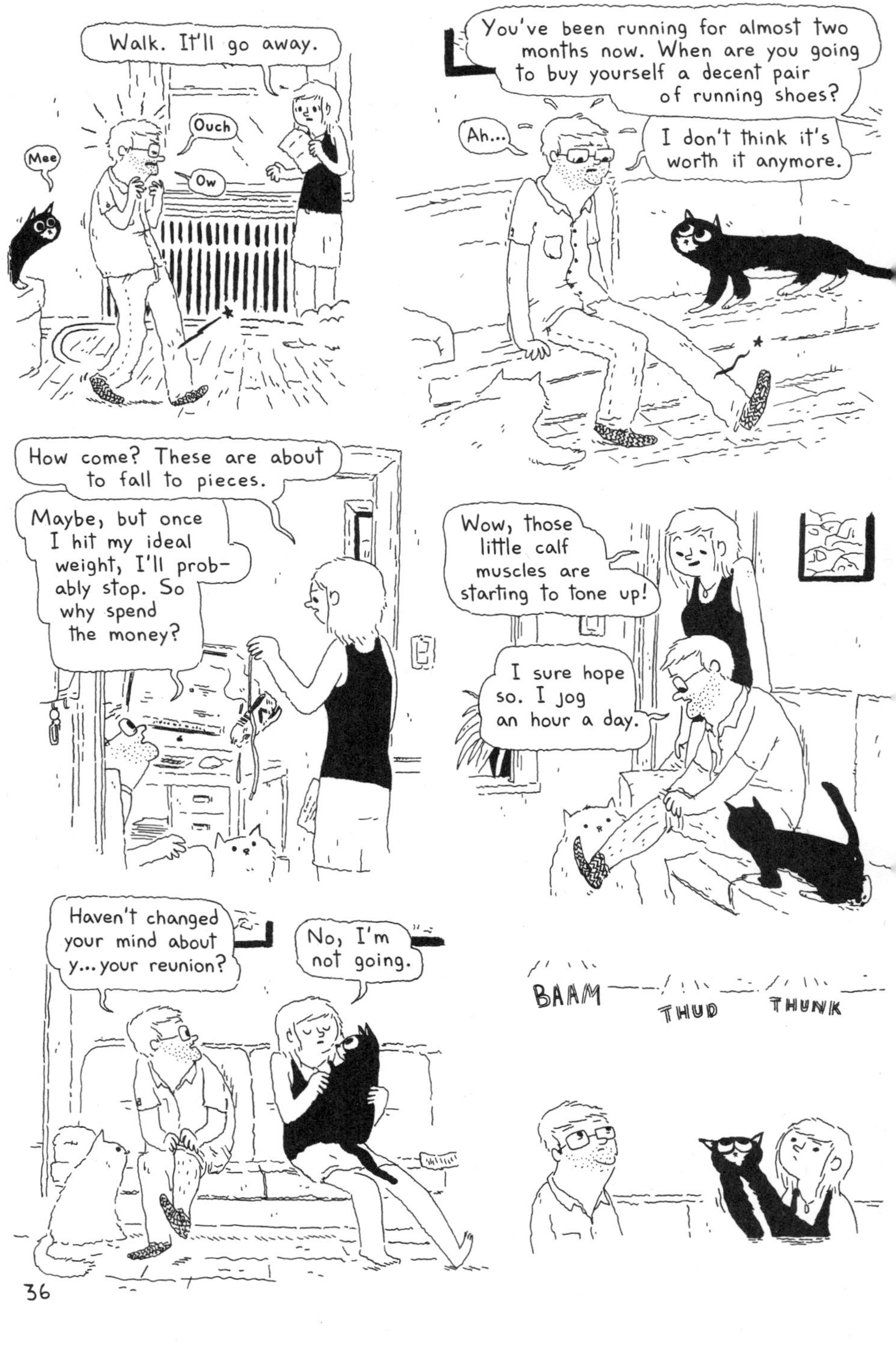
Walk. It'll go away.
Ouch
Ow
Mee
You've been running for almost two months now. When are you going to buy yourself a decent pair of running shoes?
Ah...
I don't think it's worth it anymore.
How come? These are about to fall to pieces.
Maybe, but once I hit my ideal weight, I'll probably stop. So why spend the money?
Wow, those little calf muscles are starting to tone up!
I sure hope so. I jog an hour a day.
Haven't changed your mind about y...your reunion?
No, I'm not going.
BAAM
THUD
THUNK

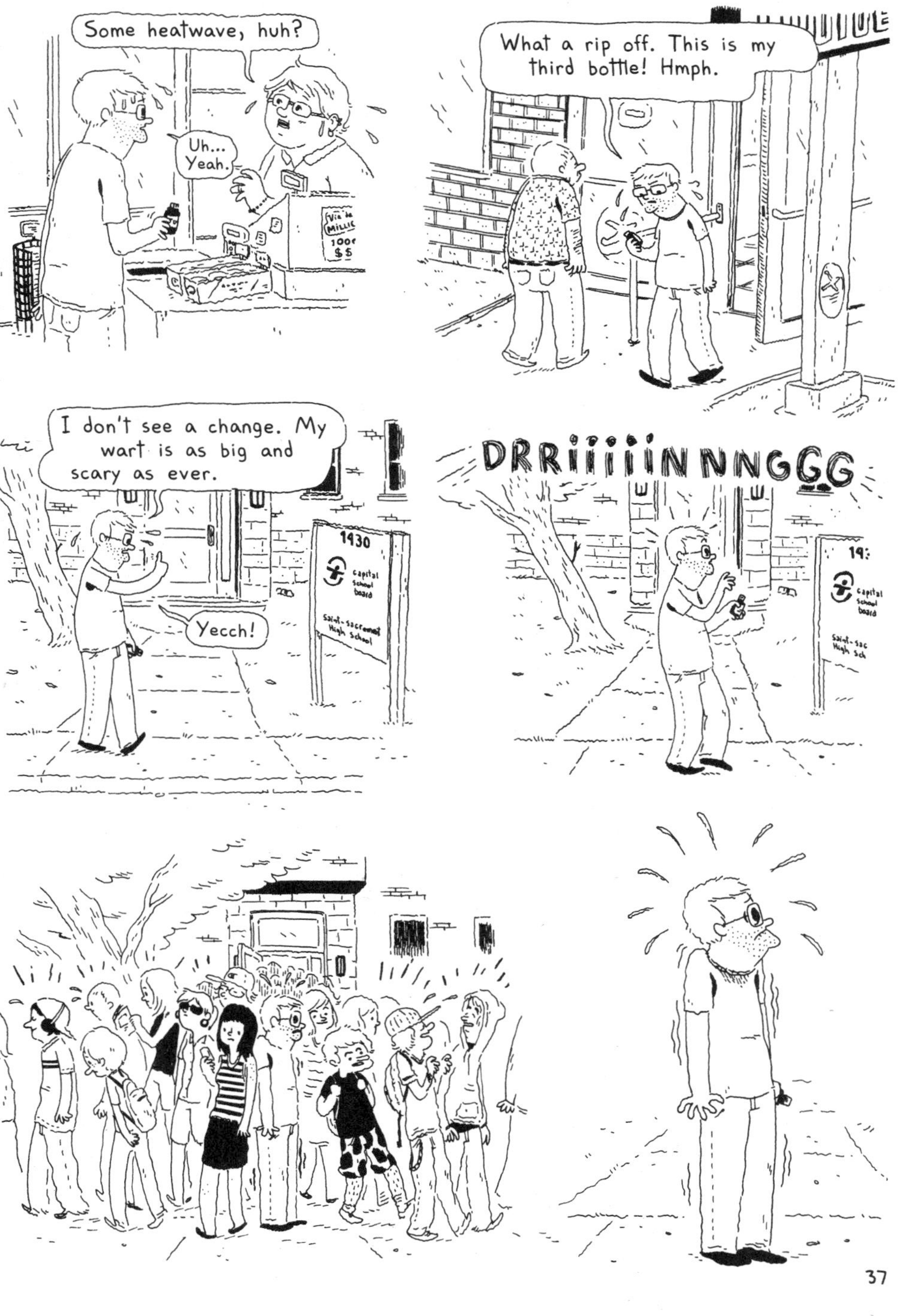
Some heatwave, huh?
Uh... Yeah.
What a rip off. This is my third bottle! Hmph.
I don't see a change. My wart is as big and scary as ever.
Yecch!
1430
capital school board
Saint-sacrement High School
DRRiiiiiiNNNGGG

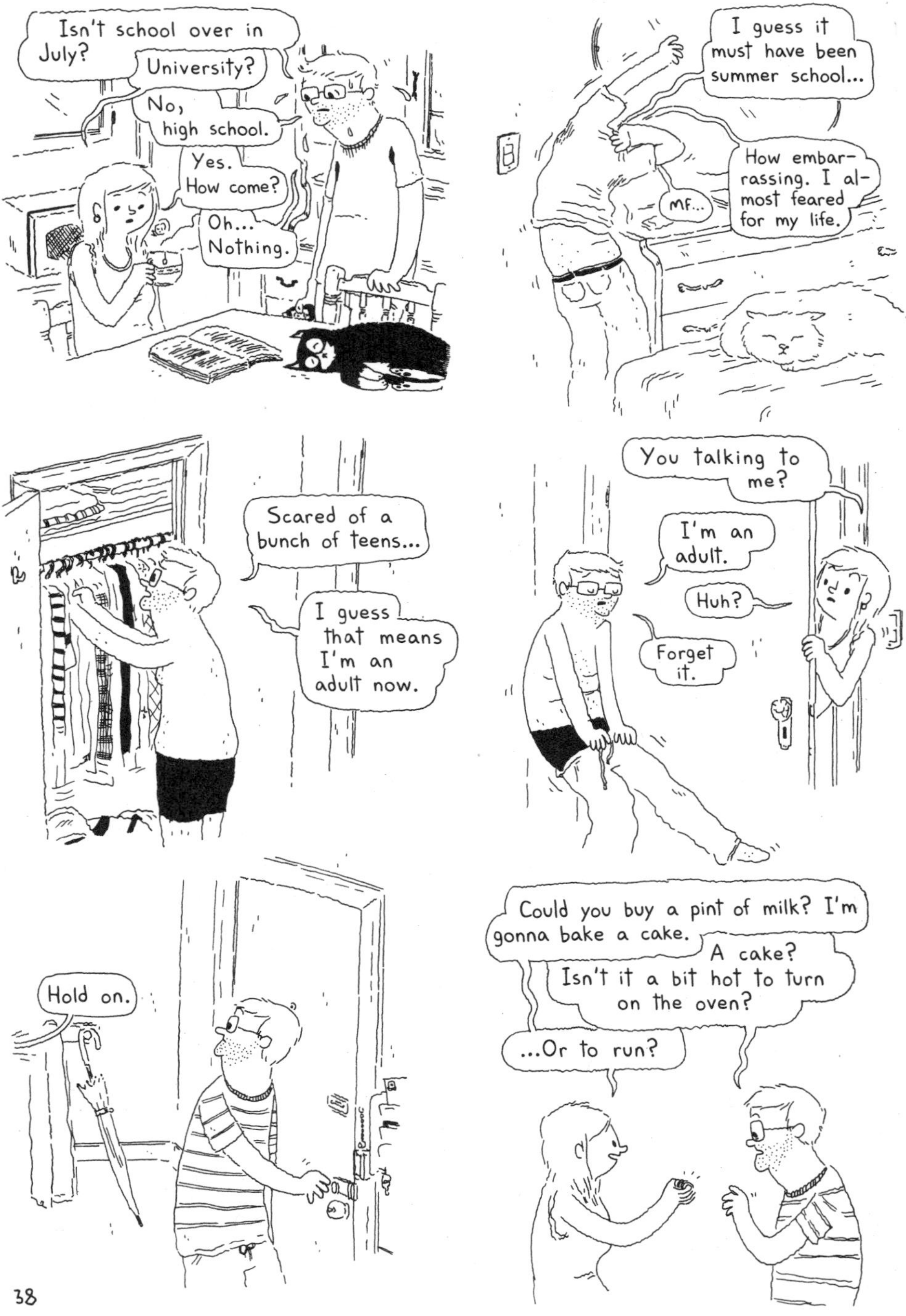
Isn't school over in July?
University?
No, high school.
Yes. How come?
Oh... Nothing.
I guess it must have been summer school...
MF...
How embar-rassing. I al-most feared for my life.
Scared of a bunch of teens...
I guess that means I'm an adult now.
You talking to me?
I'm an adult.
Huh?
Forget it.
Hold on.
Could you buy a pint of milk? I'm gonna bake a cake.
A cake? Isn't it a bit hot to turn on the oven?
...Or to run?

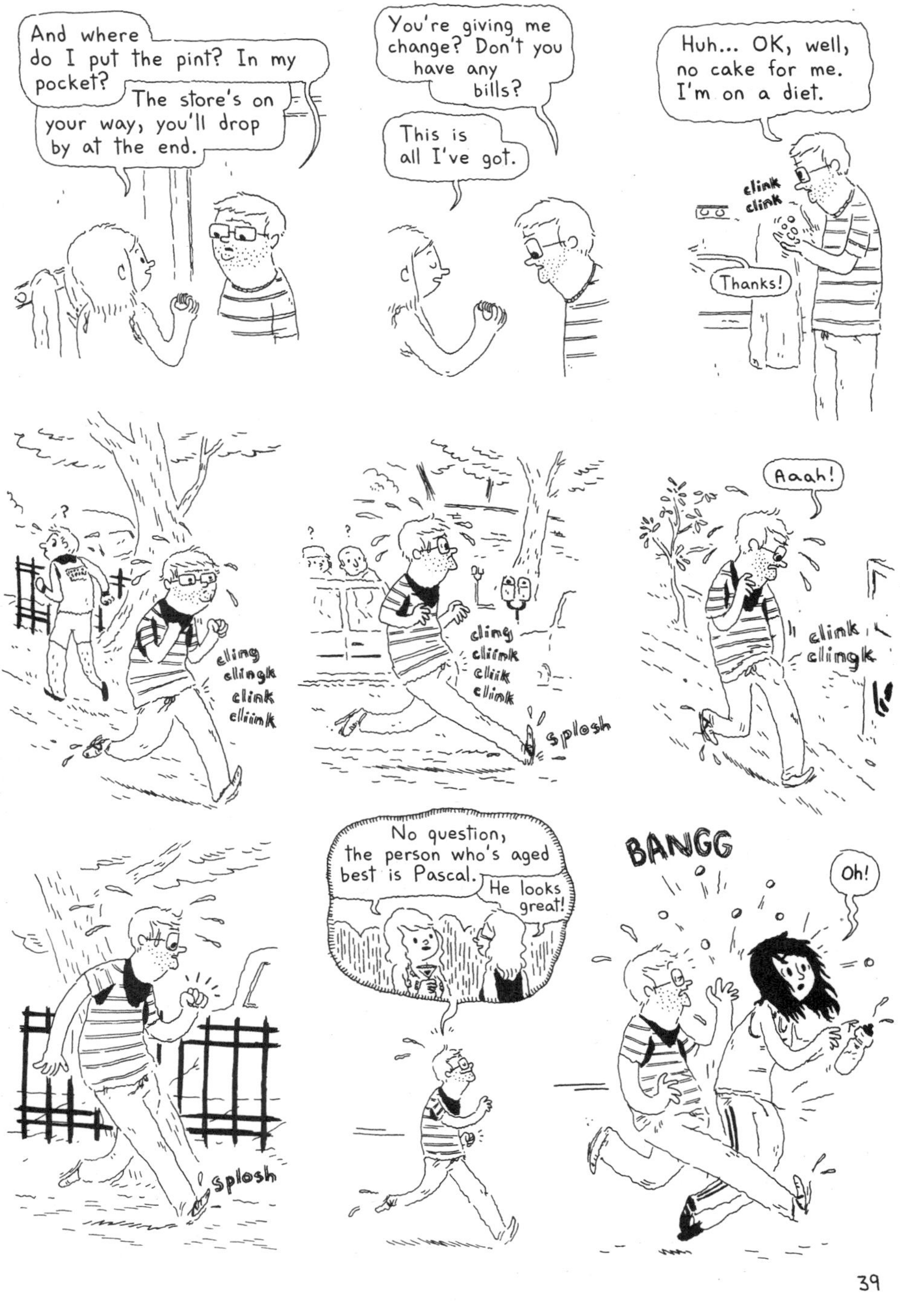

And where do I put the pint? In my pocket?
The store's on your way, you'll drop by at the end.
You're giving me change? Don't you have any bills?
This is all I've got.
Huh... OK, well, no cake for me. I'm on a diet.
clink clink
Thanks!
cling clingk clink clliink
cling cliink cliik clink
splosh
Aaah!
clink clingk
splosh
No question, the person who's aged best is Pascal.
He looks great!
BANGG
Oh!

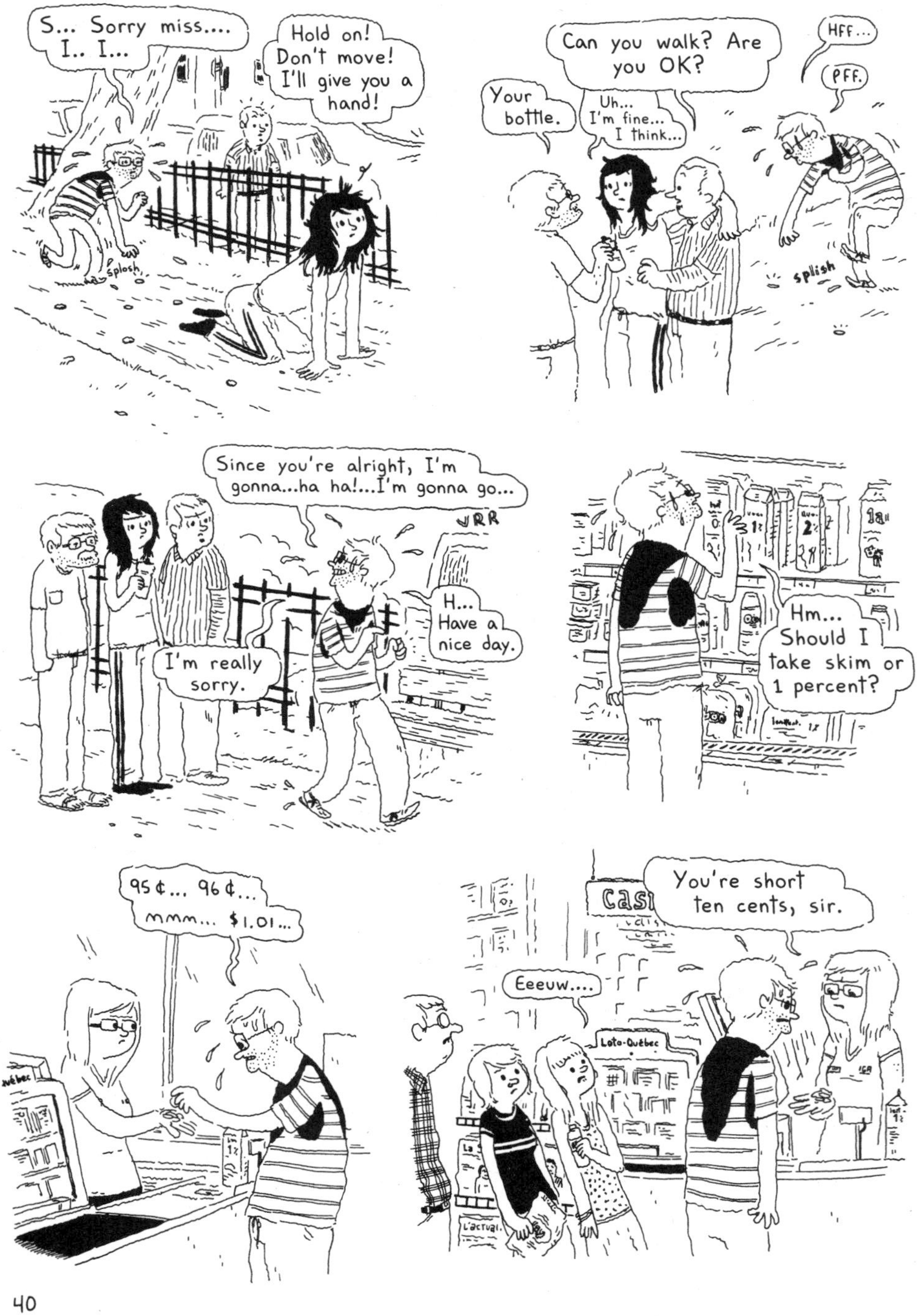
S... Sorry miss.... I.. I...
Hold on! Don't move! I'll give you a hand!
splosh
Can you walk? Are you OK?
HFF...
PFF.
Your bottle.
Uh... I'm fine... I think...
splish
Since you're alright, I'm gonna...ha ha!...I'm gonna go...
VRR
H... Have a nice day.
I'm really sorry.
Hm... Should I take skim or 1 percent?
95¢... 96¢... mmm... $1.01...
You're short ten cents, sir.
Eeeuw....
Loto-Québec

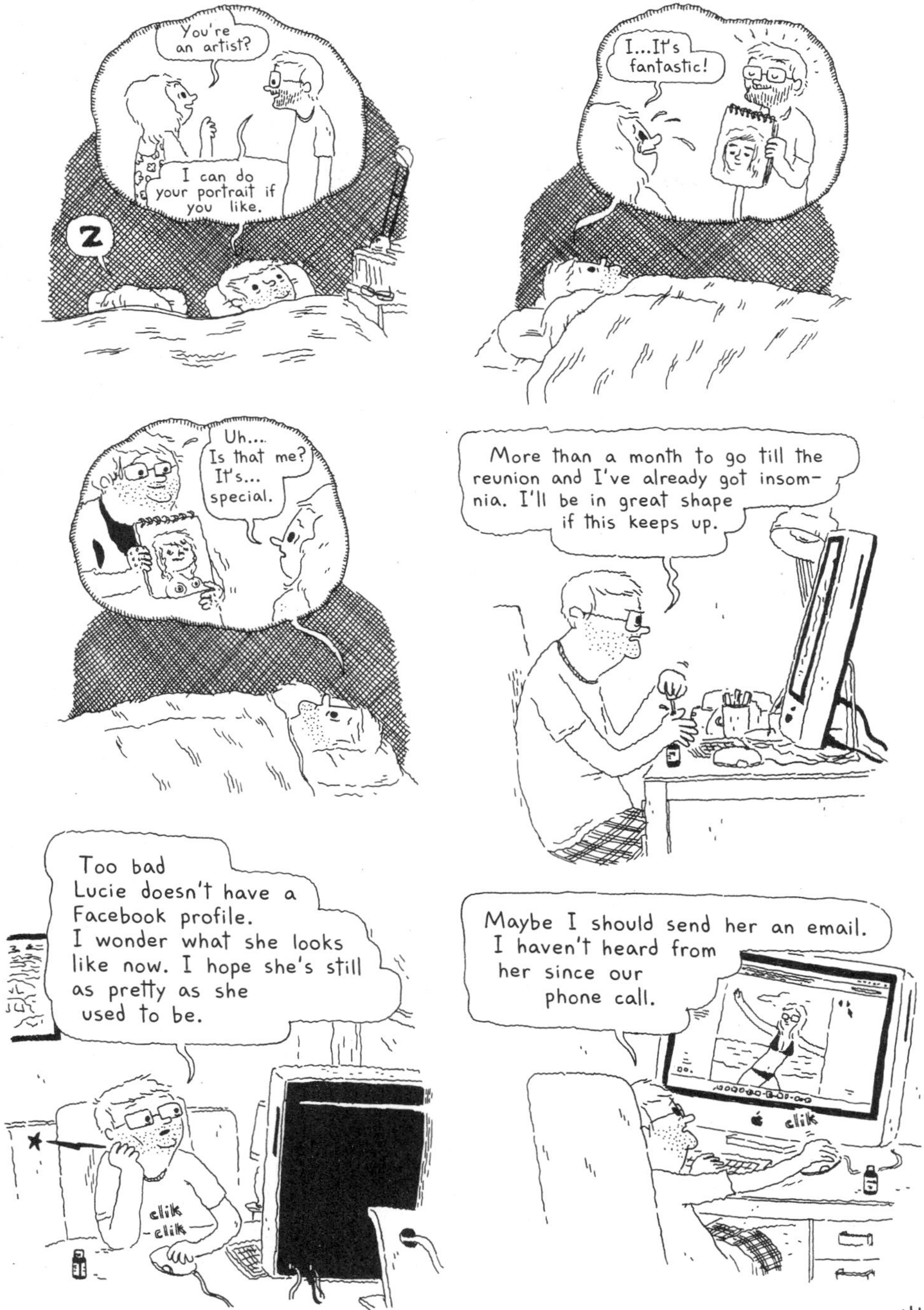
You're an artist?
I can do your portrait if you like.
Z
I...It's fantastic!
Uh... Is that me? It's... special.
More than a month to go till the reunion and I've already got insom-nia. I'll be in great shape if this keeps up.
Too bad Lucie doesn't have a Facebook profile. I wonder what she looks like now. I hope she's still as pretty as she used to be.
clik clik
Maybe I should send her an email. I haven't heard from her since our phone call.
clik

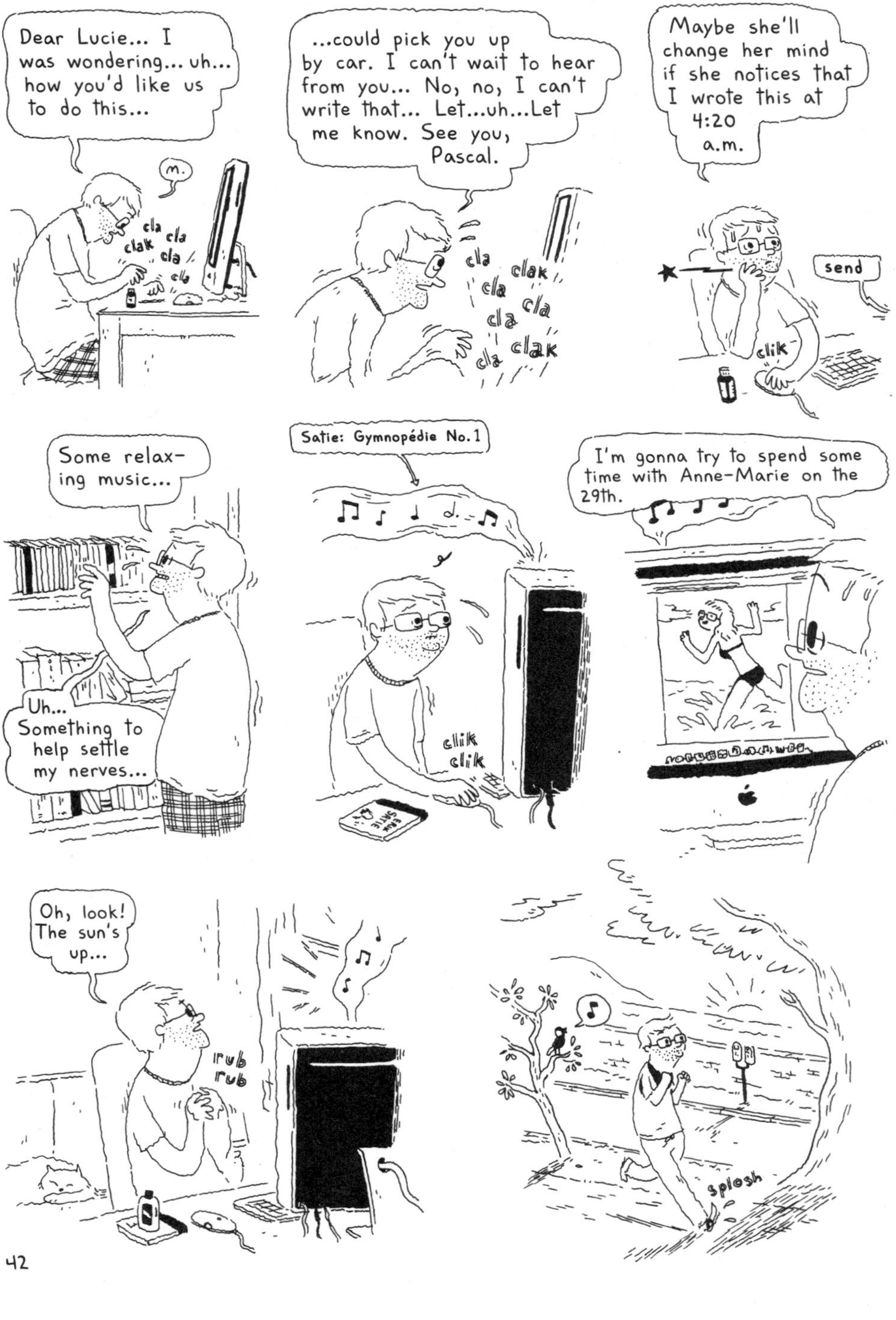
Dear Lucie... I was wondering... uh... how you'd like us to do this...
m.
cla cla clak cla cla
...could pick you up by car. I can't wait to hear from you... No, no, I can't write that... Let...uh...Let me know. See you, Pascal.
cla clak cla cla cla cla clak
Maybe she'll change her mind if she notices that I wrote this at 4:20 a.m.
send
clik
Some relax-ing music...
Uh... Something to help settle my nerves...
Satie: Gymnopédie No. 1
clik clik
I'm gonna try to spend some time with Anne-Marie on the 29th.
Oh, look! The sun's up...
rub rub
splosh

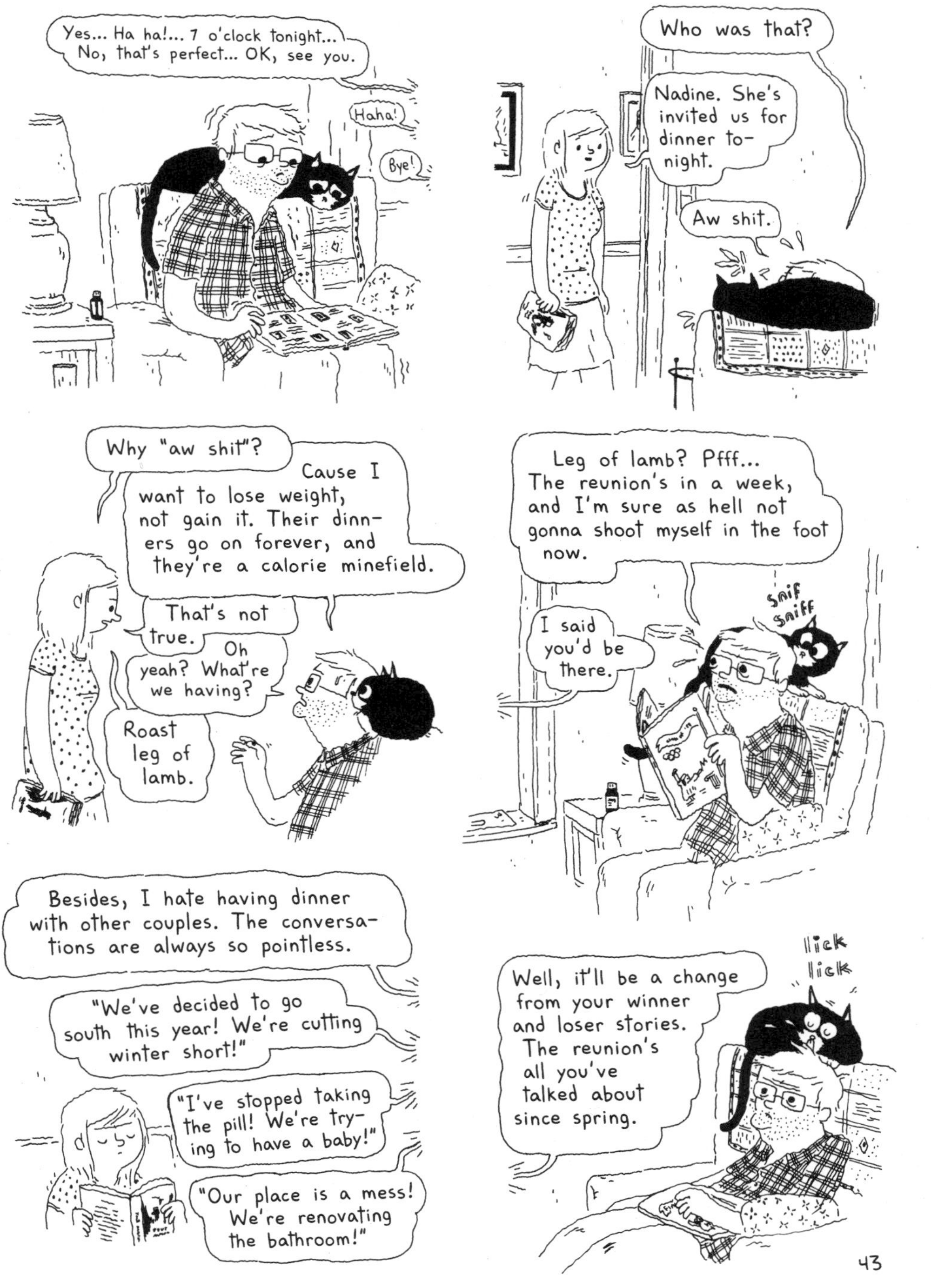
Yes... Ha ha!... 7 o'clock tonight... No, that's perfect... OK, see you.
Haha!
Bye!
Who was that?
Nadine. She's invited us for dinner to-night.
Aw shit.
Why "aw shit"?
Cause I want to lose weight, not gain it. Their dinn-ers go on forever, and they're a calorie minefield.
That's not true.
Oh yeah? What're we having?
Roast leg of lamb.
Leg of lamb? Pfff... The reunion's in a week, and I'm sure as hell not gonna shoot myself in the foot now.
snif sniff
I said you'd be there.
Besides, I hate having dinner with other couples. The conversa-tions are always so pointless.
"We've decided to go south this year! We're cutting winter short!"
"I've stopped taking the pill! We're try-ing to have a baby!"
"Our place is a mess! We're renovating the bathroom!"
lick lick
Well, it'll be a change from your winner and loser stories. The reunion's all you've talked about since spring.

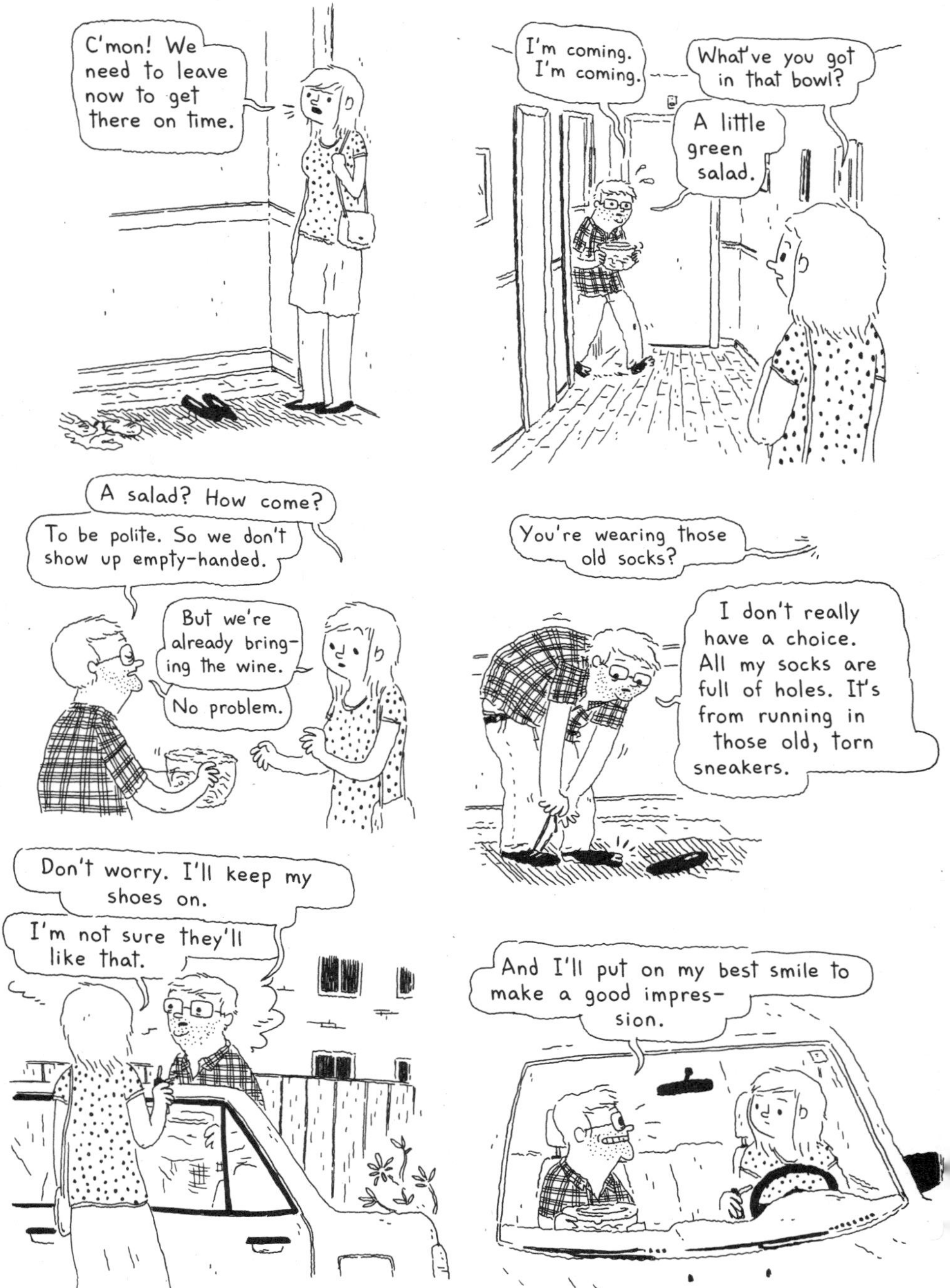
C'mon! We need to leave now to get there on time.
I'm coming. I'm coming.
What've you got in that bowl?
A little green salad.
A salad? How come?
To be polite. So we don't show up empty-handed.
But we're already bring-ing the wine.
No problem.
You're wearing those old socks?
I don't really have a choice. All my socks are full of holes. It's from running in those old, torn sneakers.
Don't worry. I'll keep my shoes on.
I'm not sure they'll like that.
And I'll put on my best smile to make a good impres-sion.

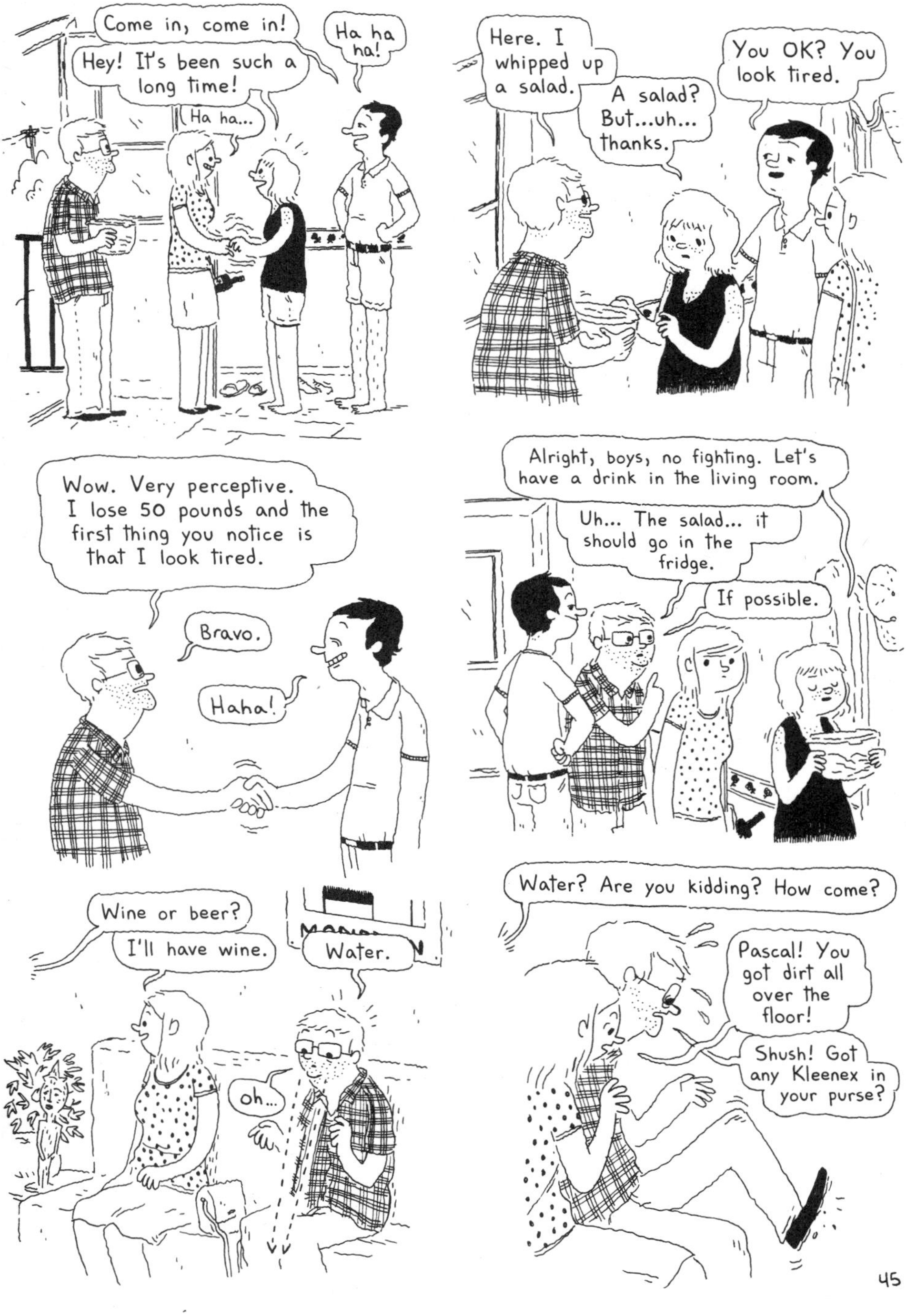
Come in, come in!
Hey! It's been such a long time!
Ha ha ha!
Ha ha...
Here. I whipped up a salad.
A salad? But...uh... thanks.
You OK? You look tired.
Wow. Very perceptive. I lose 50 pounds and the first thing you notice is that I look tired.
Bravo.
Haha!
Alright, boys, no fighting. Let's have a drink in the living room.
Uh... The salad... it should go in the fridge.
If possible.
Wine or beer?
I'll have wine.
Water.
oh...
Water? Are you kidding? How come?
Pascal! You got dirt all over the floor!
Shush! Got any Kleenex in your purse?

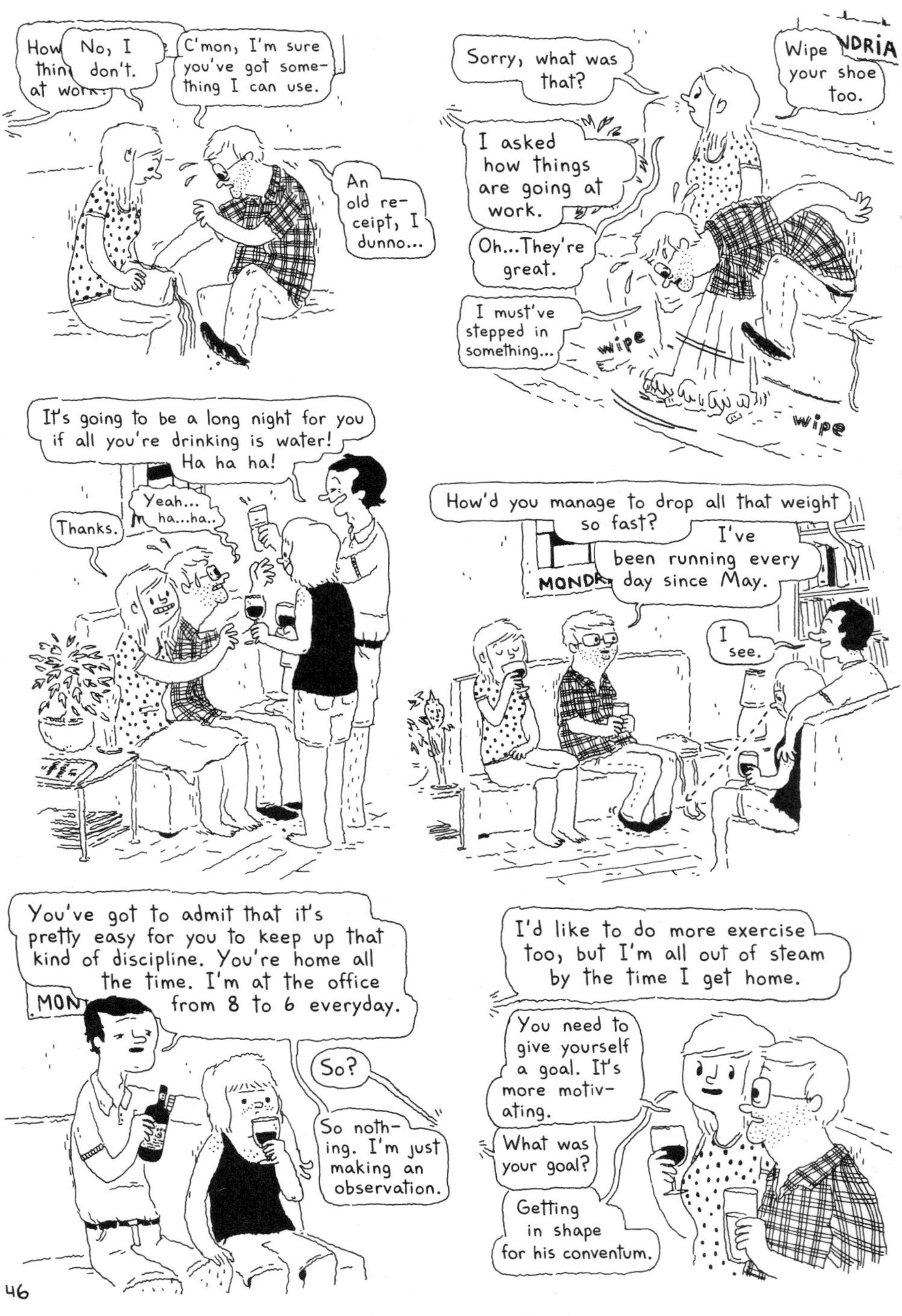

No, I don't.
C'mon, I'm sure you've got something I can use.
An old receipt, I dunno...
Sorry, what was that?
Wipe your shoe too.
I asked how things are going at work.
Oh...They're great.
I must've stepped in something...
wipe
wipe
It's going to be a long night for you if all you're drinking is water! Ha ha ha!
Yeah... ha...ha..
Thanks.
How'd you manage to drop all that weight so fast?
I've been running every day since May.
I see.
You've got to admit that it's pretty easy for you to keep up that kind of discipline. You're home all the time. I'm at the office from 8 to 6 everyday.
So?
So nothing. I'm just making an observation.
I'd like to do more exercise too, but I'm all out of steam by the time I get home.
You need to give yourself a goal. It's more motivating.
What was your goal?
Getting in shape for his conventum.

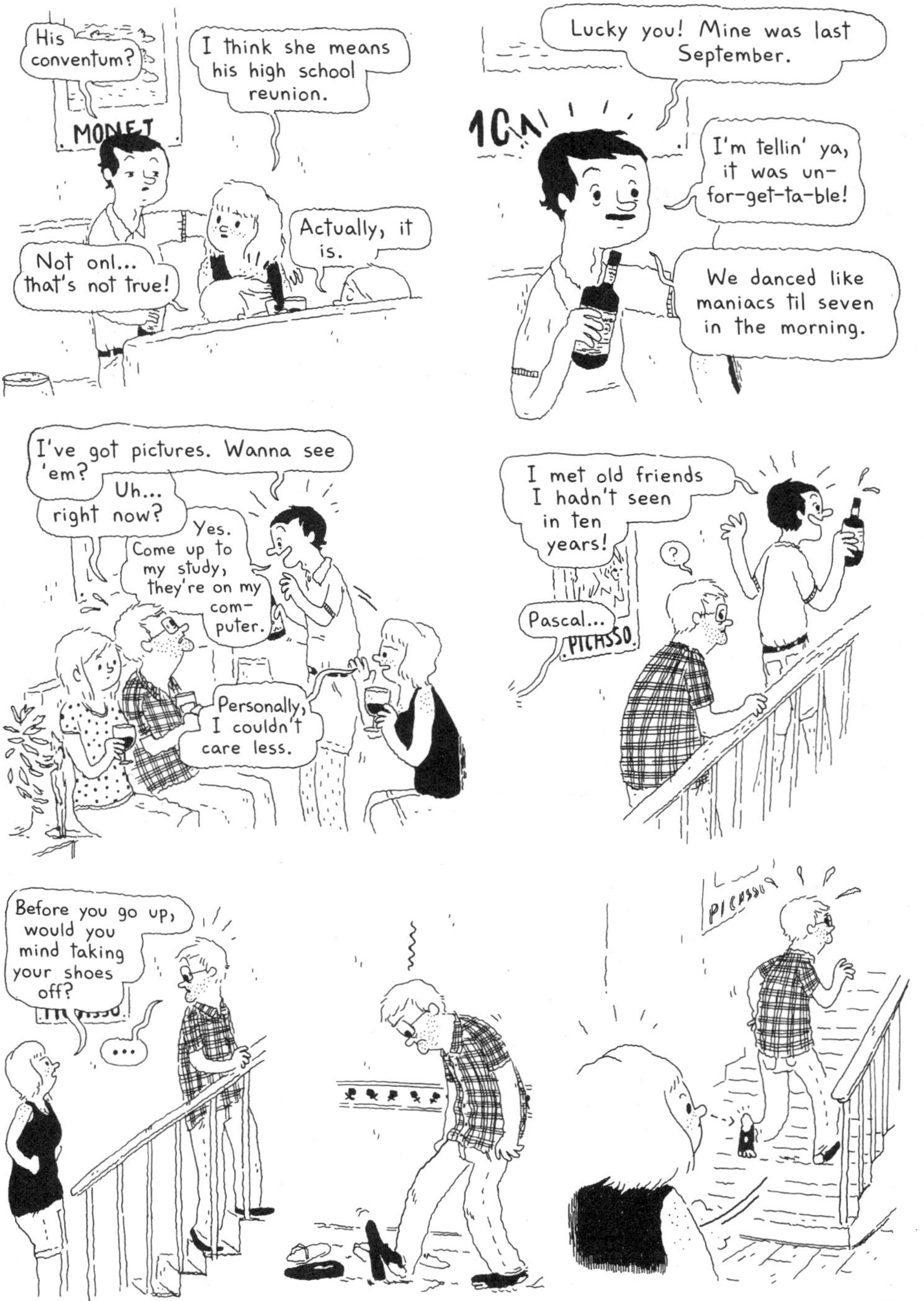

MONET
His conventum?
I think she means his high school reunion.
Not onl... that's not true!
Actually, it is.
Lucky you! Mine was last September.
I'm tellin' ya, it was un-for-get-ta-ble!
We danced like maniacs til seven in the morning.
I've got pictures. Wanna see 'em?
Uh... right now?
Yes. Come up to my study, they're on my com-puter.
Personally, I couldn't care less.
I met old friends I hadn't seen in ten years!
?
Pascal...
PICASSO
Before you go up, would you mind taking your shoes off?
...
PICASSO

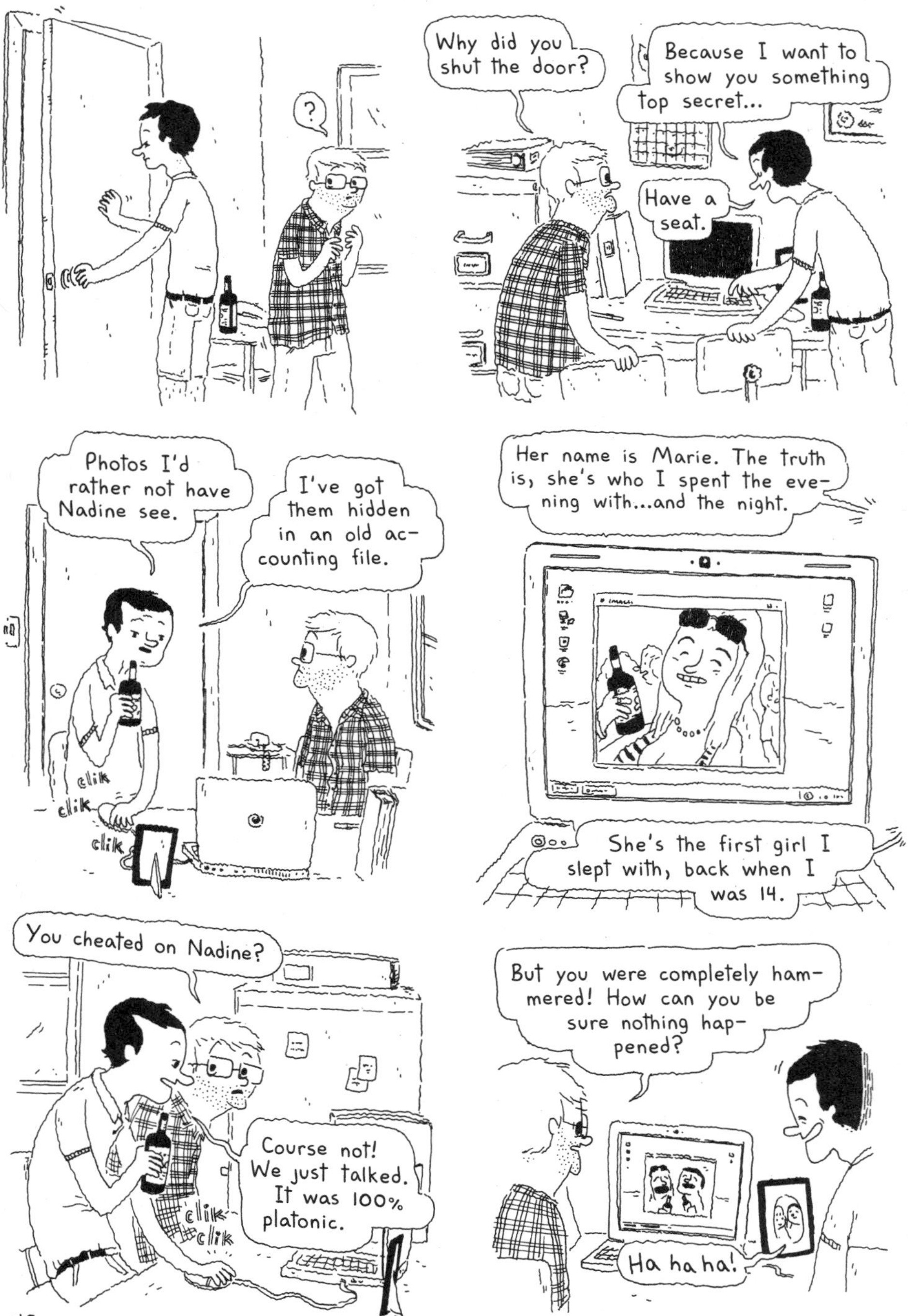
?
Why did you shut the door?
Because I want to show you something top secret...
Have a seat.
Photos I'd rather not have Nadine see.
I've got them hidden in an old accounting file.
clik
clik
clik
Her name is Marie. The truth is, she's who I spent the evening with...and the night.
She's the first girl I slept with, back when I was 14.
You cheated on Nadine?
Course not! We just talked. It was 100% platonic.
clik
clik
But you were completely hammered! How can you be sure nothing happened?
Ha ha ha!

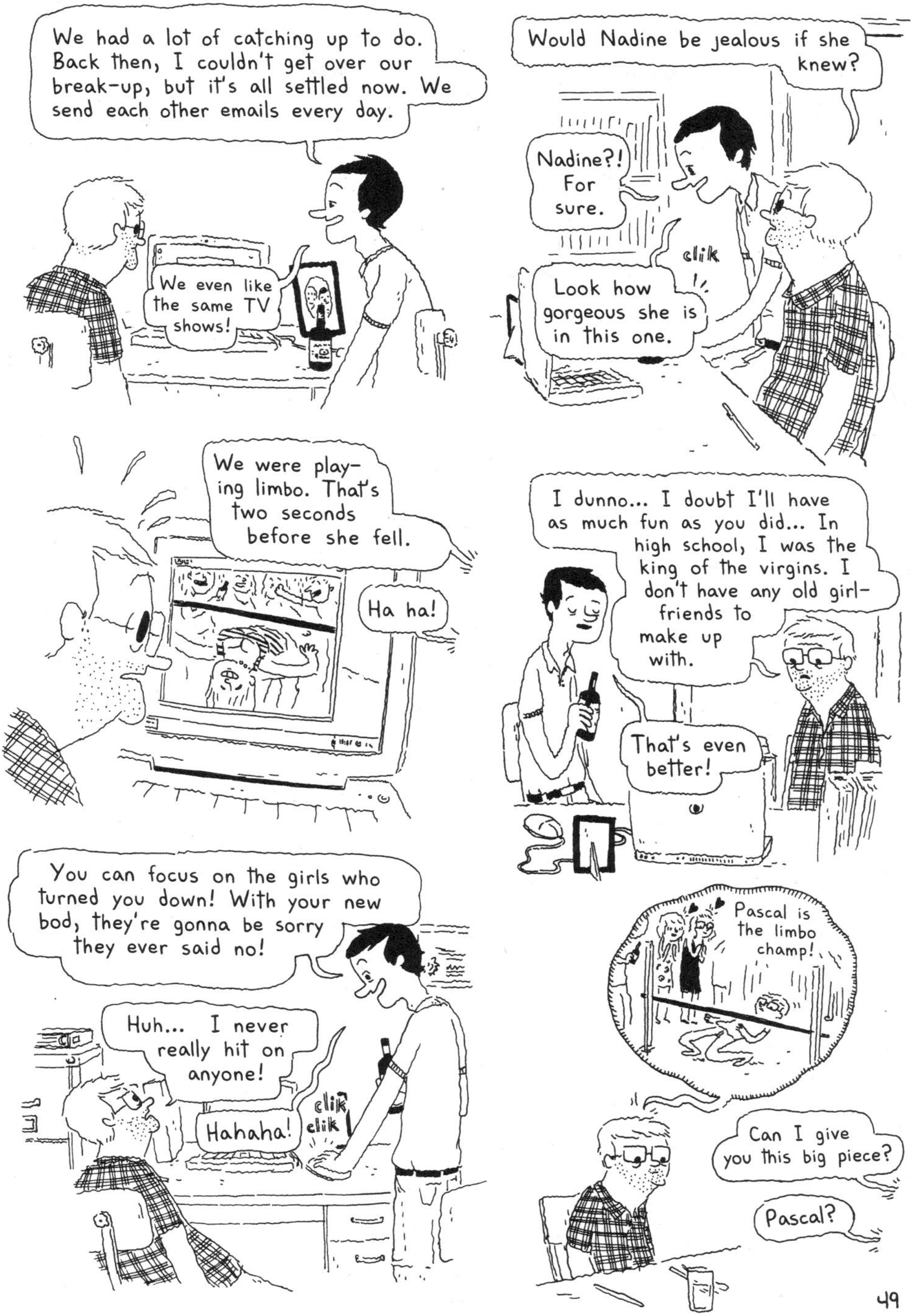

We had a lot of catching up to do. Back then, I couldn't get over our break-up, but it's all settled now. We send each other emails every day.
We even like the same TV shows!
Would Nadine be jealous if she knew?
Nadine?! For sure.
clik
Look how gorgeous she is in this one.
We were playing limbo. That's two seconds before she fell.
Ha ha!
I dunno... I doubt I'll have as much fun as you did... In high school, I was the king of the virgins. I don't have any old girlfriends to make up with.
That's even better!
You can focus on the girls who turned you down! With your new bod, they're gonna be sorry they ever said no!
Huh... I never really hit on anyone!
Hahaha!
clik
clik
Pascal is the limbo champ!
Can I give you this big piece?
Pascal?

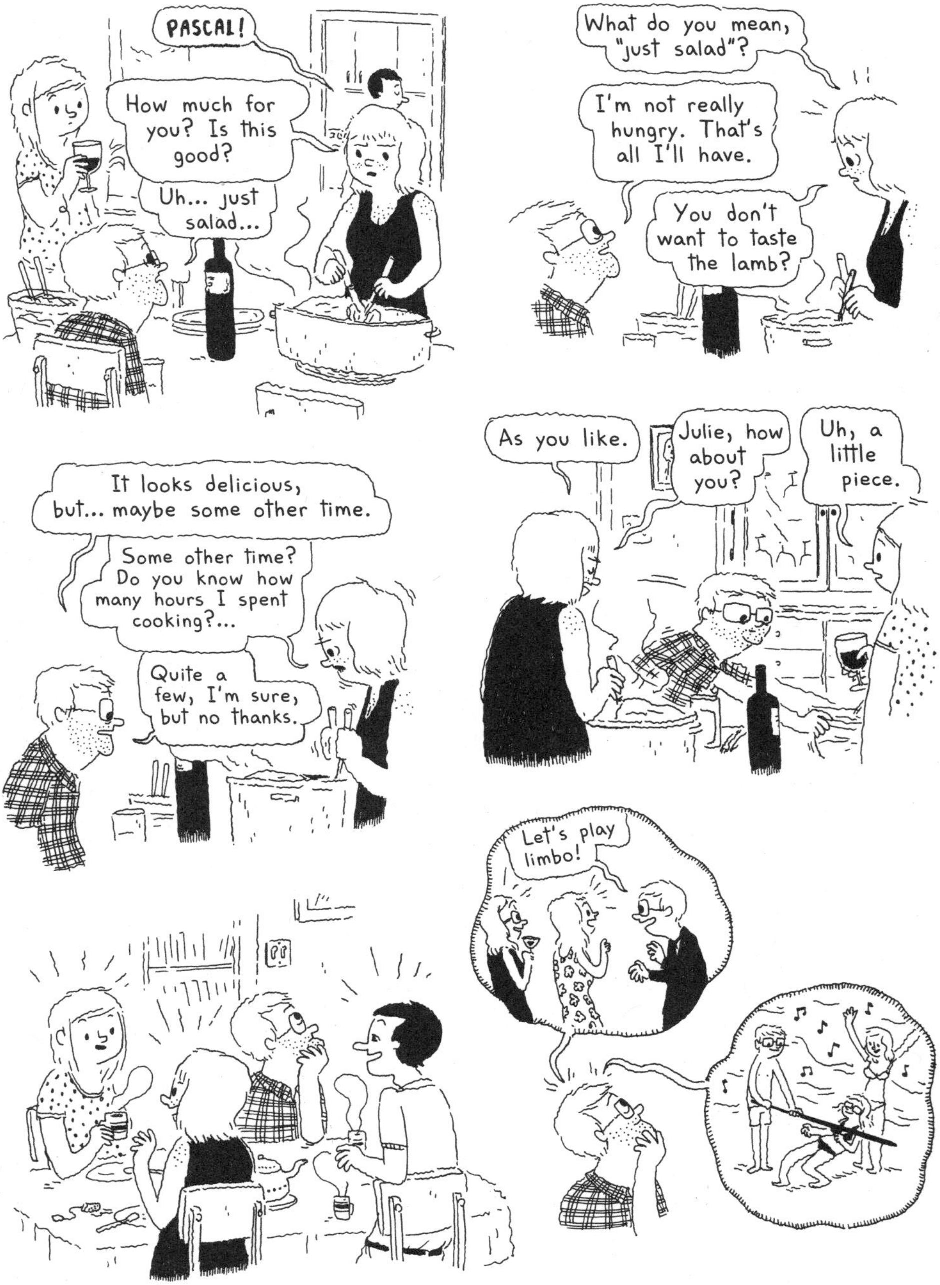
PASCAL!
How much for you? Is this good?
Uh... just salad...
What do you mean, "just salad"?
I'm not really hungry. That's all I'll have.
You don't want to taste the lamb?
It looks delicious, but... maybe some other time.
Some other time? Do you know how many hours I spent cooking?...
Quite a few, I'm sure, but no thanks.
As you like.
Julie, how about you?
Uh, a little piece.
Let's play limbo!

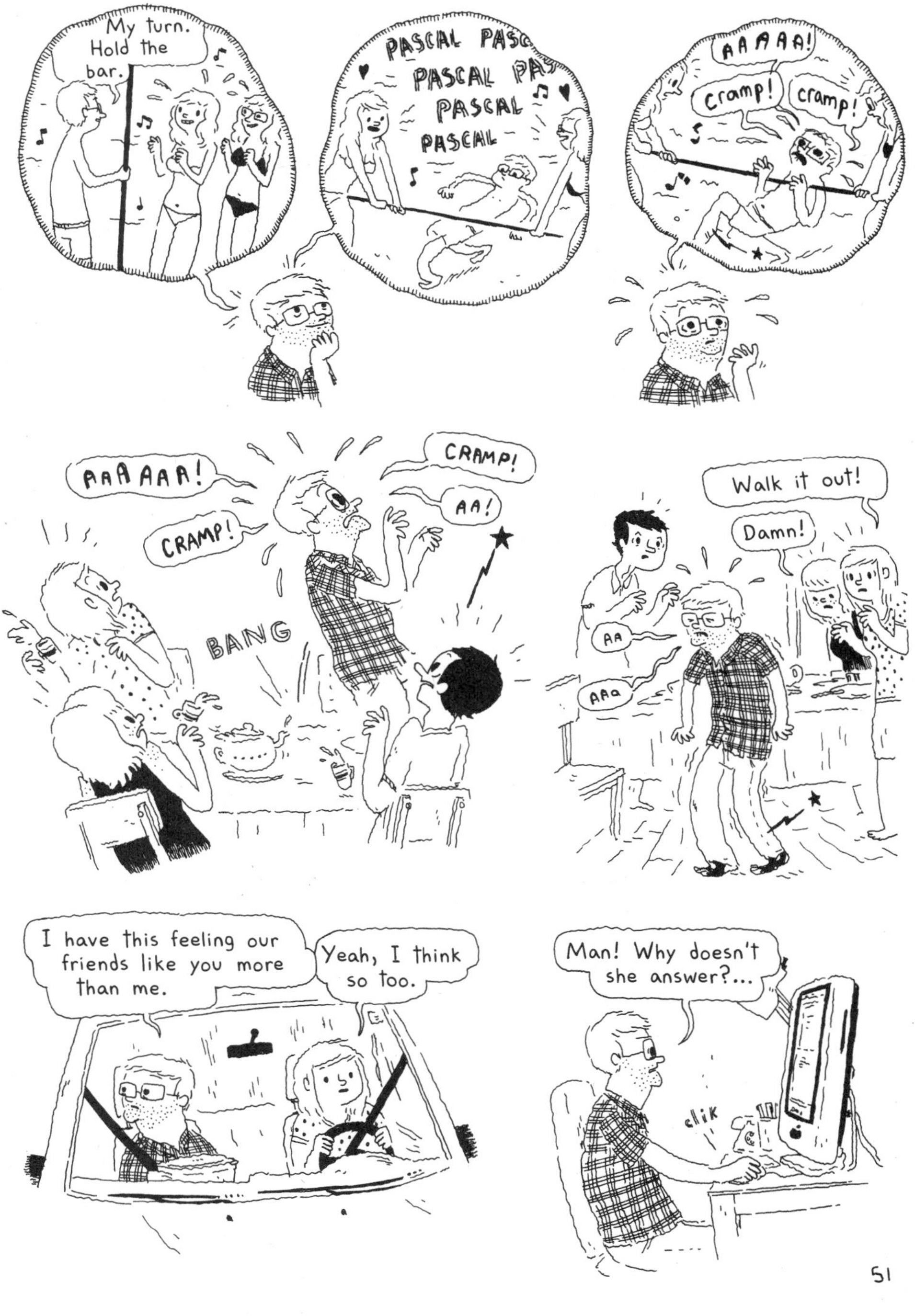
My turn. Hold the bar.
PASCAL PASC
PASCAL PAS
PASCAL
PASCAL
AAAAA!
Cramp!
cramp!
AAAAAA!
CRAMP!
CRAMP!
AA!
BANG
Walk it out!
Damn!
AA
AAa
I have this feeling our friends like you more than me.
Yeah, I think so too.
Man! Why doesn't she answer?...
clik

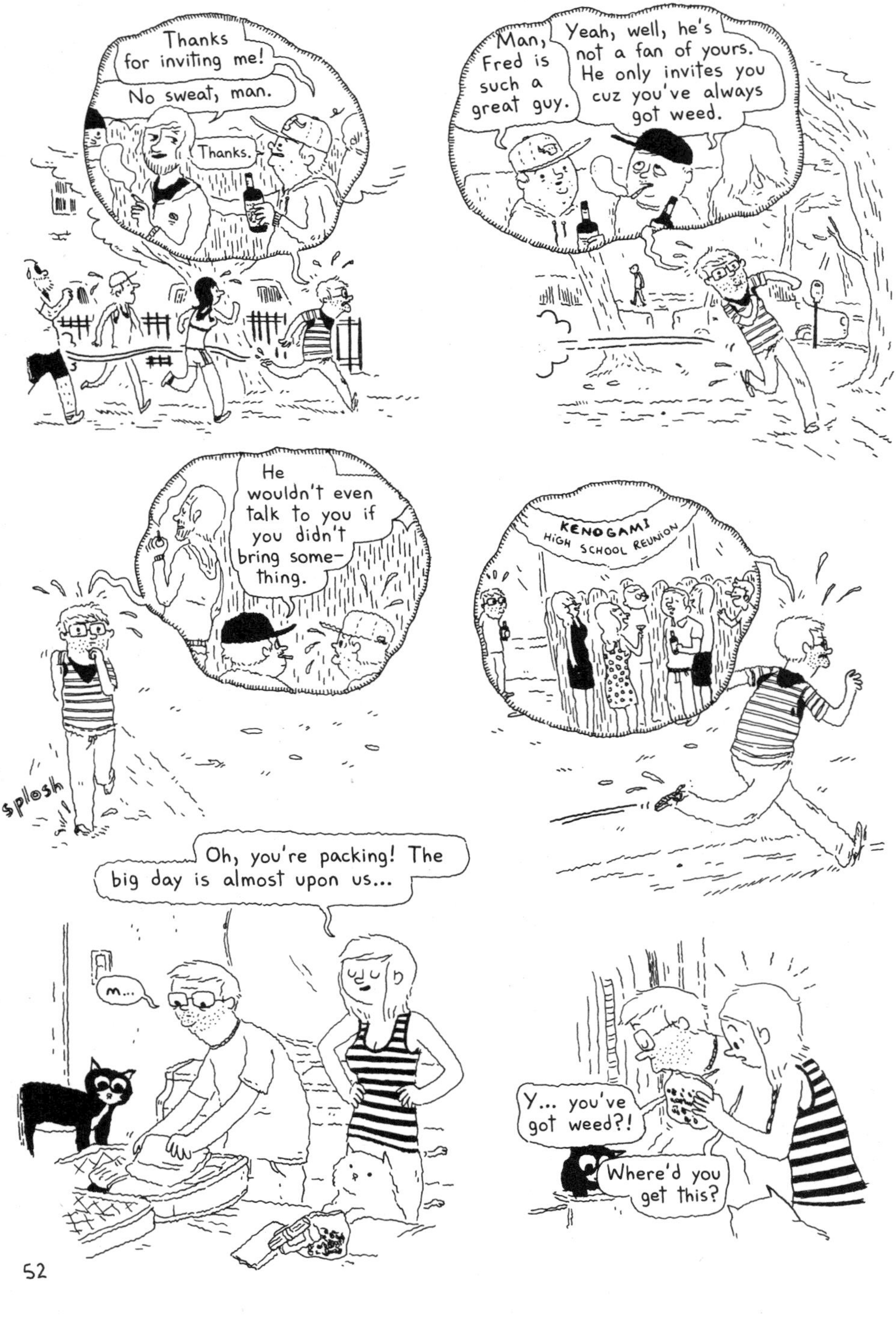
Thanks for inviting me!
No sweat, man.
Thanks.
Man, Fred is such a great guy.
Yeah, well, he's not a fan of yours. He only invites you cuz you've always got weed.
He wouldn't even talk to you if you didn't bring some-thing.
splosh
KENOGAMI HIGH SCHOOL REUNION
Oh, you're packing! The big day is almost upon us...
m...
Y... you've got weed?!
Where'd you get this?

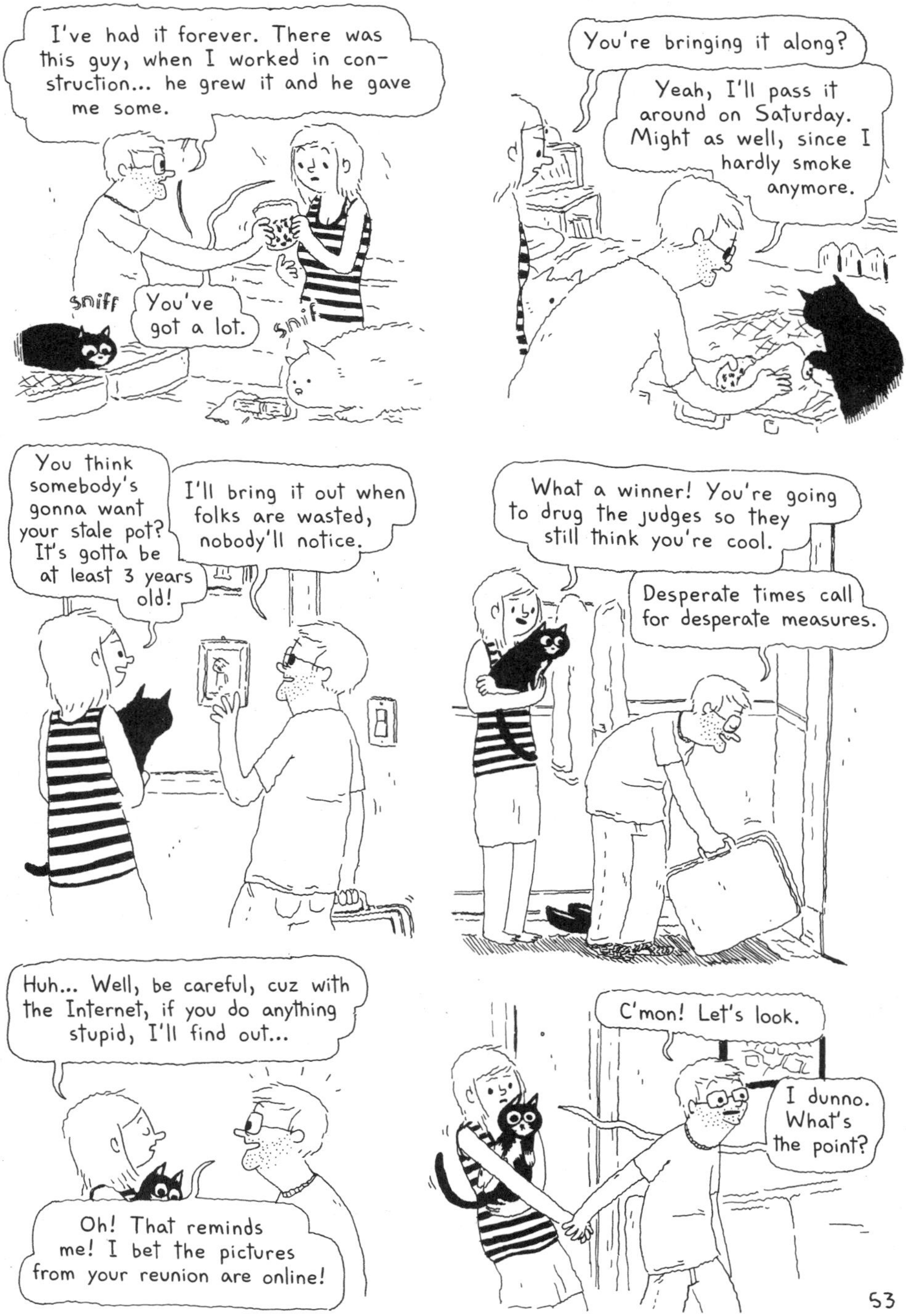
I've had it forever. There was this guy, when I worked in construction... he grew it and he gave me some.
sniff
You've got a lot.
snif
You're bringing it along?
Yeah, I'll pass it around on Saturday. Might as well, since I hardly smoke anymore.
You think somebody's gonna want your stale pot? It's gotta be at least 3 years old!
I'll bring it out when folks are wasted, nobody'll notice.
What a winner! You're going to drug the judges so they still think you're cool.
Desperate times call for desperate measures.
Huh... Well, be careful, cuz with the Internet, if you do anything stupid, I'll find out...
Oh! That reminds me! I bet the pictures from your reunion are online!
C'mon! Let's look.
I dunno. What's the point?

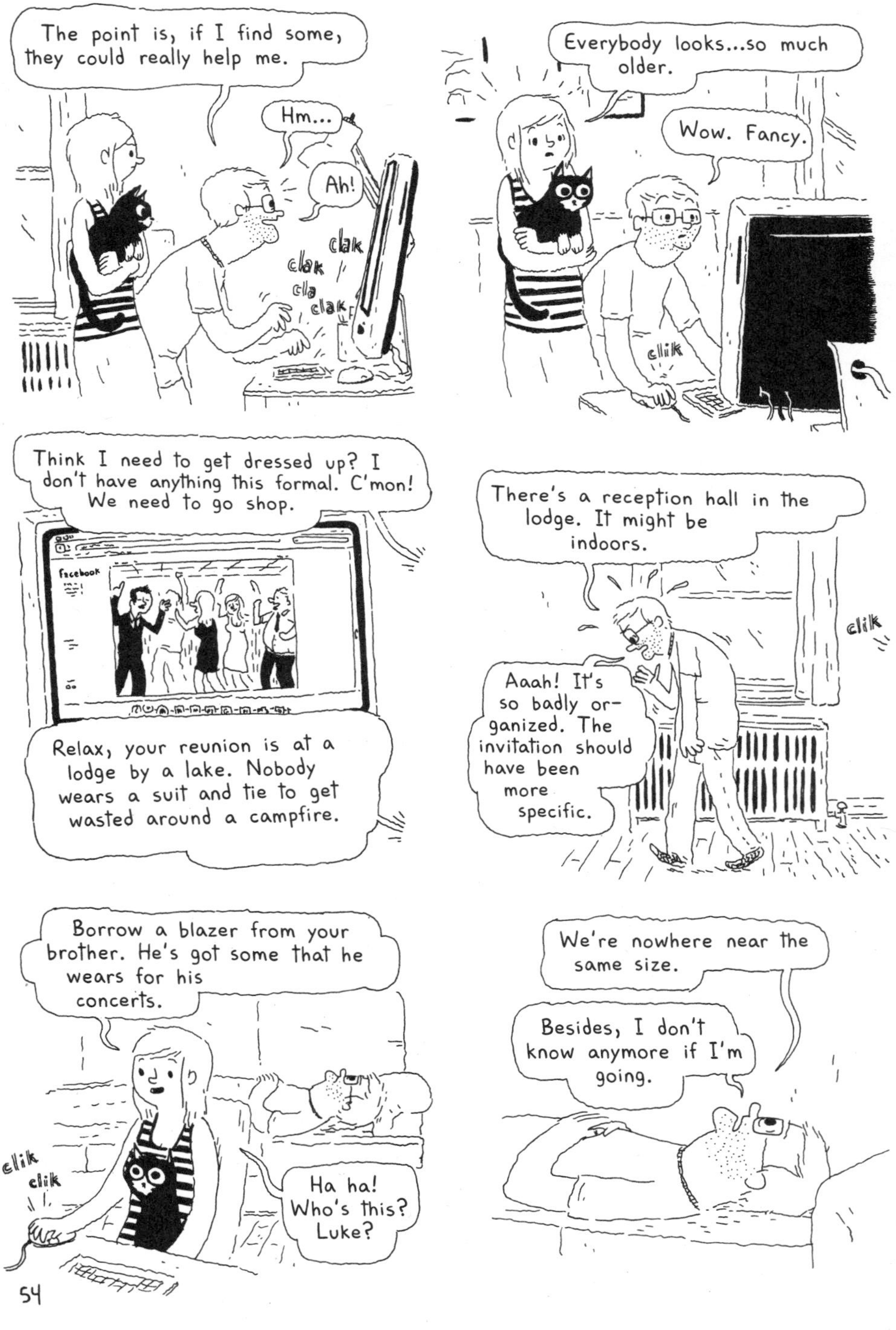
The point is, if I find some, they could really help me.
Hm...
Ah!
clak
clak
cla
clak
Everybody looks...so much older.
Wow. Fancy.
clik
Think I need to get dressed up? I don't have anything this formal. C'mon! We need to go shop.
facebook
Relax, your reunion is at a lodge by a lake. Nobody wears a suit and tie to get wasted around a campfire.
There's a reception hall in the lodge. It might be indoors.
clik
Aaah! It's so badly organized. The invitation should have been more specific.
Borrow a blazer from your brother. He's got some that he wears for his concerts.
clik
clik
Ha ha! Who's this? Luke?
We're nowhere near the same size.
Besides, I don't know anymore if I'm going.

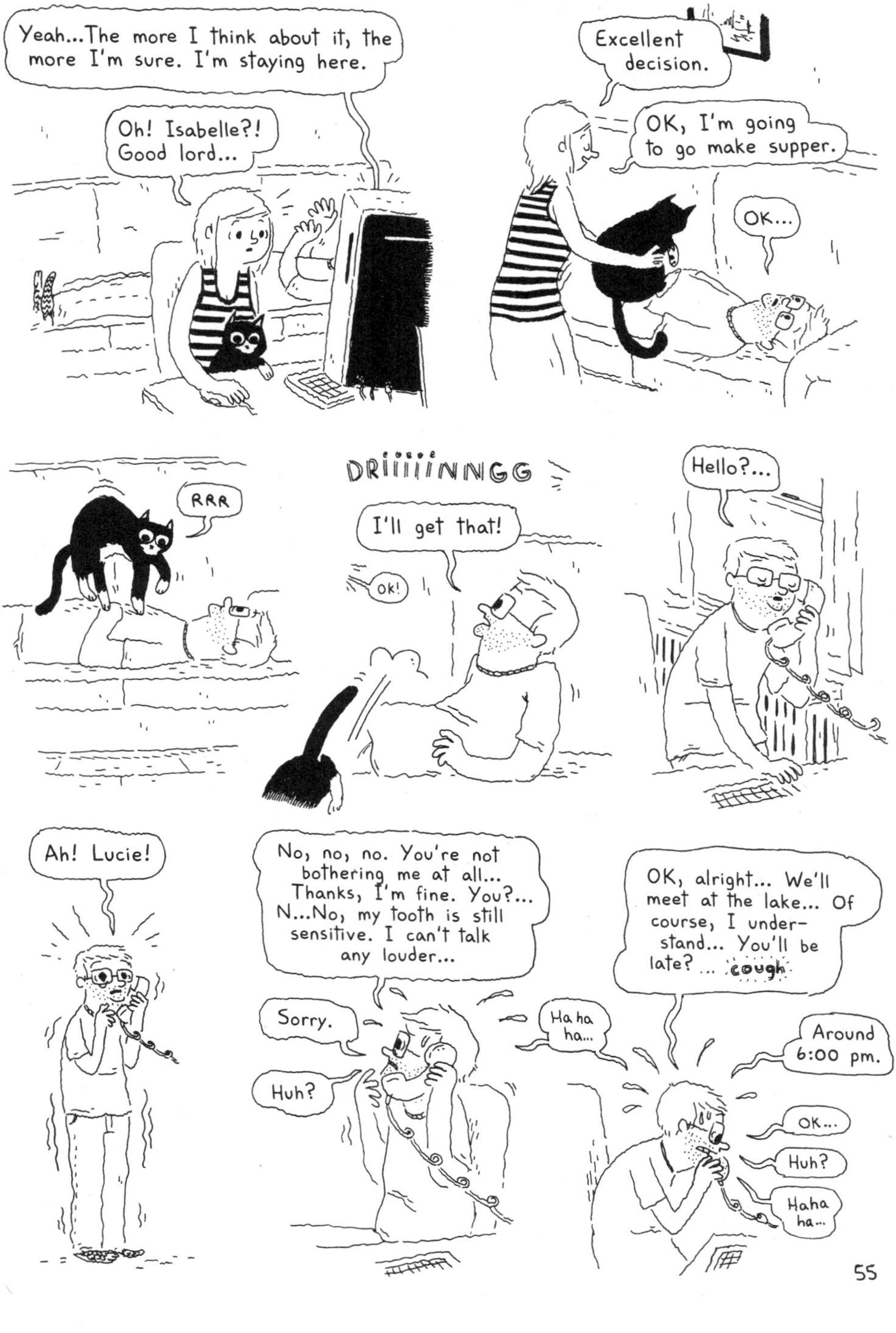
Yeah...The more I think about it, the more I'm sure. I'm staying here.
Oh! Isabelle?! Good lord...
Excellent decision.
OK, I'm going to go make supper.
OK...
RRR
DRiiiiiNNGG
I'll get that!
Ok!
Hello?...
Ah! Lucie!
No, no, no. You're not bothering me at all... Thanks, I'm fine. You?... N...No, my tooth is still sensitive. I can't talk any louder...
Sorry.
Huh?
Ha ha ha...
OK, alright... We'll meet at the lake... Of course, I under-stand... You'll be late? ... cough
Around 6:00 pm.
OK...
Huh?
Haha ha...

Uh...I...I think
I'll regret it if I don't go
Aah!
Z
Z
THUNK
?
BANG
CLIK
CLAK
CLICK
CLIK
BANG
CLIK
CLAK
Mmf...
BANG
CLAK

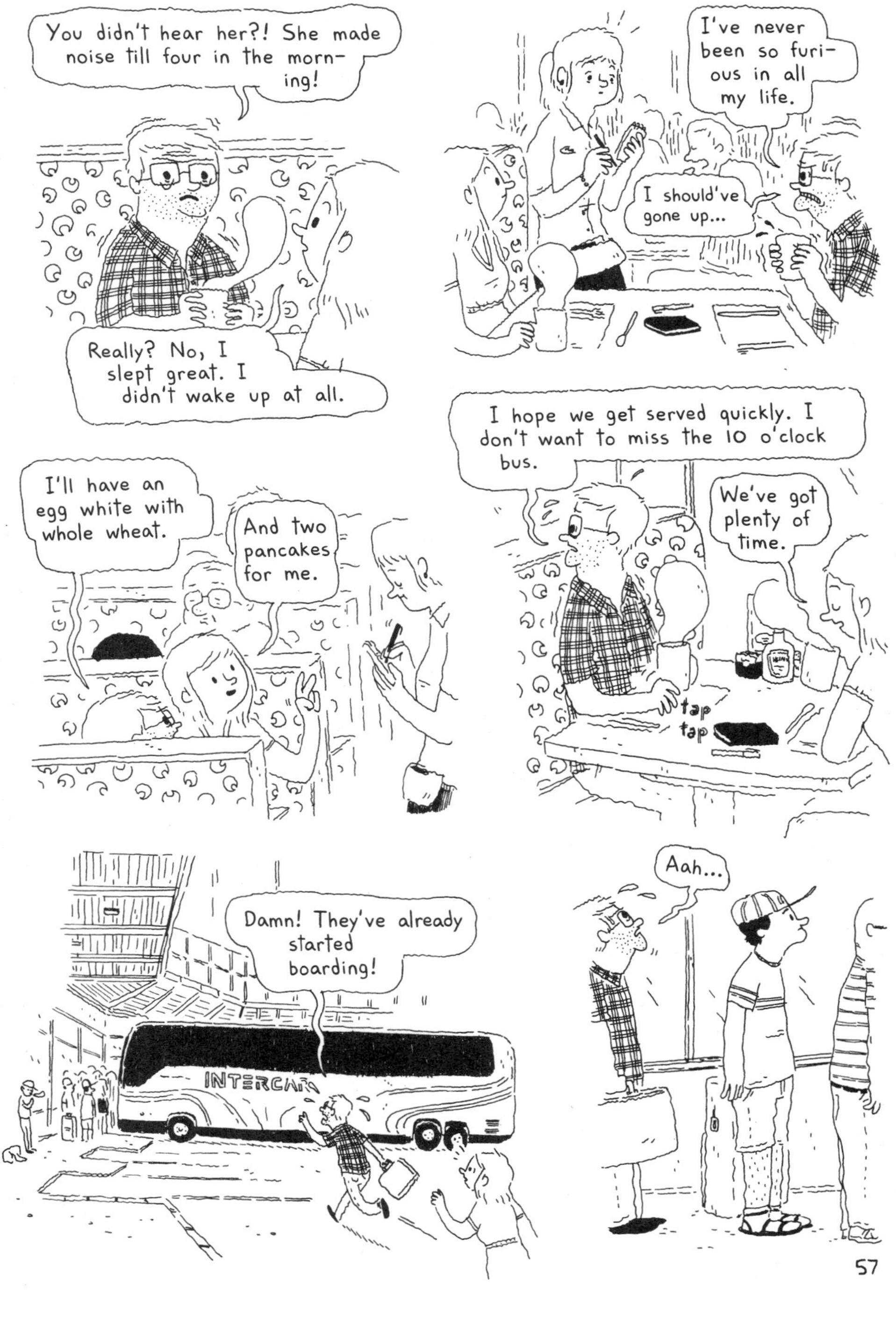
You didn't hear her?! She made noise till four in the morn-ing!
Really? No, I slept great. I didn't wake up at all.
I've never been so furi-ous in all my life.
I should've gone up...
I'll have an egg white with whole wheat.
And two pancakes for me.
I hope we get served quickly. I don't want to miss the 10 o'clock bus.
We've got plenty of time.
tap tap
Damn! They've already started boarding!
INTERCAR
Aah...

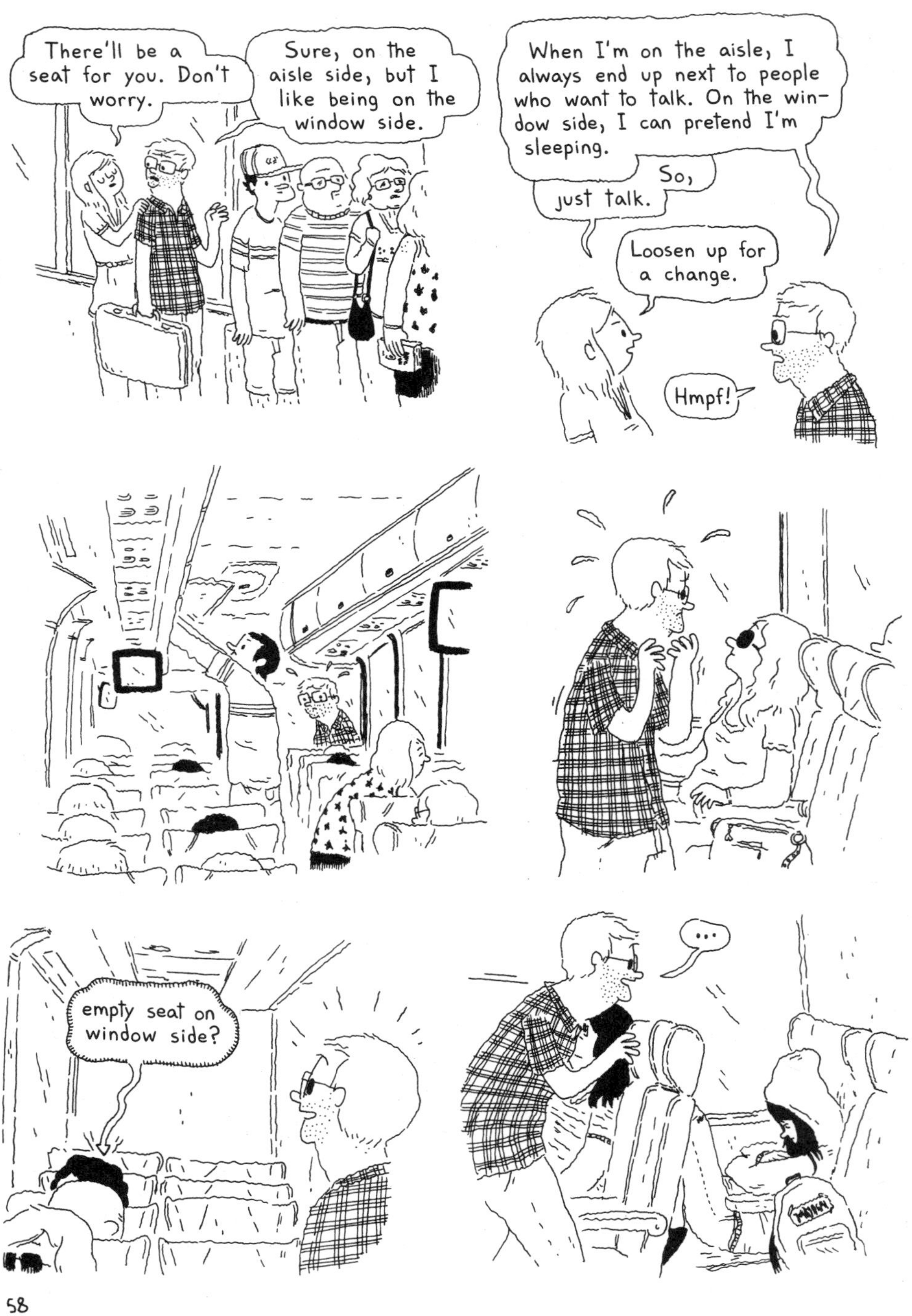
There'll be a seat for you. Don't worry.
Sure, on the aisle side, but I like being on the window side.
When I'm on the aisle, I always end up next to people who want to talk. On the window side, I can pretend I'm sleeping.
So, just talk.
Loosen up for a change.
Hmpf!
empty seat on window side?
...

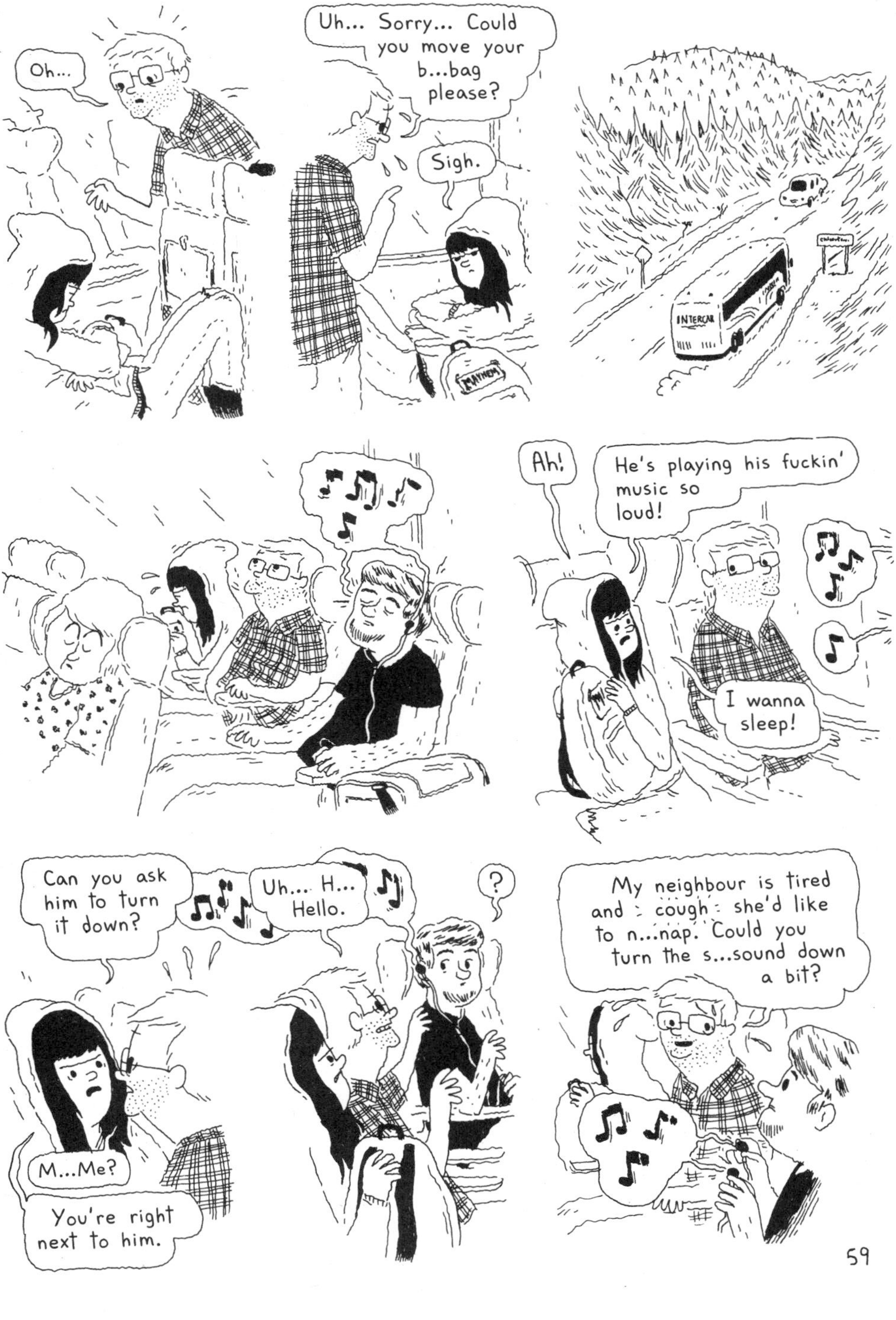
Oh...
Uh... Sorry... Could you move your b...bag please?
Sigh.
Ah!
He's playing his fuckin' music so loud!
I wanna sleep!
Can you ask him to turn it down?
M...Me?
You're right next to him.
Uh... H... Hello.
?
My neighbour is tired and cough she'd like to n...nap. Could you turn the s...sound down a bit?

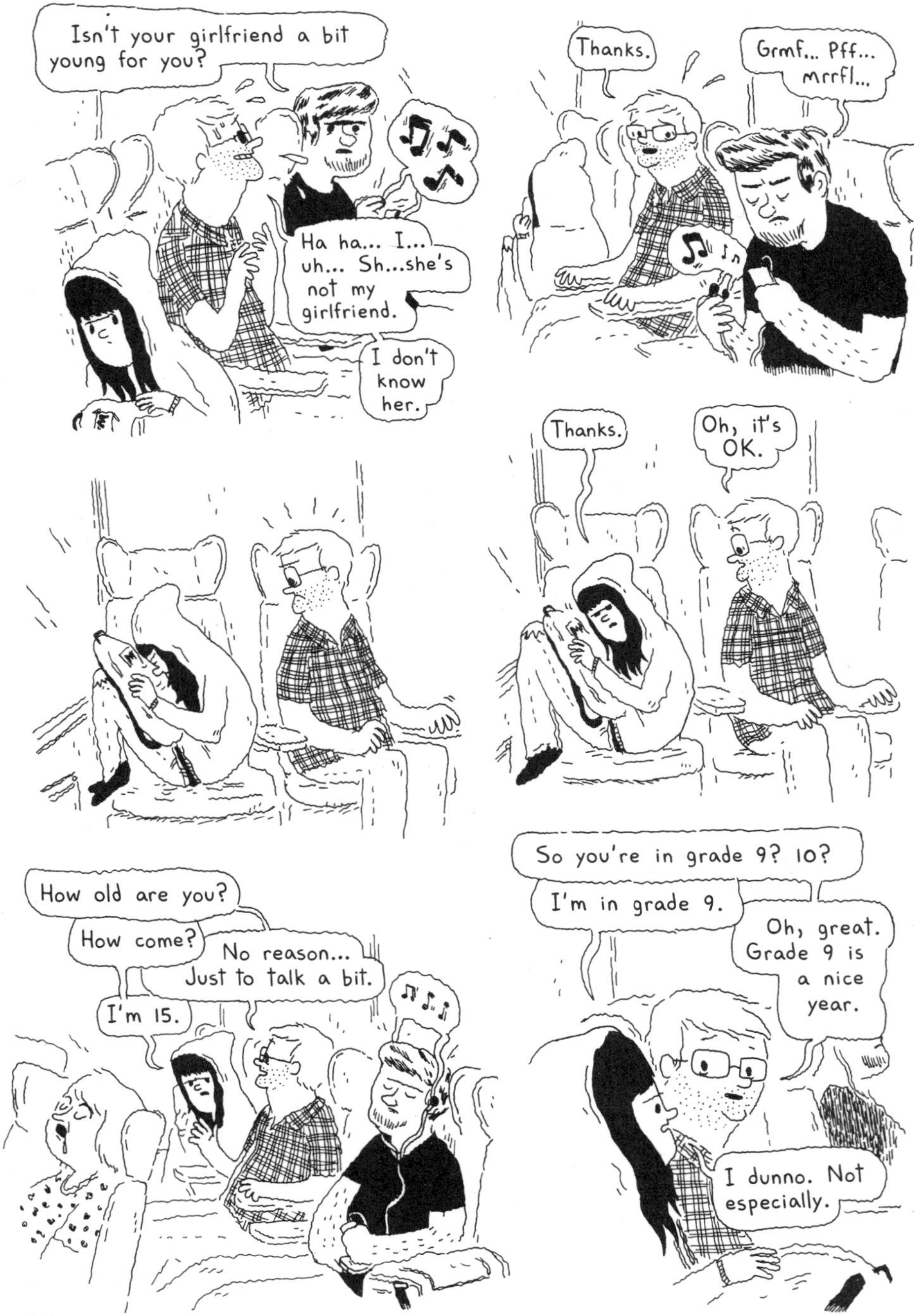
Isn't your girlfriend a bit young for you?
Ha ha... I... uh... Sh...she's not my girlfriend.
I don't know her.
Thanks.
Grmf... Pff... mrrfl...
Thanks.
Oh, it's OK.
How old are you?
How come?
No reason... Just to talk a bit.
I'm 15.
So you're in grade 9? 10?
I'm in grade 9.
Oh, great. Grade 9 is a nice year.
I dunno. Not especially.

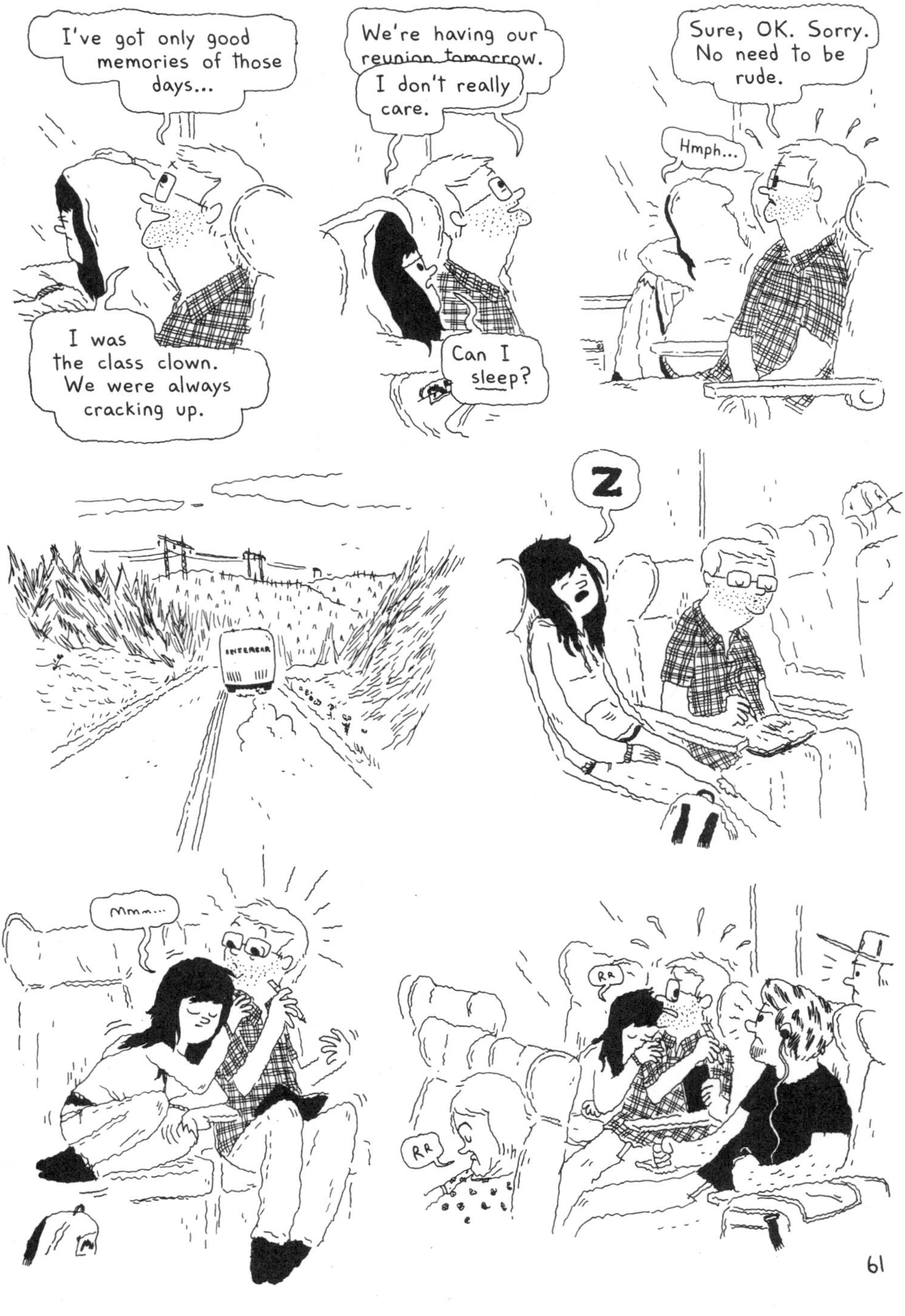
I've got only good memories of those days...
I was the class clown. We were always cracking up.
We're having our reunion tomorrow.
I don't really care.
Can I sleep?
Sure, OK. Sorry. No need to be rude.
Hmph...
Z
Mmm...
RR
RR

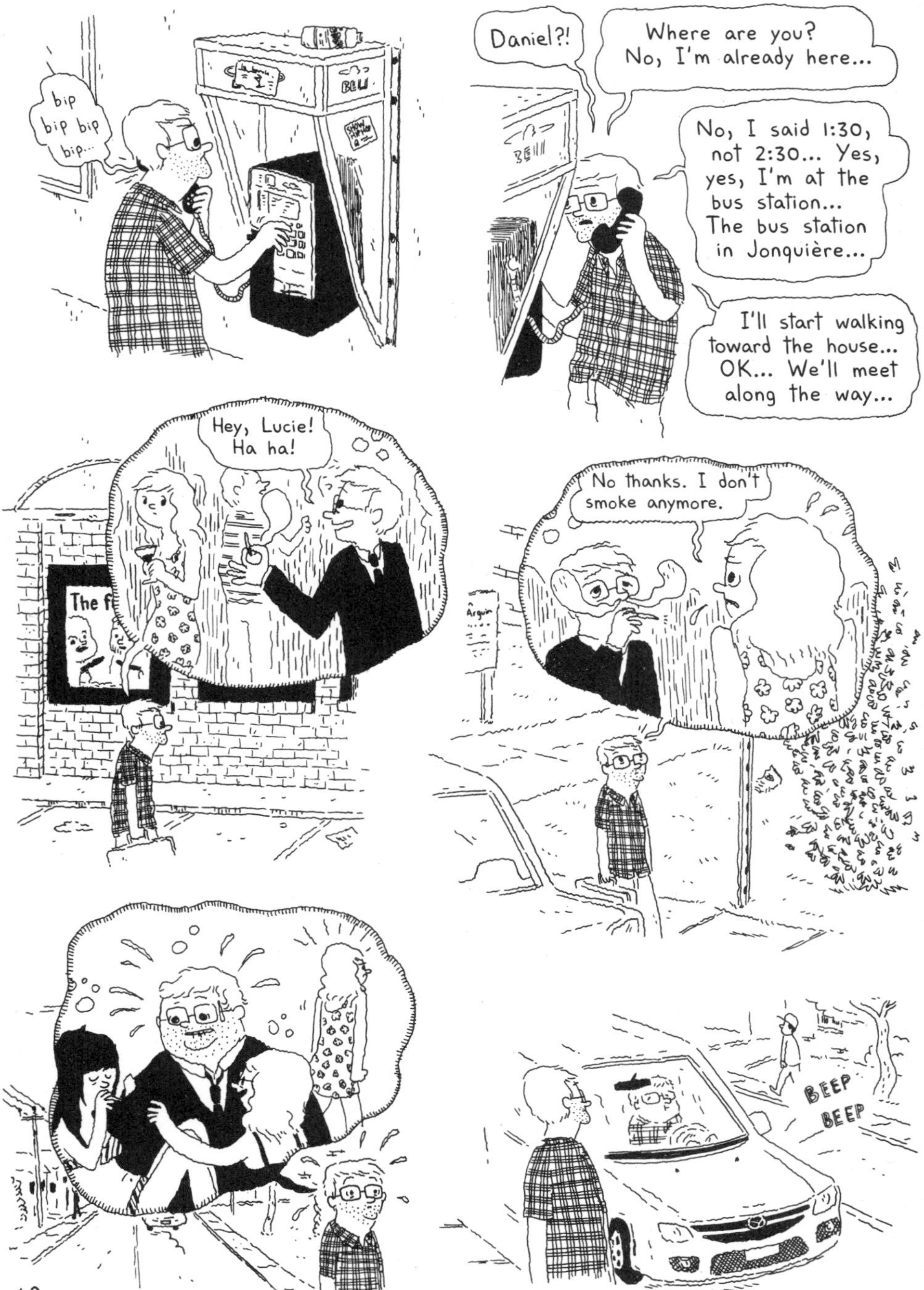

bip bip bip bip...
Daniel?!
Where are you? No, I'm already here...
No, I said 1:30, not 2:30... Yes, yes, I'm at the bus station... The bus station in Jonquière...
I'll start walking toward the house... OK... We'll meet along the way...
Hey, Lucie! Ha ha!
No thanks. I don't smoke anymore.
BEEP BEEP

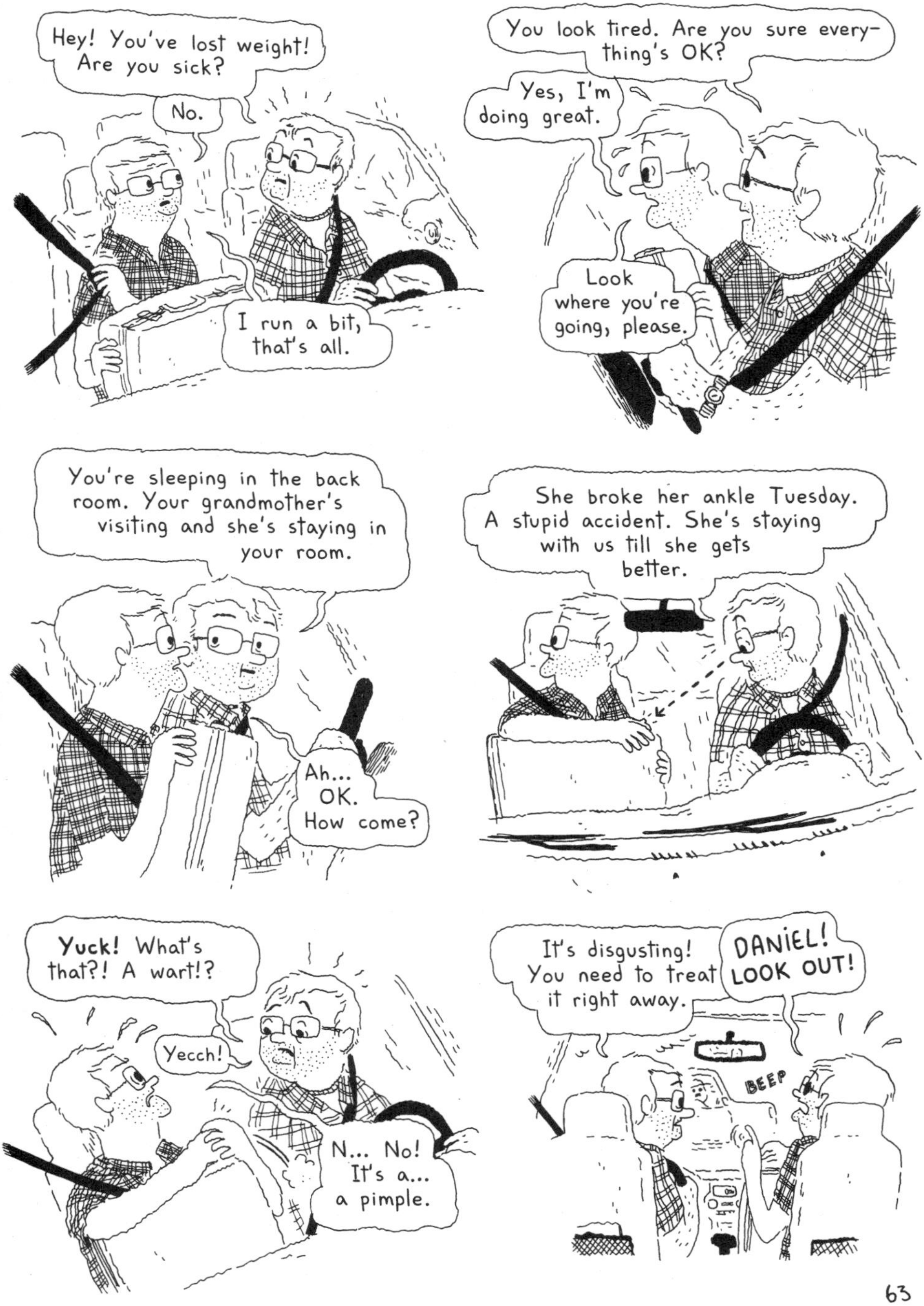
Hey! You've lost weight! Are you sick?
No.
I run a bit, that's all.
You look tired. Are you sure every-thing's OK?
Yes, I'm doing great.
Look where you're going, please.
You're sleeping in the back room. Your grandmother's visiting and she's staying in your room.
Ah... OK. How come?
She broke her ankle Tuesday. A stupid accident. She's staying with us till she gets better.
Yuck! What's that?! A wart!?
Yecch!
N... No! It's a... a pimple.
It's disgusting! You need to treat it right away.
DANIEL! LOOK OUT!
BEEP

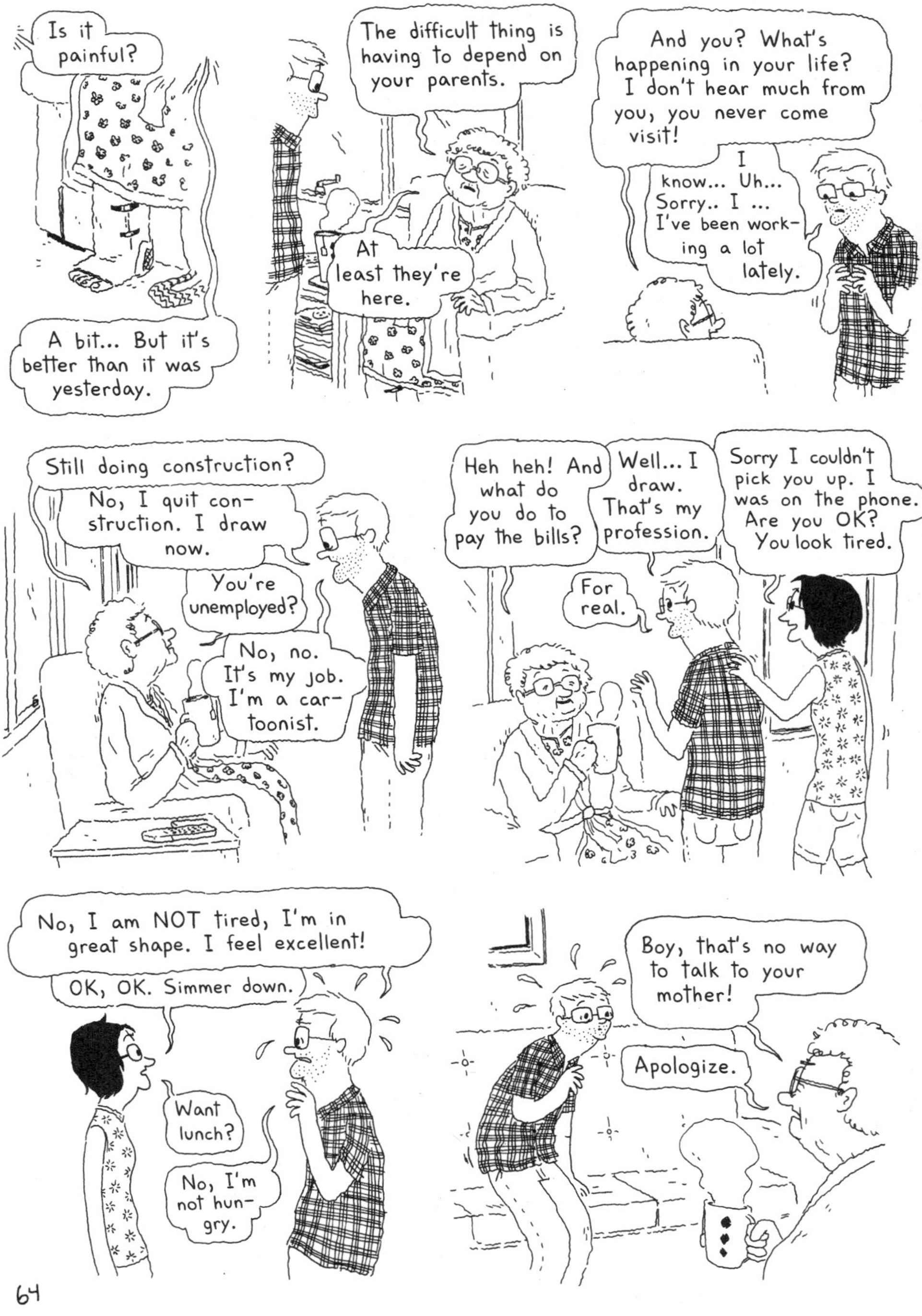
Is it painful?
A bit... But it's better than it was yesterday.
The difficult thing is having to depend on your parents.
At least they're here.
And you? What's happening in your life? I don't hear much from you, you never come visit!
I know... Uh... Sorry.. I ... I've been working a lot lately.
Still doing construction?
No, I quit construction. I draw now.
You're unemployed?
No, no. It's my job. I'm a cartoonist.
Heh heh! And what do you do to pay the bills?
Well... I draw. That's my profession.
For real.
Sorry I couldn't pick you up. I was on the phone. Are you OK? You look tired.
No, I am NOT tired, I'm in great shape. I feel excellent!
OK, OK. Simmer down.
Want lunch?
No, I'm not hungry.
Boy, that's no way to talk to your mother!
Apologize.

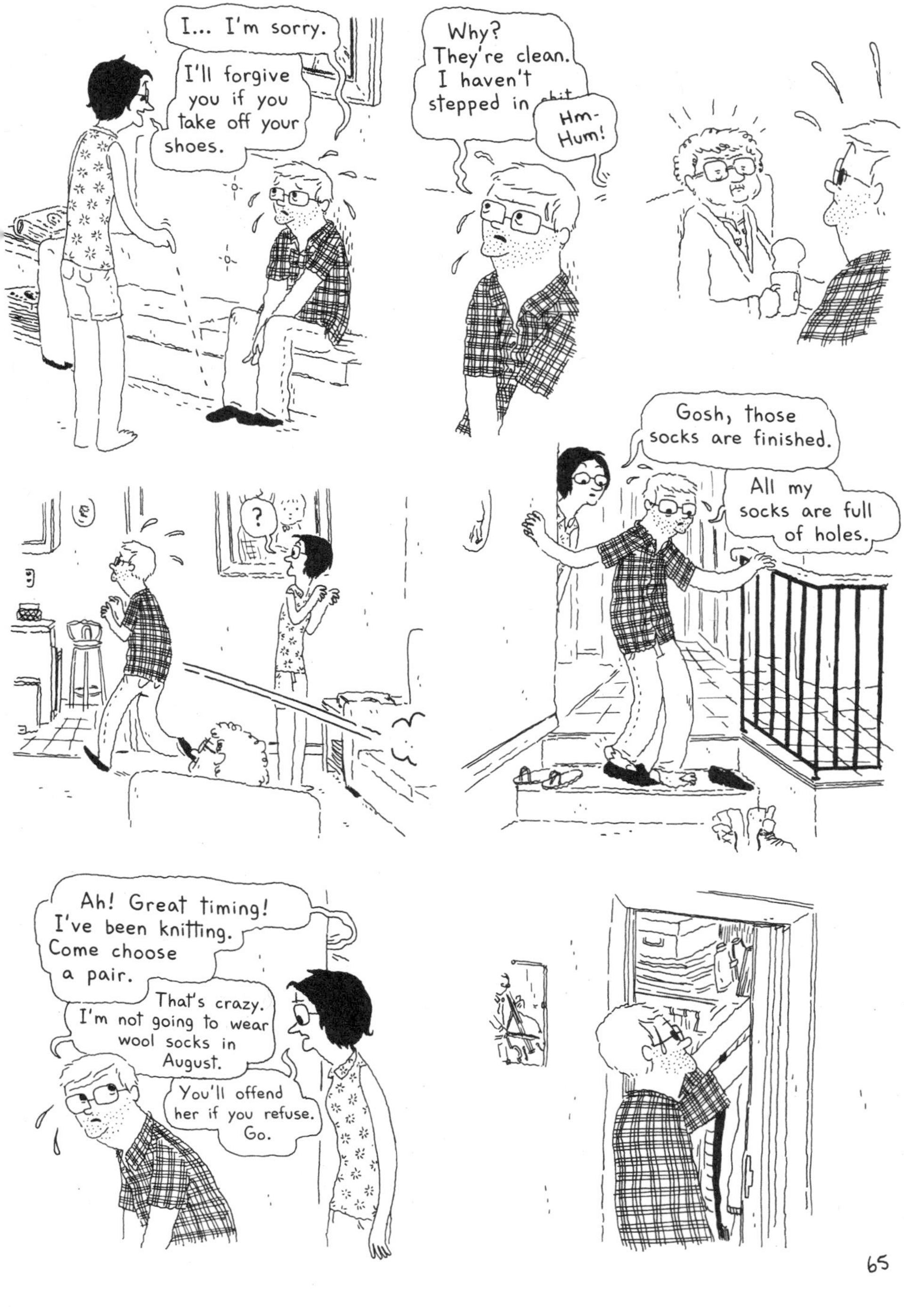
I... I'm sorry.
I'll forgive you if you take off your shoes.
Why? They're clean. I haven't stepped in
Hm-Hum!
?
Gosh, those socks are finished.
All my socks are full of holes.
Ah! Great timing! I've been knitting. Come choose a pair.
That's crazy. I'm not going to wear wool socks in August.
You'll offend her if you refuse. Go.

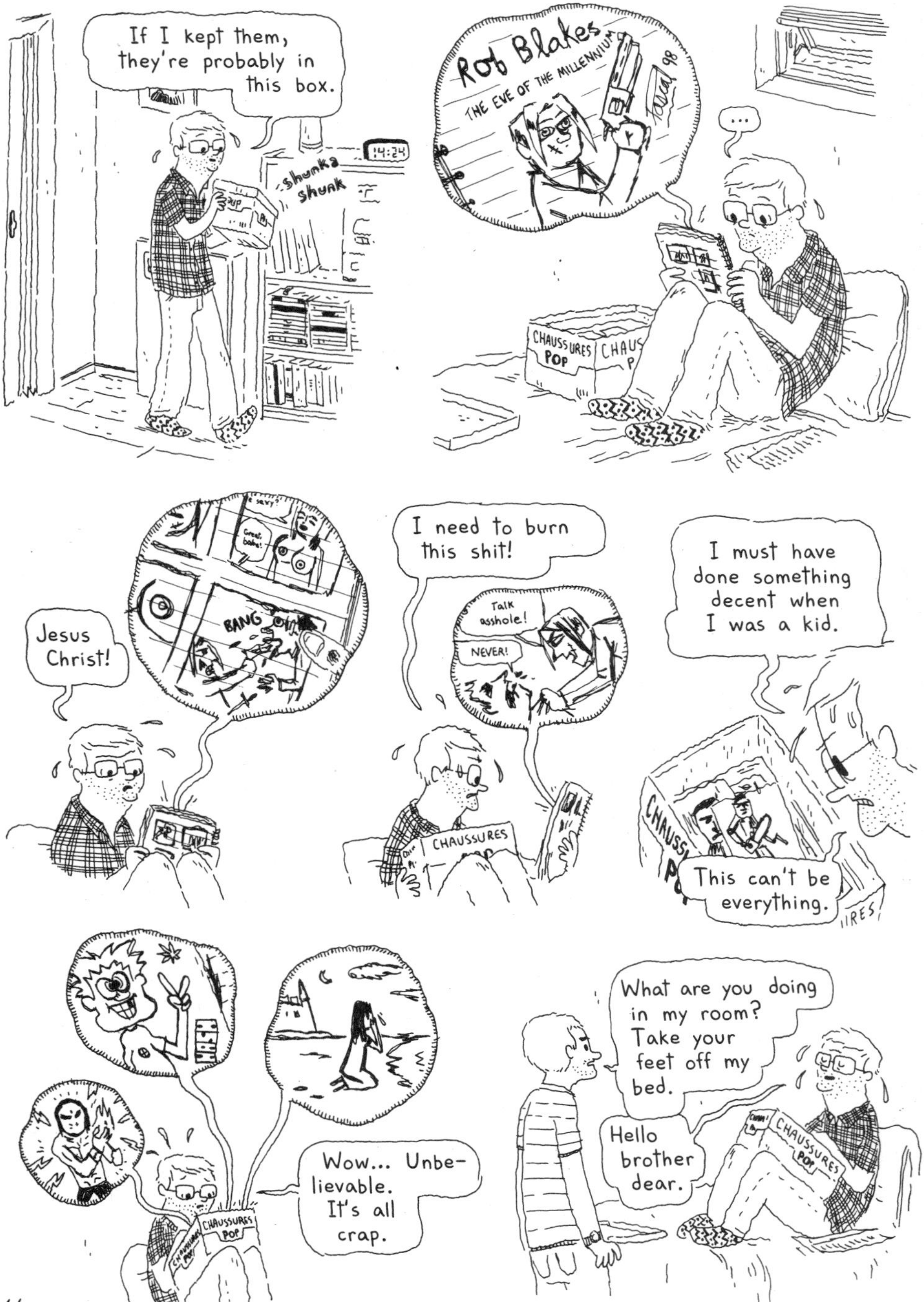

If I kept them, they're probably in this box.
14:24
shunka shunk
Rob Blakes
THE EVE OF THE MILLENNIUM
98
...
CHAUSSURES POP
Jesus Christ!
Great, babe!
BANG
I need to burn this shit!
Talk asshole!
NEVER!
CHAUSSURES
I must have done something decent when I was a kid.
This can't be everything.
Wow... Unbe-lievable. It's all crap.
CHAUSSURES POP
What are you doing in my room? Take your feet off my bed.
Hello brother dear.
CHAUSSURES POP

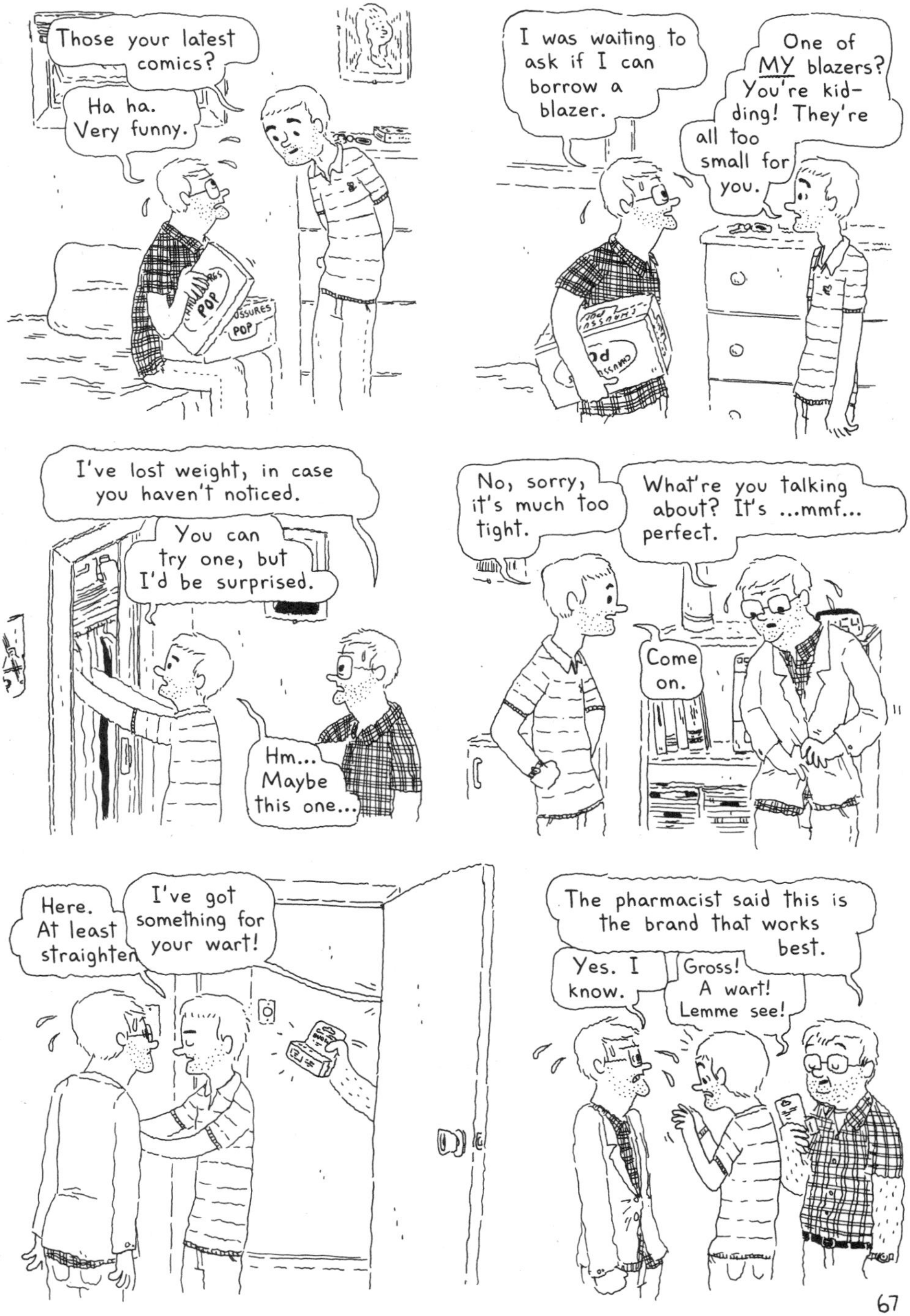
Those your latest comics?
Ha ha. Very funny.
CHAUSSURES POP
CHAUSSURES POP
I was waiting to ask if I can borrow a blazer.
One of MY blazers? You're kidding! They're all too small for you.
I've lost weight, in case you haven't noticed.
You can try one, but I'd be surprised.
Hm... Maybe this one...
No, sorry, it's much too tight.
What're you talking about? It's ...mmf... perfect.
Come on.
Here. At least straighten
I've got something for your wart!
The pharmacist said this is the brand that works best.
Yes. I know.
Gross! A wart! Lemme see!

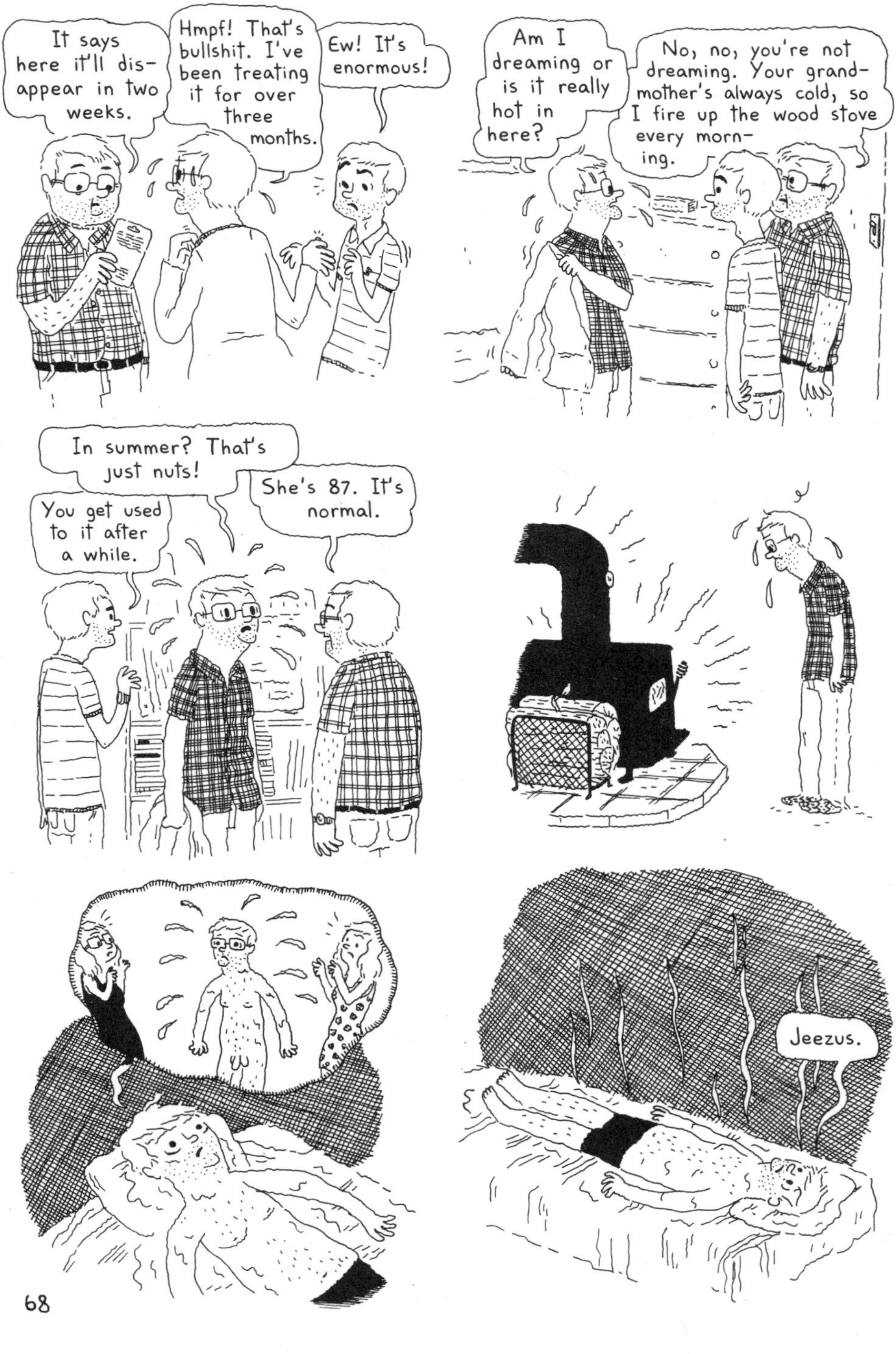

It says here it'll dis-appear in two weeks.
Hmpf! That's bullshit. I've been treating it for over three months.
Ew! It's enormous!
Am I dreaming or is it really hot in here?
No, no, you're not dreaming. Your grand-mother's always cold, so I fire up the wood stove every morn-ing.
In summer? That's just nuts!
You get used to it after a while.
She's 87. It's normal.
Jeezus.

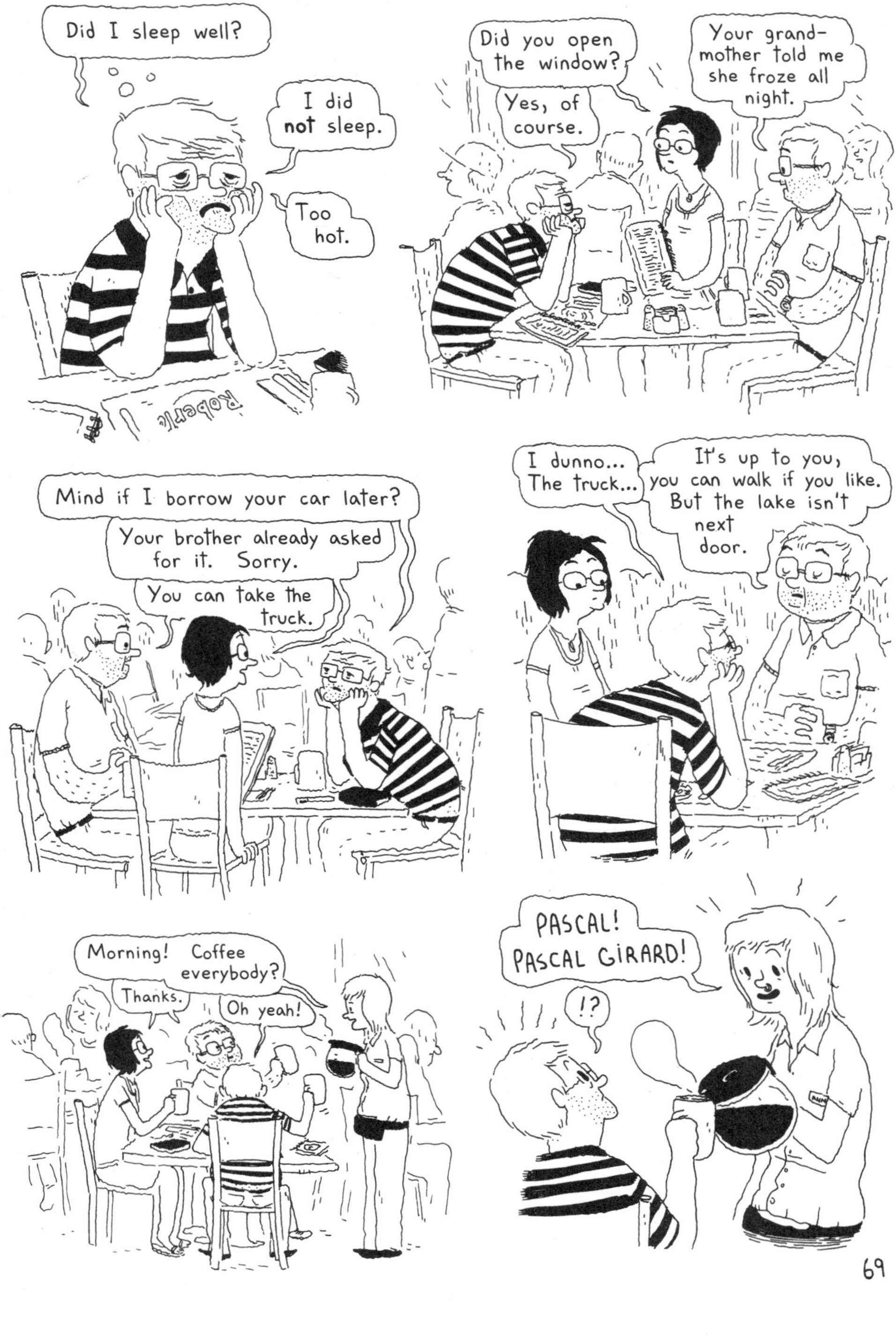
Did I sleep well?
I did **not** sleep.
Too hot.
Did you open the window?
Yes, of course.
Your grandmother told me she froze all night.
Mind if I borrow your car later?
Your brother already asked for it. Sorry.
You can take the truck.
I dunno... The truck...
It's up to you, you can walk if you like. But the lake isn't next door.
Morning! Coffee everybody?
Thanks.
Oh yeah!
PASCAL! PASCAL GIRARD!
!?

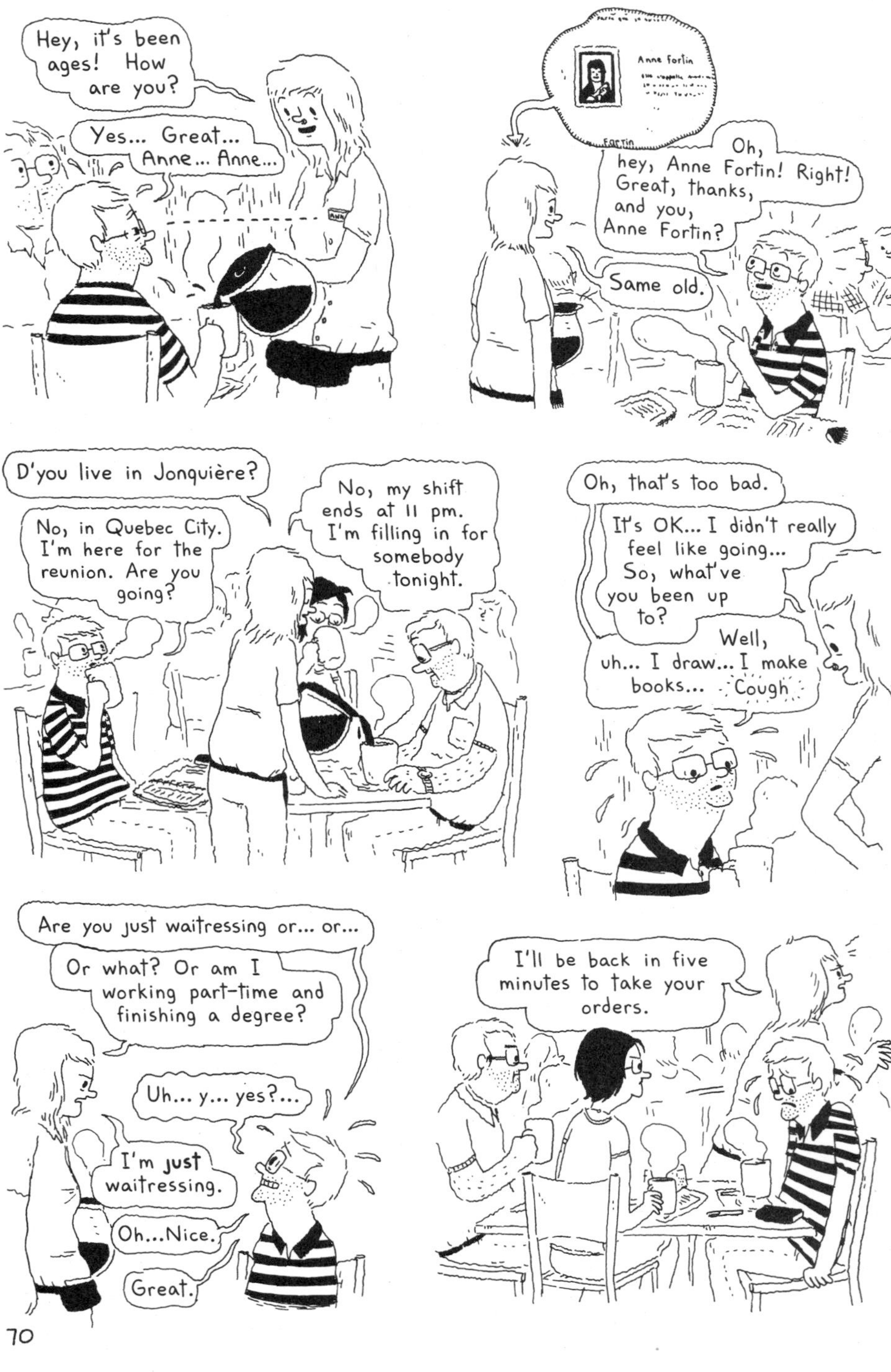
Hey, it's been ages! How are you?
Yes... Great... Anne... Anne...
Anne Fortin
Oh, hey, Anne Fortin! Right! Great, thanks, and you, Anne Fortin?
Same old.
D'you live in Jonquière?
No, in Quebec City. I'm here for the reunion. Are you going?
No, my shift ends at 11 pm. I'm filling in for somebody tonight.
Oh, that's too bad.
It's OK... I didn't really feel like going... So, what've you been up to?
Well, uh... I draw... I make books... Cough
Are you just waitressing or... or...
Or what? Or am I working part-time and finishing a degree?
Uh... y... yes?...
I'm **just** waitressing.
Oh...Nice.
Great.
I'll be back in five minutes to take your orders.

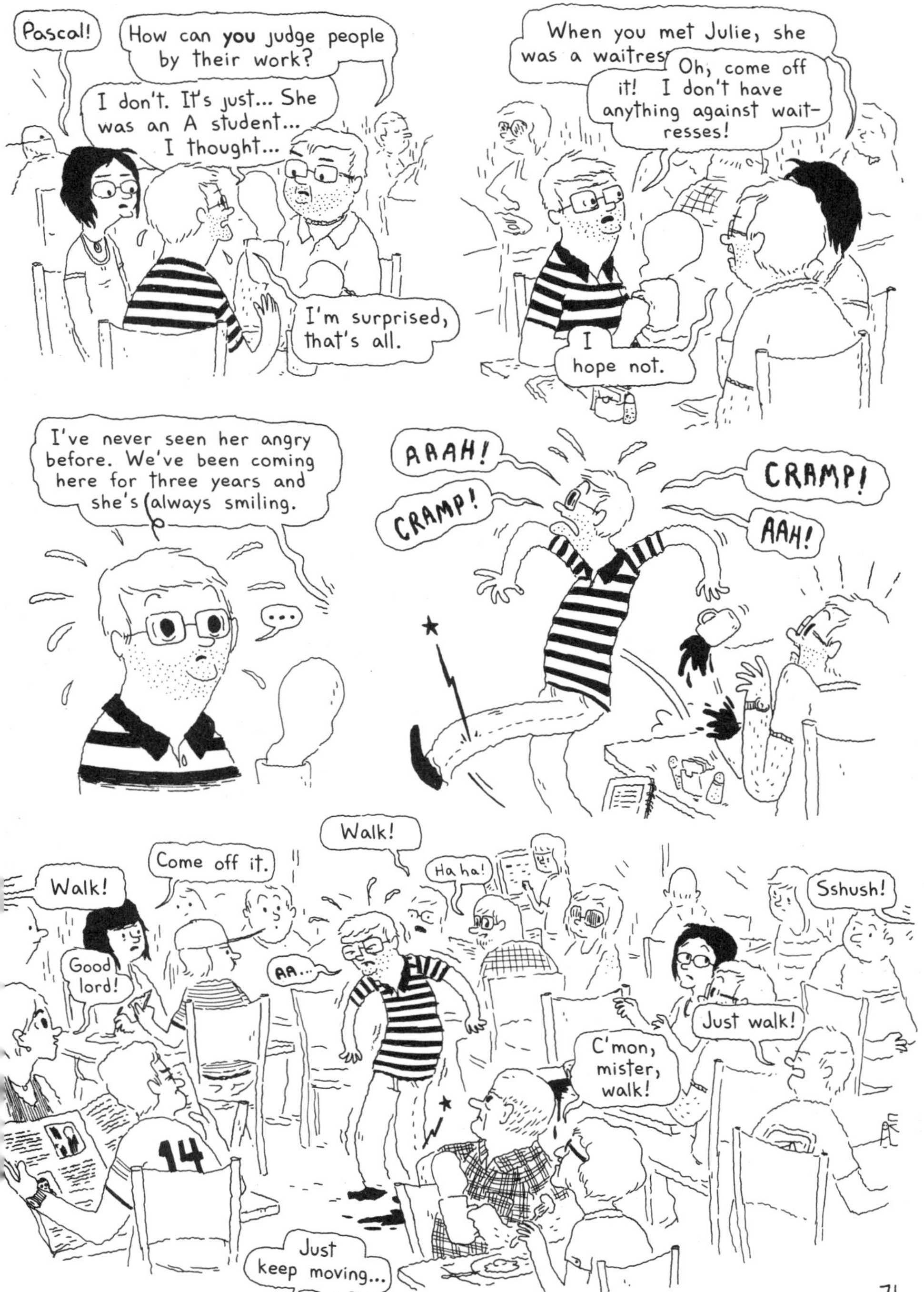
Pascal!
How can you judge people by their work?
I don't. It's just... She was an A student... I thought...
I'm surprised, that's all.
When you met Julie, she was a waitress
Oh, come off it! I don't have anything against waitresses!
I hope not.
I've never seen her angry before. We've been coming here for three years and she's always smiling.
...
AAAH!
CRAMP!
CRAMP!
AAH!
Walk!
Come off it.
Walk!
Ha ha!
Sshush!
Good lord!
AA...
Just walk!
C'mon, mister, walk!
Just keep moving...

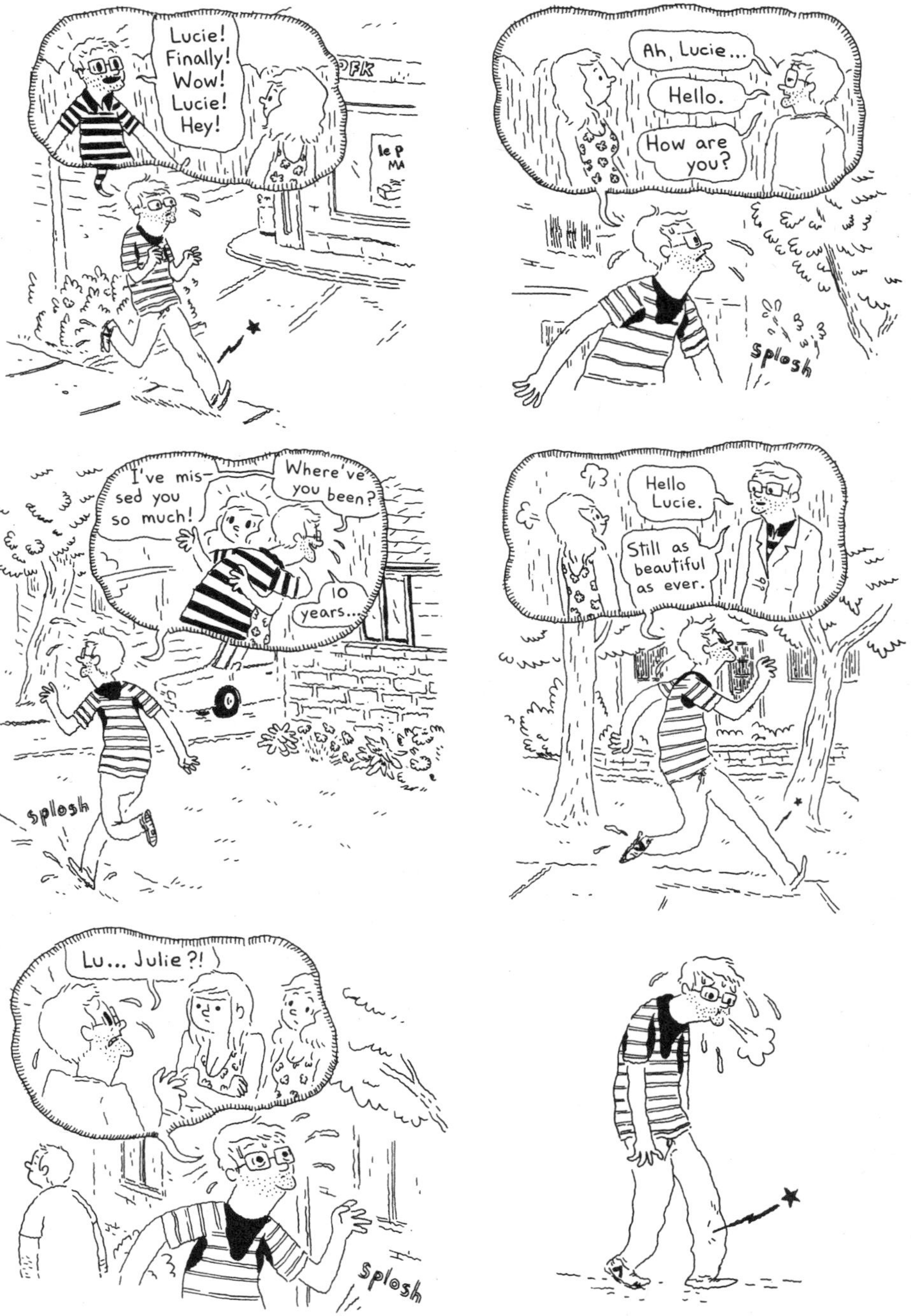
Lucie! Finally! Wow! Lucie! Hey!
Ah, Lucie...
Hello.
How are you?
splosh
I've mis-sed you so much!
Where've you been?
10 years...
splosh
Hello Lucie.
Still as beautiful as ever.
Lu... Julie?!
Splosh

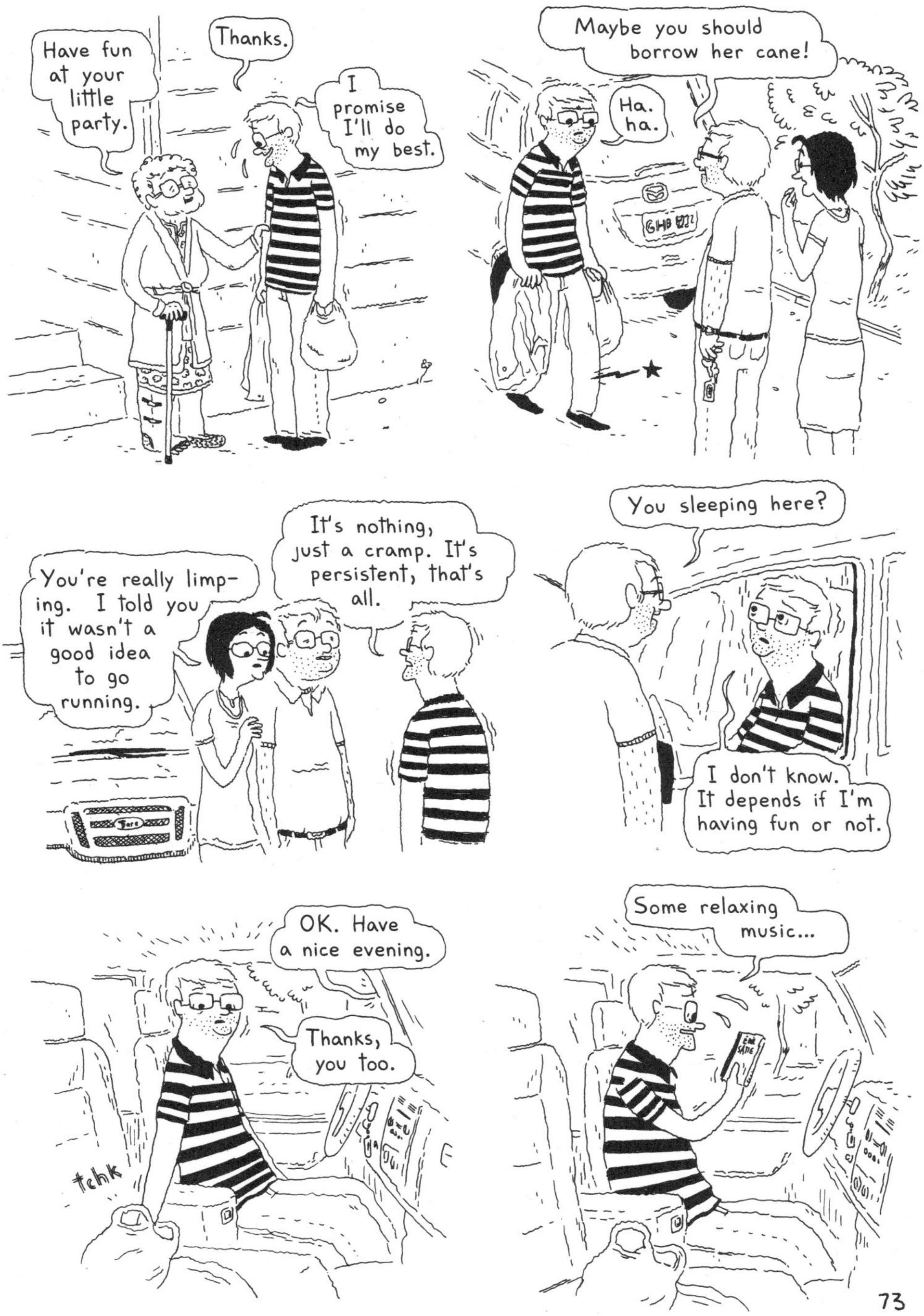
Have fun at your little party.
Thanks.
I promise I'll do my best.
Maybe you should borrow her cane!
Ha. ha.
You're really limp-ing. I told you it wasn't a good idea to go running.
It's nothing, just a cramp. It's persistent, that's all.
You sleeping here?
I don't know. It depends if I'm having fun or not.
OK. Have a nice evening.
Thanks, you too.
tchk
Some relaxing music...

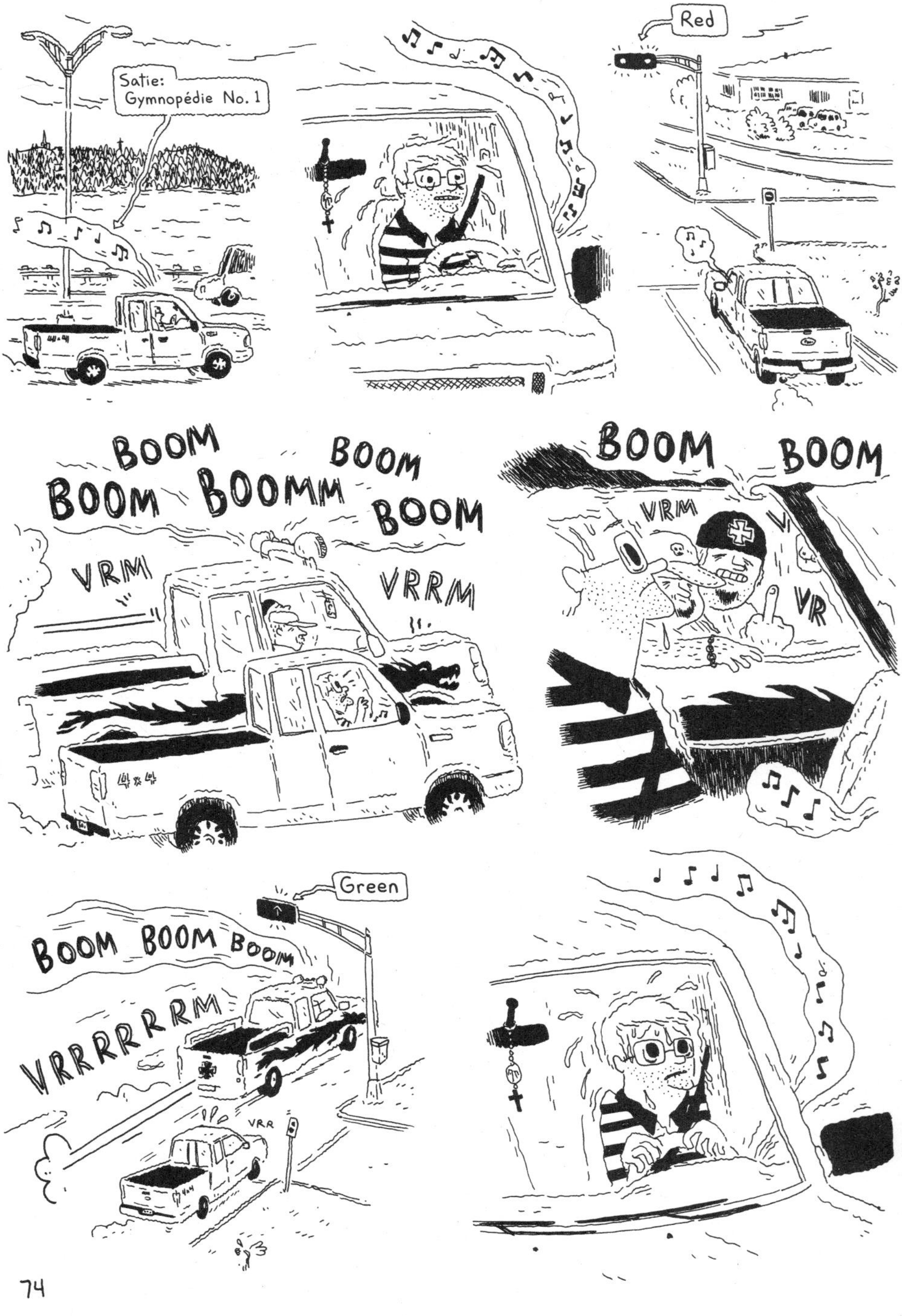
Satie:
Gymnopédie No. 1
Red
BOOM
BOOM BOOMM
BOOM
BOOM
VRM
VRRM
BOOM BOOM
VRM
VR
Green
BOOM BOOM BOOM
VRRRRRRM
VRR

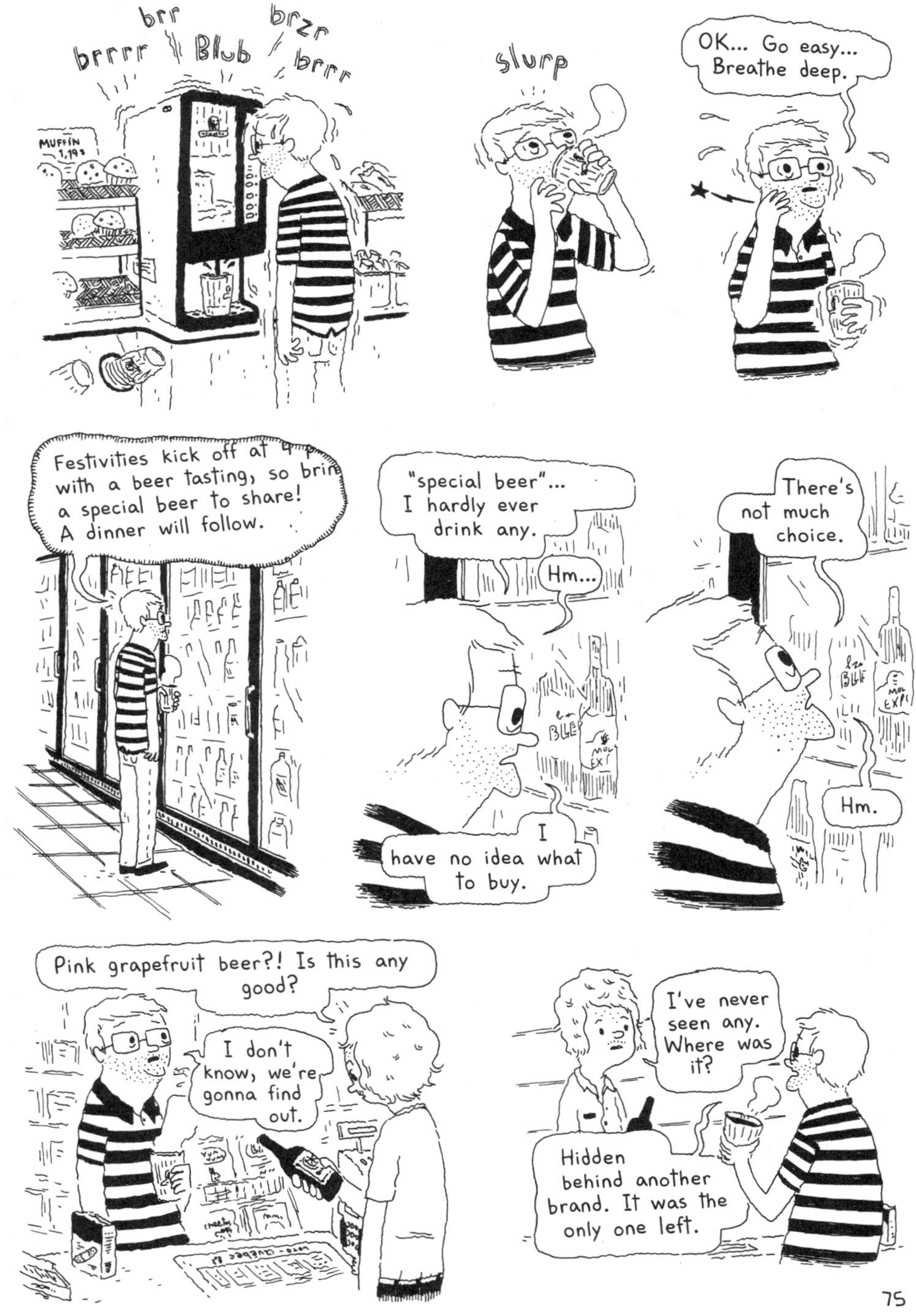
brrrr
brr
Blub
brzr
brrr
MUFFIN
slurp
OK... Go easy... Breathe deep.
Festivities kick off at 4 p with a beer tasting, so brin a special beer to share! A dinner will follow.
"special beer"... I hardly ever drink any.
Hm...
I have no idea what to buy.
There's not much choice.
Hm.
Pink grapefruit beer?! Is this any good?
I don't know, we're gonna find out.
I've never seen any. Where was it?
Hidden behind another brand. It was the only one left.

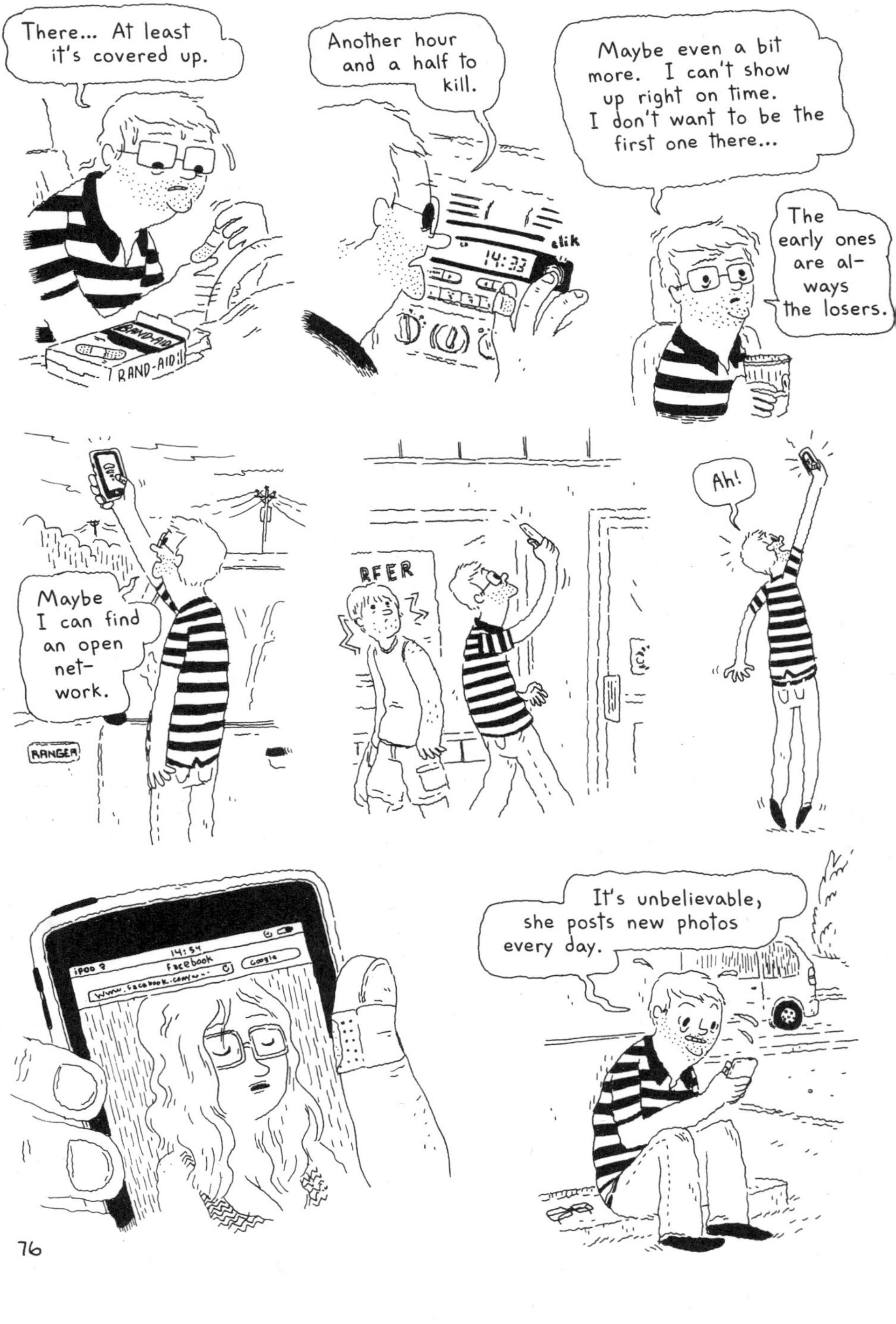
There... At least it's covered up.
BAND-AID
BAND-AID
Another hour and a half to kill.
14:33
clik
Maybe even a bit more. I can't show up right on time. I don't want to be the first one there...
The early ones are always the losers.
Maybe I can find an open network.
RANGER
RFER
Ah!
14:54
Facebook
Google
www.facebook.com
It's unbelievable, she posts new photos every day.

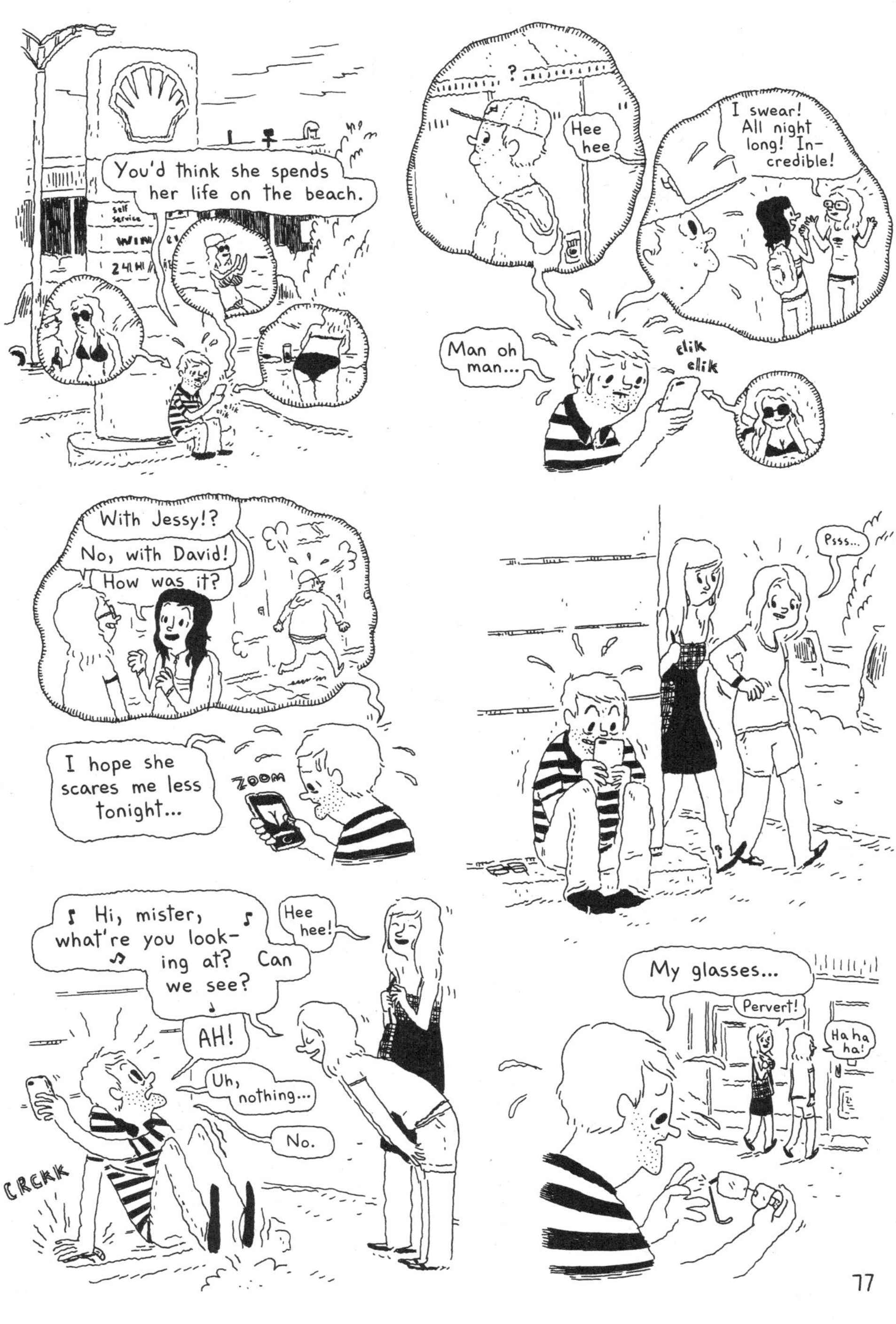
You'd think she spends her life on the beach.
Self Service
24 H
?
Hee hee
I swear! All night long! In-credible!
Man oh man...
clik clik
With Jessy!?
No, with David!
How was it?
I hope she scares me less tonight...
ZOOM
Psss...
Hi, mister, what're you look-ing at? Can we see?
Hee hee!
AH!
Uh, nothing...
No.
CRCKK
My glasses...
Pervert!
Ha ha ha!

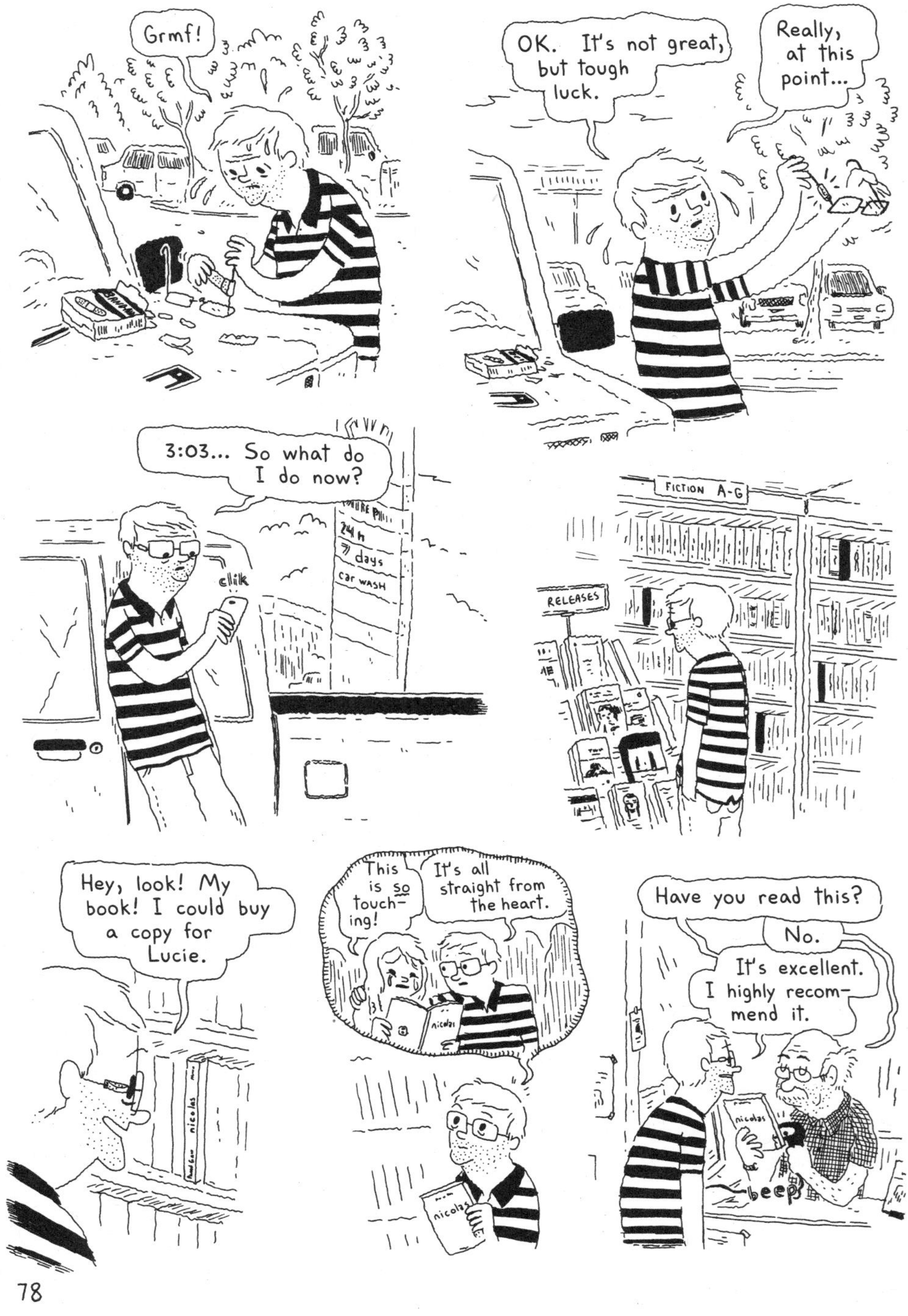
Grmf!
OK. It's not great, but tough luck.
Really, at this point...
3:03... So what do I do now?
24 h
7 days
car WASH
clik
FICTION A-G
RELEASES
Hey, look! My book! I could buy a copy for Lucie.
nicolas
This is so touching!
It's all straight from the heart.
nicolas
nicolas
Have you read this?
No.
It's excellent. I highly recommend it.
nicolas
beep

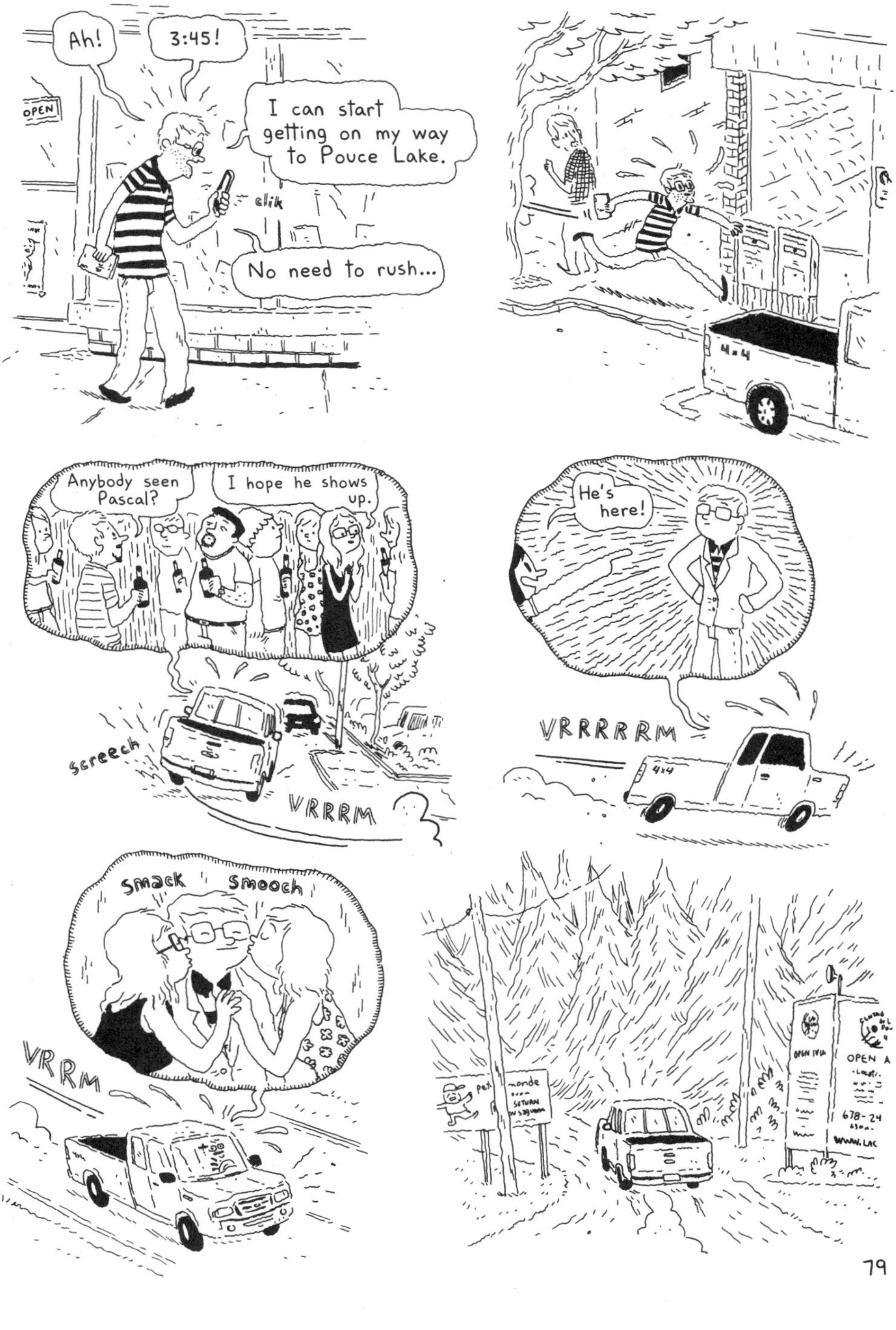
Ah!
3:45!
I can start getting on my way to Pouce Lake.
clik
No need to rush...
OPEN
4x4
Anybody seen Pascal?
I hope he shows up.
screech
VRRRM
He's here!
VRRRRRRM
4x4
Smack
Smooch
VRRM
OPEN
678-24

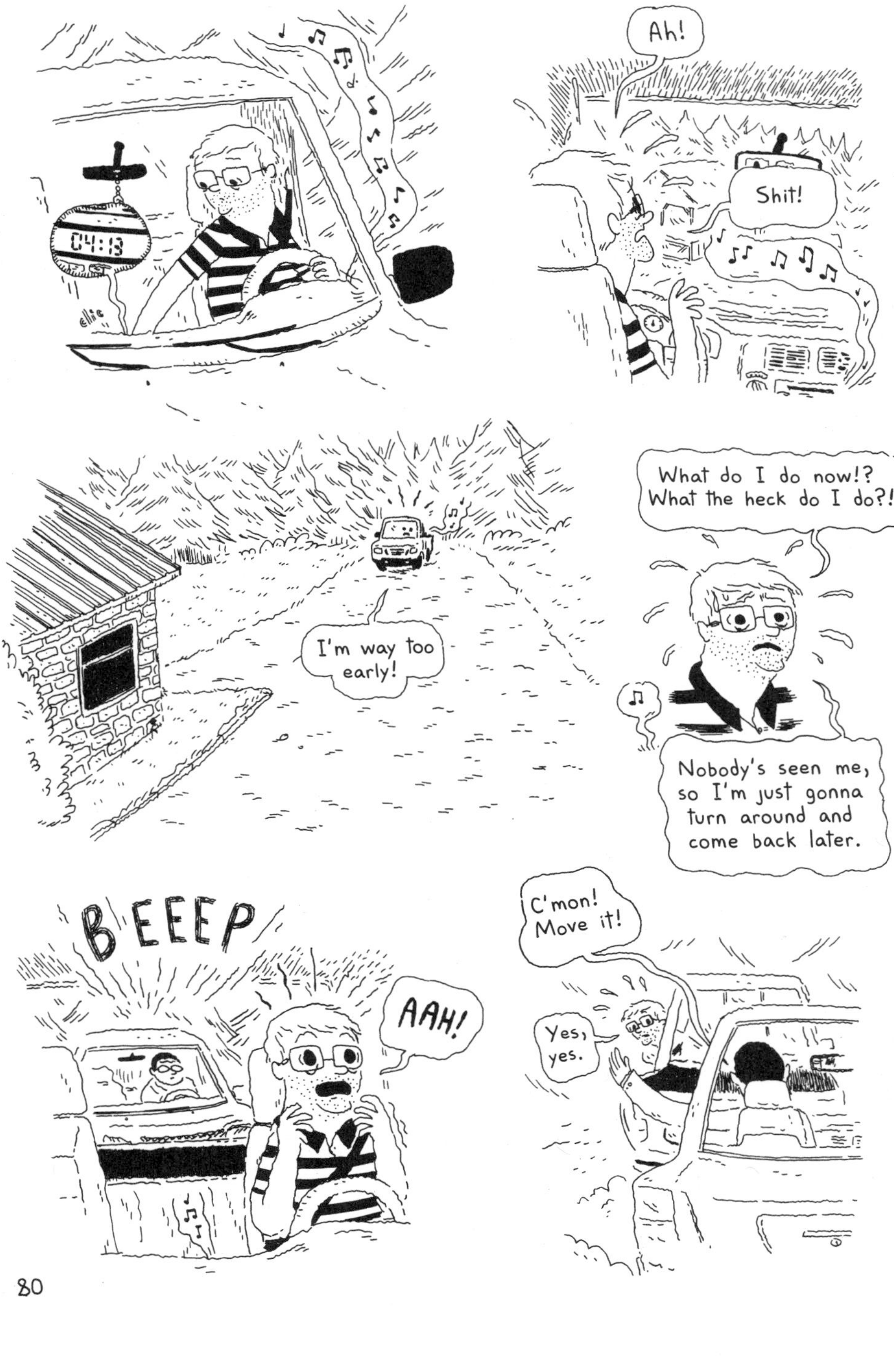
04:13
Ah!
Shit!
I'm way too early!
What do I do now!? What the heck do I do?!
Nobody's seen me, so I'm just gonna turn around and come back later.
BEEEP
AAH!
C'mon! Move it!
Yes, yes.

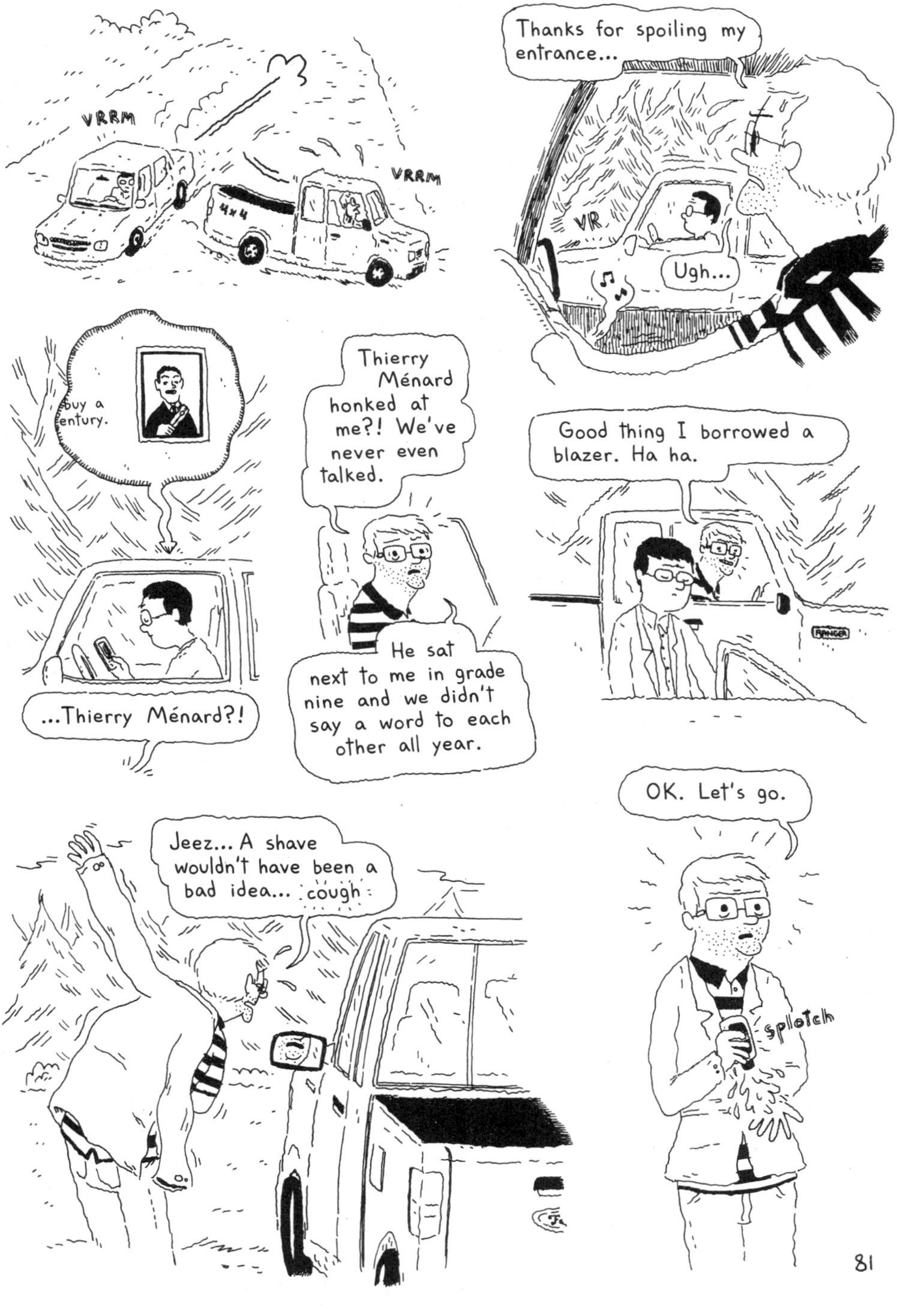
VRRM
VRRM
Thanks for spoiling my entrance...
VR
Ugh...
...Thierry Ménard?!
Thierry Ménard honked at me?! We've never even talked.
He sat next to me in grade nine and we didn't say a word to each other all year.
Good thing I borrowed a blazer. Ha ha.
RANGER
Jeez... A shave wouldn't have been a bad idea... cough
OK. Let's go.
splotch

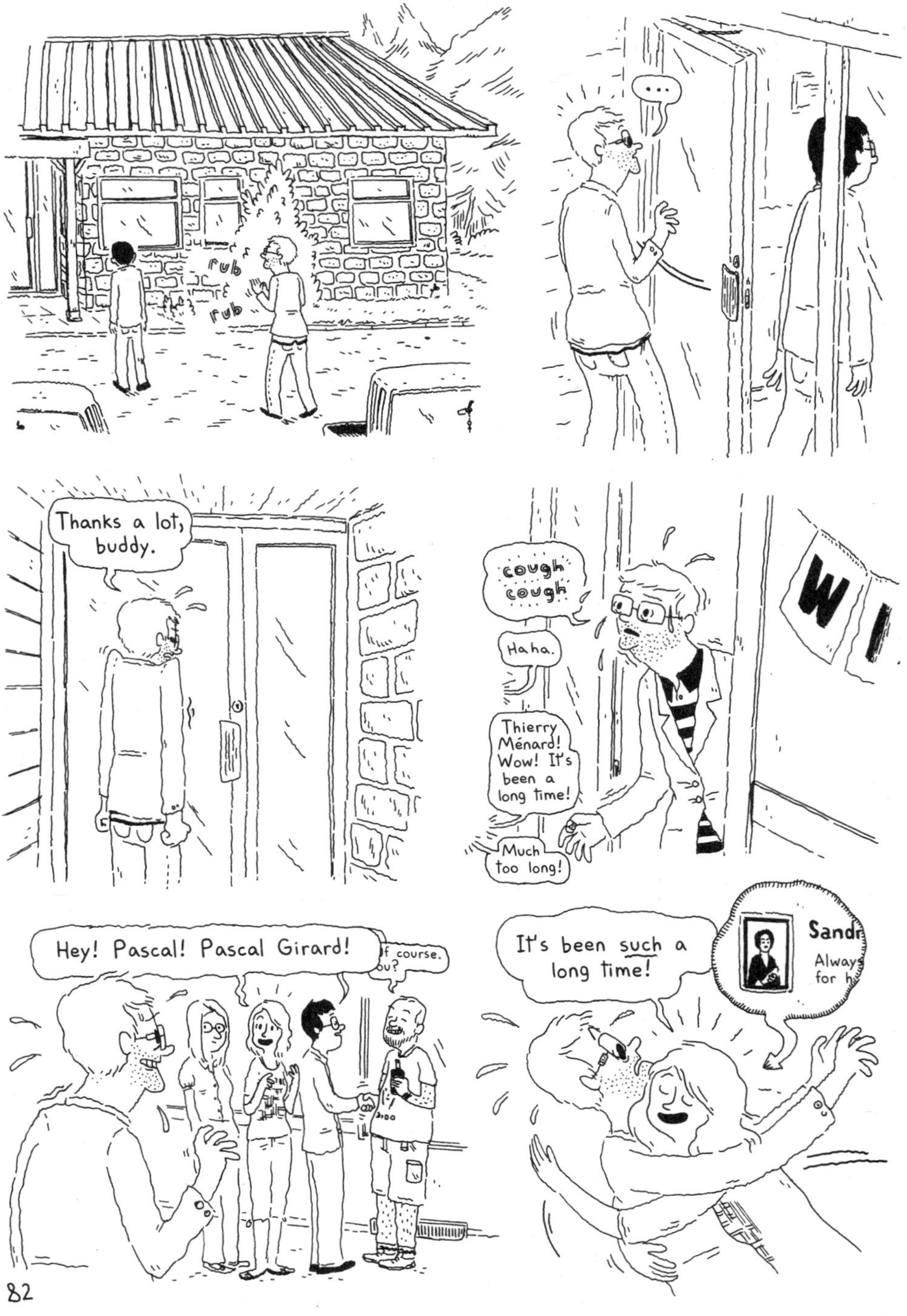
rub
rub
...
Thanks a lot, buddy.
cough cough
Haha.
Thierry Ménard! Wow! It's been a long time!
Much too long!
Hey! Pascal! Pascal Girard!
It's been such a long time!

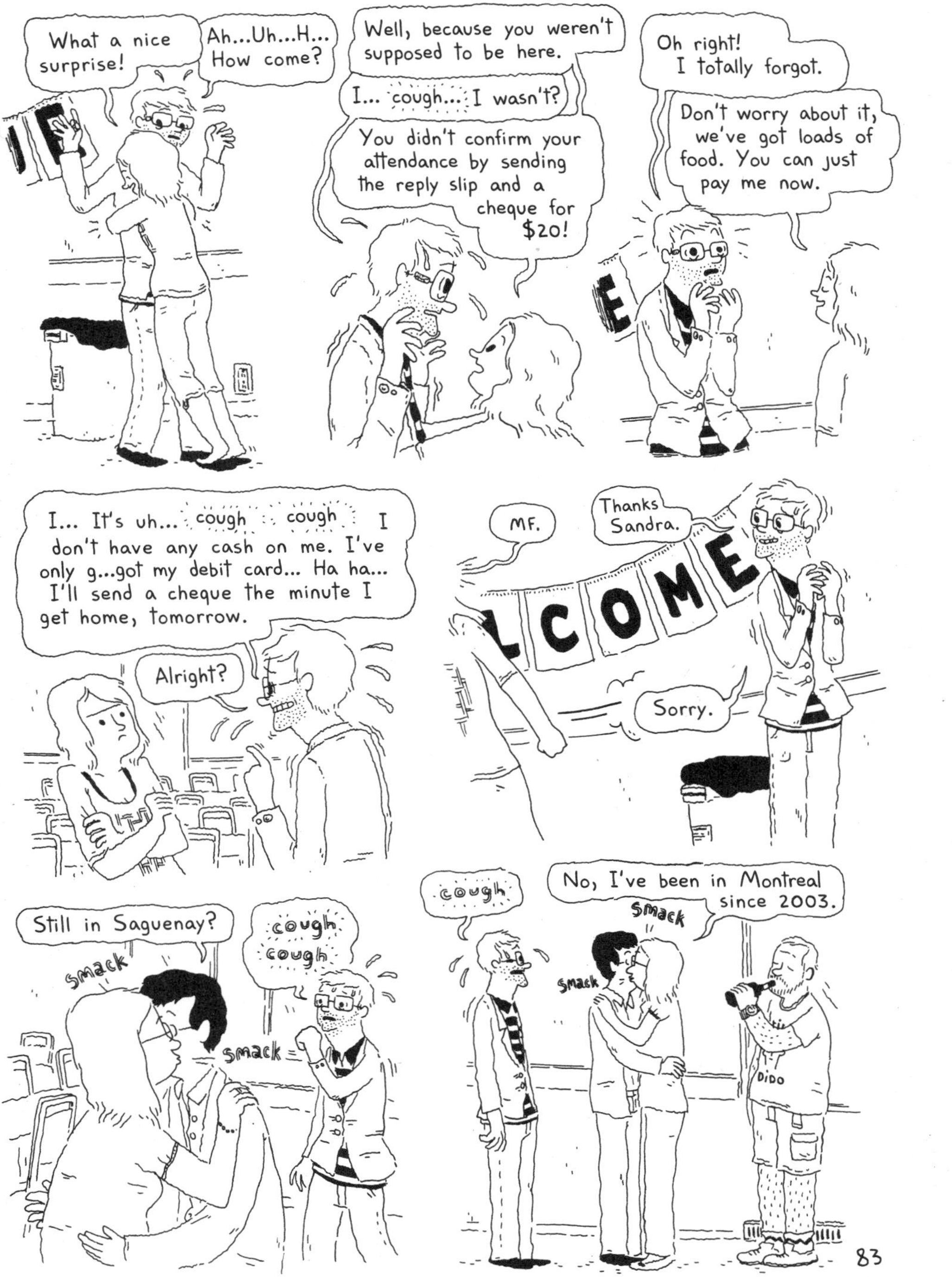
What a nice surprise!
Ah...Uh...H... How come?
Well, because you weren't supposed to be here.
I... cough... I wasn't?
You didn't confirm your attendance by sending the reply slip and a cheque for $20!
Oh right! I totally forgot.
Don't worry about it, we've got loads of food. You can just pay me now.
I... It's uh... cough cough I don't have any cash on me. I've only g...got my debit card... Ha ha... I'll send a cheque the minute I get home, tomorrow.
Alright?
MF.
Thanks Sandra.
LCOME
Sorry.
Still in Saguenay?
smack
smack
cough cough
cough
No, I've been in Montreal since 2003.
smack
smack
DIDO

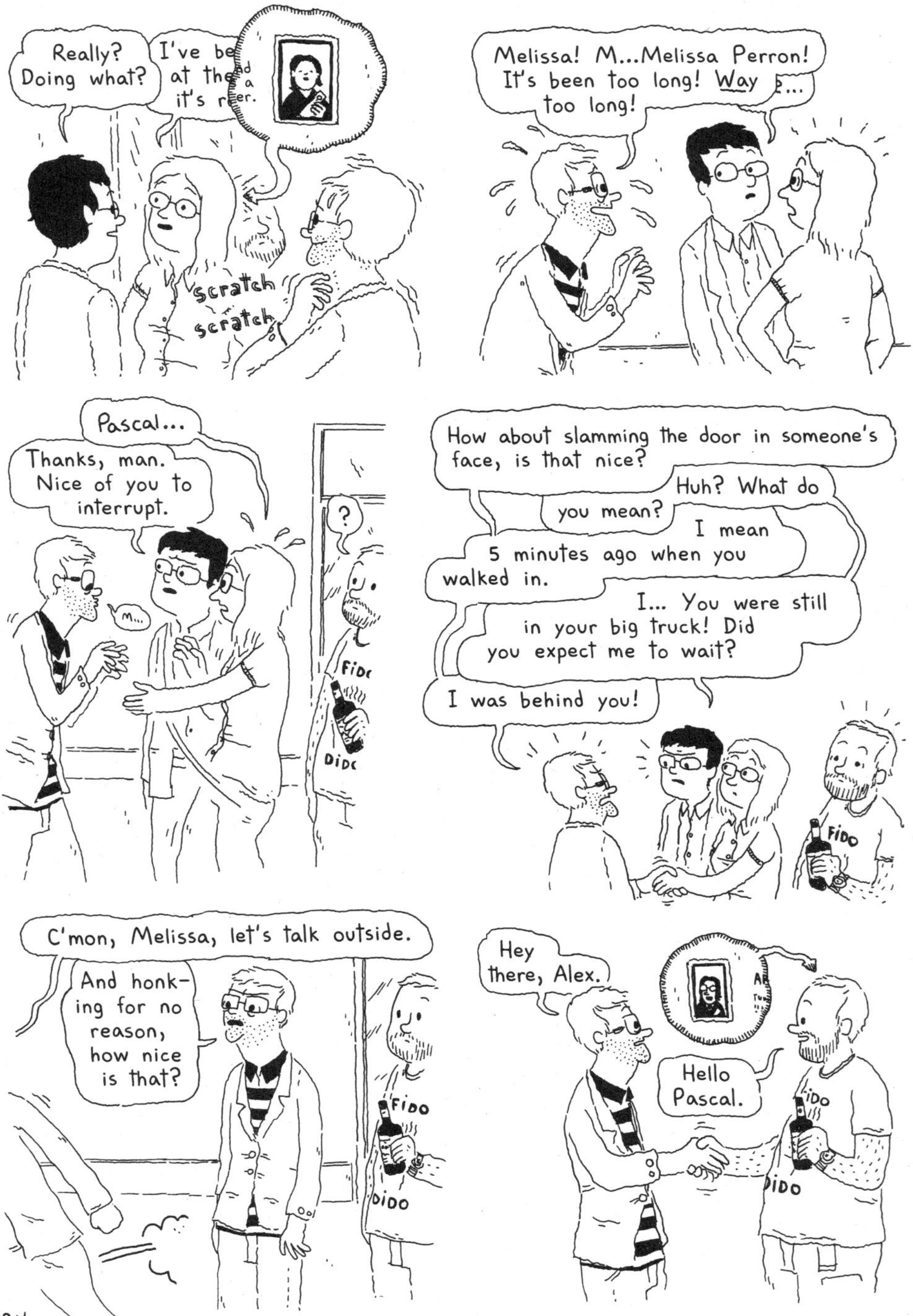
Really? Doing what?
I've be at the it's r er.
scratch scratch
Melissa! M...Melissa Perron! It's been too long! Way too long!
Pascal...
Thanks, man. Nice of you to interrupt.
M...
?
FIDO
DIDO
How about slamming the door in someone's face, is that nice?
Huh? What do you mean?
I mean 5 minutes ago when you walked in.
I... You were still in your big truck! Did you expect me to wait?
I was behind you!
FIDO
C'mon, Melissa, let's talk outside.
And honking for no reason, how nice is that?
FIDO
DIDO
Hey there, Alex.
Hello Pascal.
FIDO
DIDO

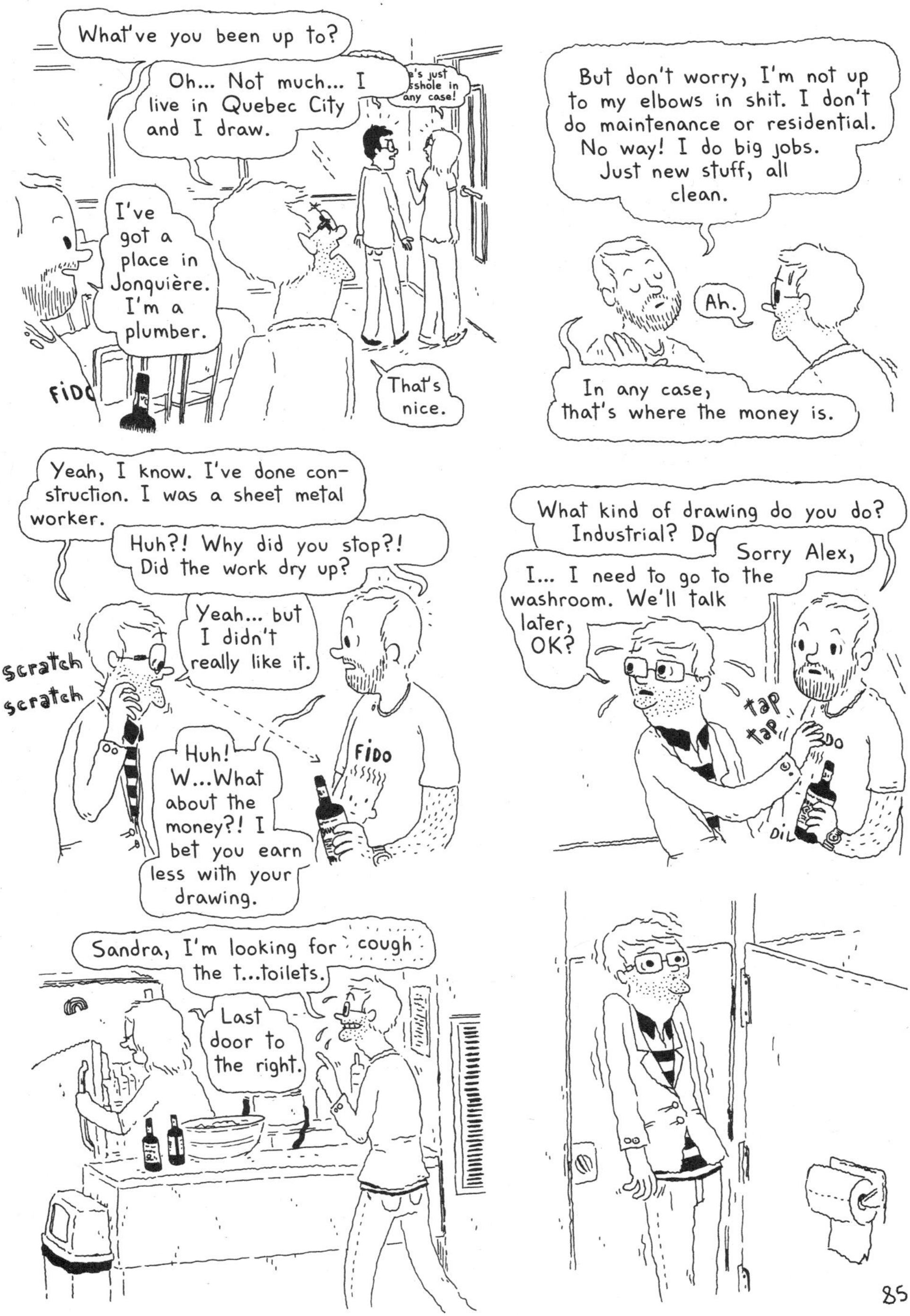
What've you been up to?
Oh... Not much... I live in Quebec City and I draw.
e's just sshole in any case!
I've got a place in Jonquière. I'm a plumber.
FIDO
That's nice.
But don't worry, I'm not up to my elbows in shit. I don't do maintenance or residential. No way! I do big jobs. Just new stuff, all clean.
Ah.
In any case, that's where the money is.
Yeah, I know. I've done construction. I was a sheet metal worker.
Huh?! Why did you stop?! Did the work dry up?
Yeah... but I didn't really like it.
scratch scratch
FIDO
Huh! W...What about the money?! I bet you earn less with your drawing.
What kind of drawing do you do? Industrial? Do
Sorry Alex, I... I need to go to the washroom. We'll talk later, OK?
tap tap
Sandra, I'm looking for cough the t...toilets.
Last door to the right.

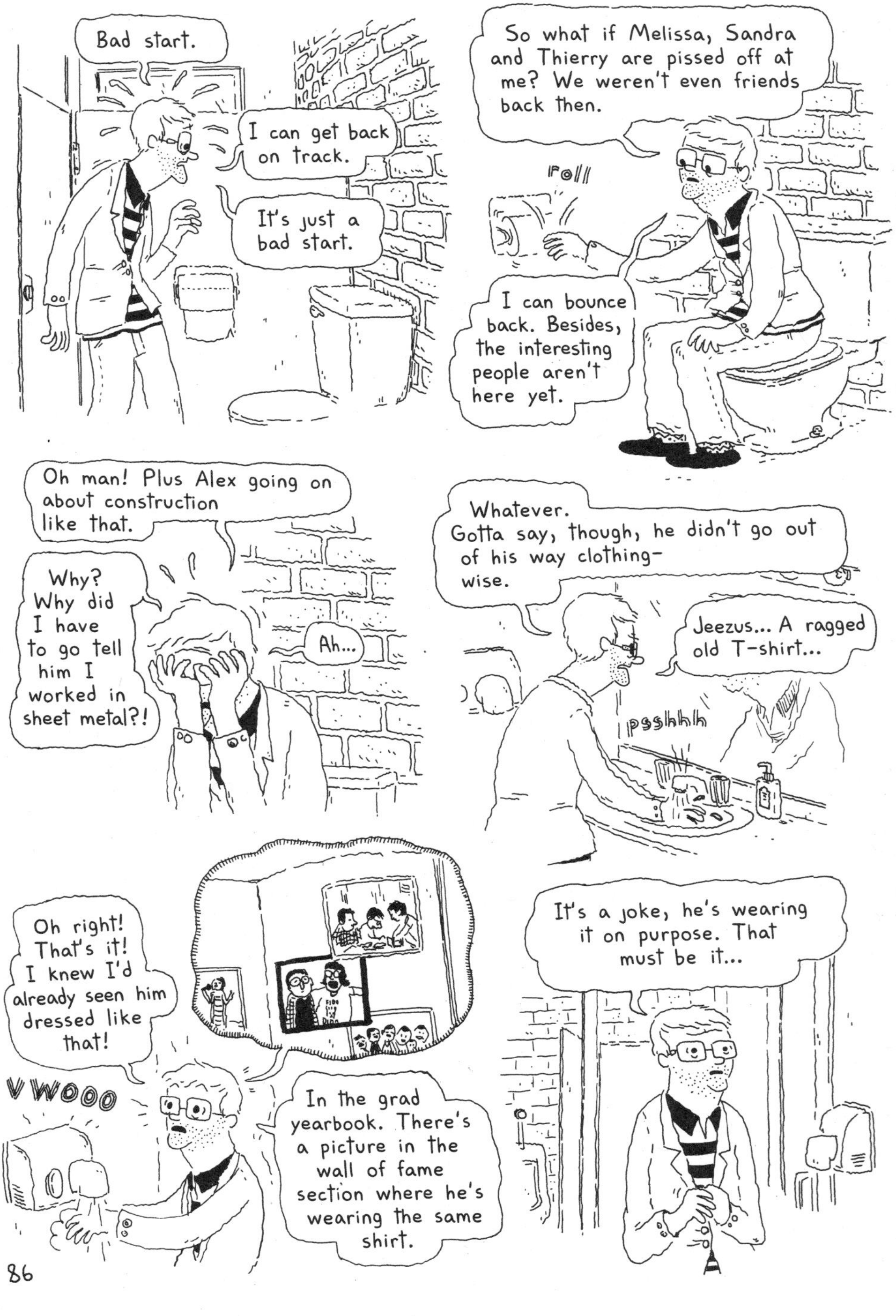
Bad start.
I can get back on track.
It's just a bad start.
So what if Melissa, Sandra and Thierry are pissed off at me? We weren't even friends back then.
roll
I can bounce back. Besides, the interesting people aren't here yet.
Oh man! Plus Alex going on about construction like that.
Why? Why did I have to go tell him I worked in sheet metal?!
Ah...
Whatever. Gotta say, though, he didn't go out of his way clothing-wise.
Jeezus... A ragged old T-shirt...
psshhh
Oh right! That's it! I knew I'd already seen him dressed like that!
VWOOO
In the grad yearbook. There's a picture in the wall of fame section where he's wearing the same shirt.
It's a joke, he's wearing it on purpose. That must be it...

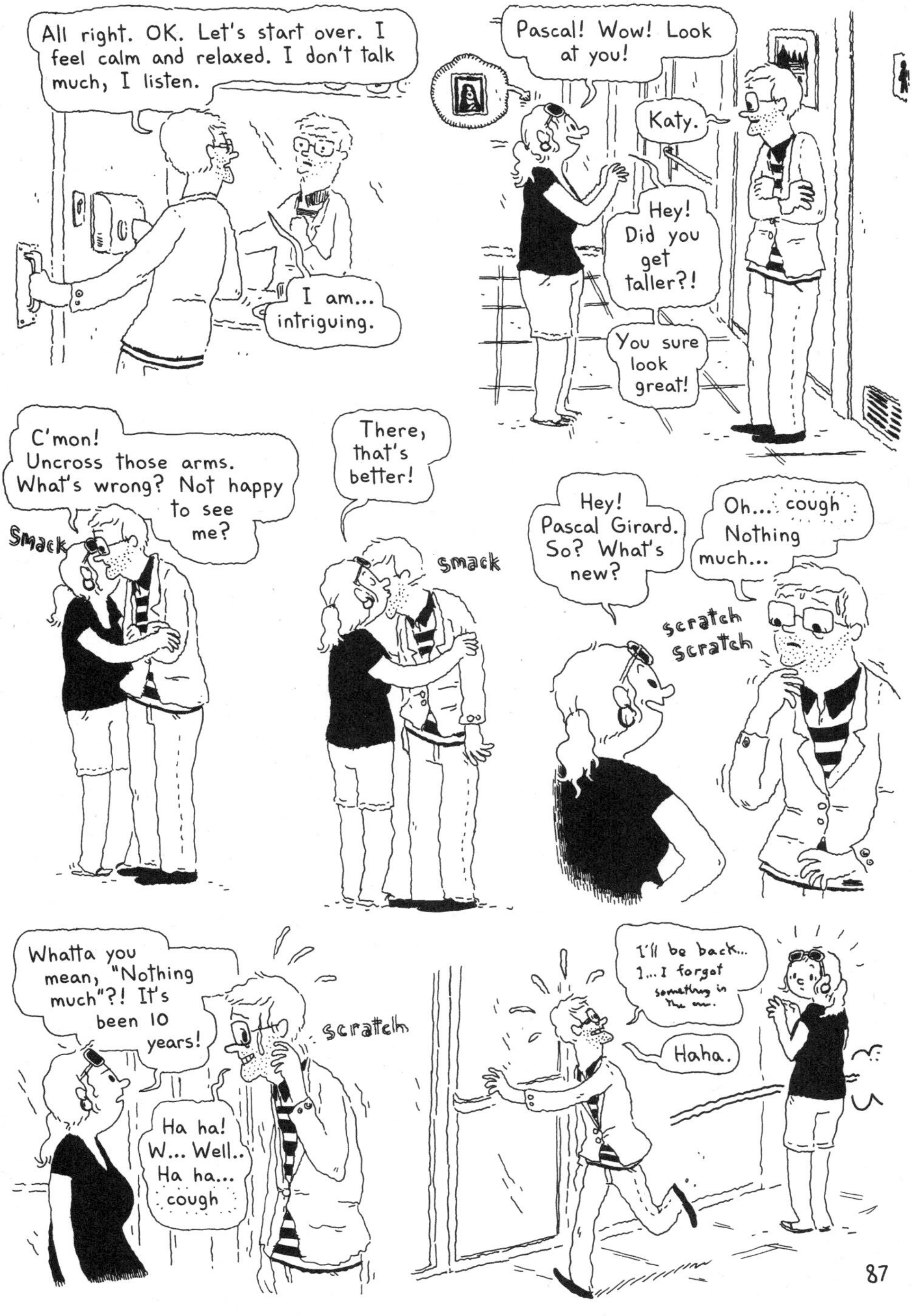
All right. OK. Let's start over. I feel calm and relaxed. I don't talk much, I listen.
I am... intriguing.
Pascal! Wow! Look at you!
Katy.
Hey! Did you get taller?!
You sure look great!
C'mon! Uncross those arms. What's wrong? Not happy to see me?
Smack
There, that's better!
smack
Hey! Pascal Girard. So? What's new?
Oh... cough Nothing much...
scratch scratch
Whatta you mean, "Nothing much"?! It's been 10 years!
scratch
Ha ha! W... Well.. Ha ha... cough
I'll be back... I... I forgot something in the car.
Haha.

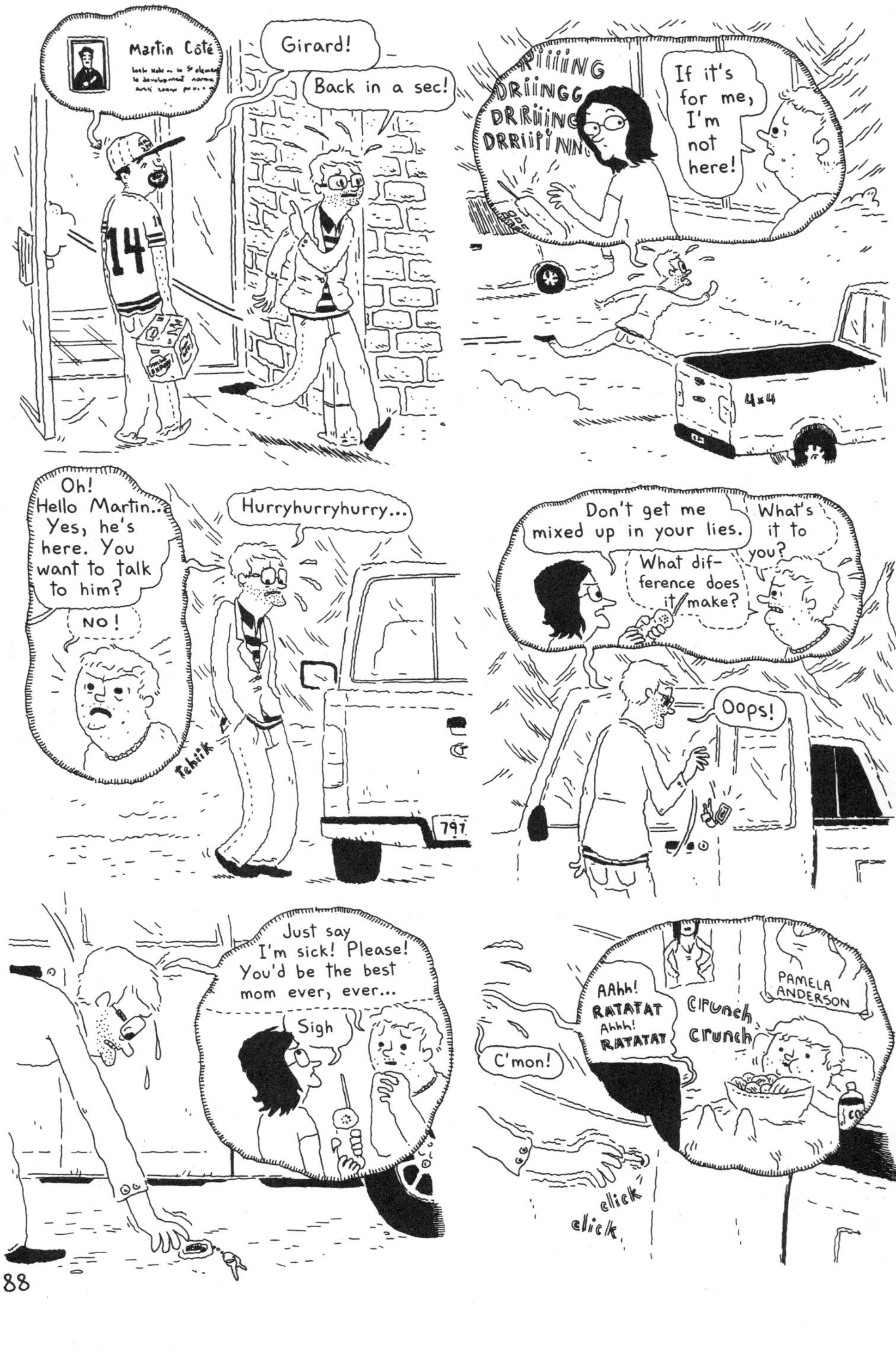
Martin Côté
Girard!
Back in a sec!
DRIIING
DRIINGG
DRRIIING
DRRIIINNN
If it's for me, I'm not here!
Oh! Hello Martin... Yes, he's here. You want to talk to him?
NO!
tchiik
Hurryhurryhurry...
Don't get me mixed up in your lies.
What's it to you?
What difference does it make?
Oops!
Just say I'm sick! Please! You'd be the best mom ever, ever...
Sigh
AAhh!
RATATAT
Ahhh!
RATATAT
Crunch
Crunch
PAMELA ANDERSON
C'mon!
click
click

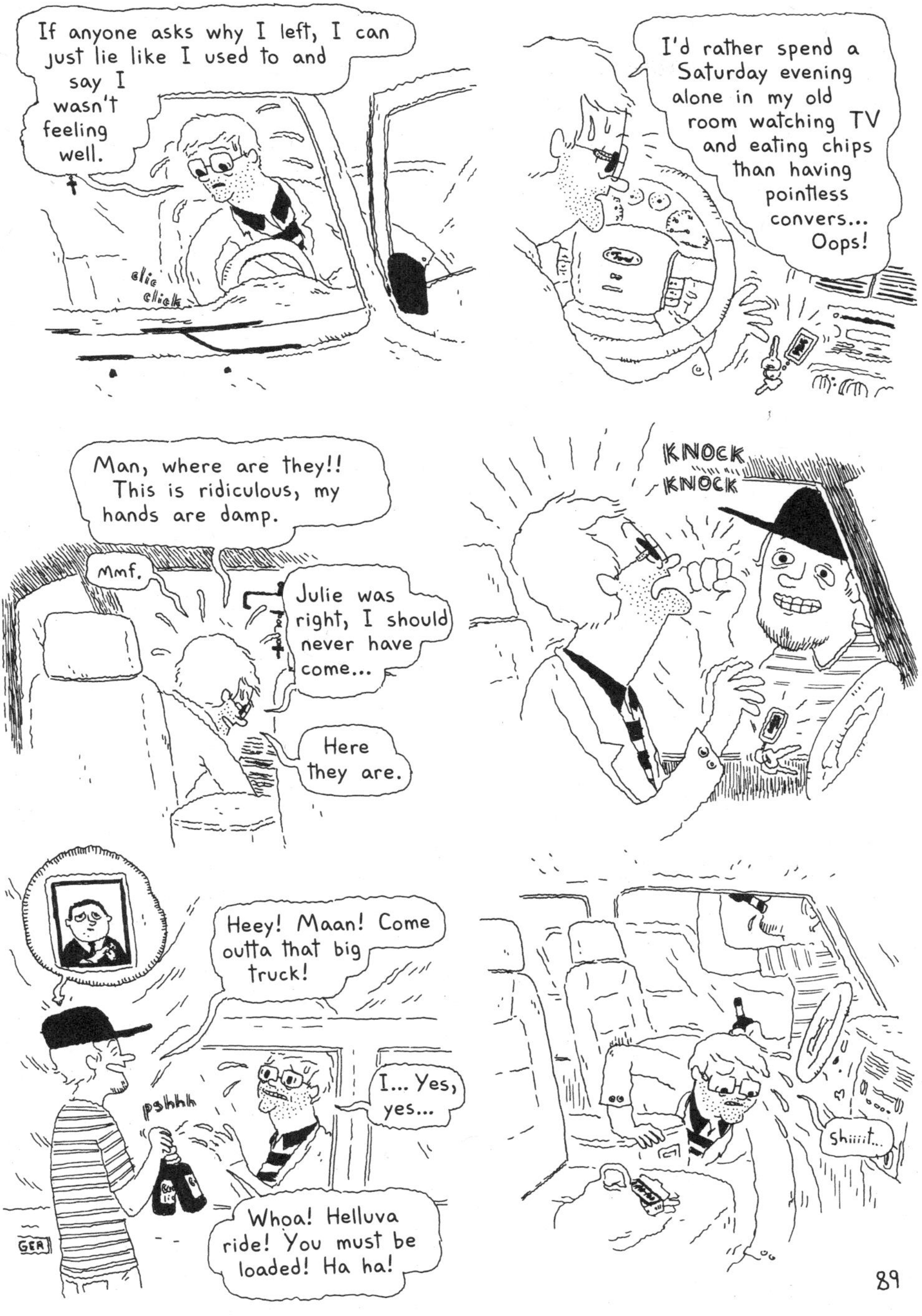
If anyone asks why I left, I can just lie like I used to and say I wasn't feeling well.
clic click
I'd rather spend a Saturday evening alone in my old room watching TV and eating chips than having pointless convers... Oops!
Man, where are they!! This is ridiculous, my hands are damp.
Mmf.
Julie was right, I should never have come...
Here they are.
KNOCK KNOCK
Heey! Maan! Come outta that big truck!
pshhh
I... Yes, yes...
Whoa! Helluva ride! You must be loaded! Ha ha!
GER
Shiiiit...

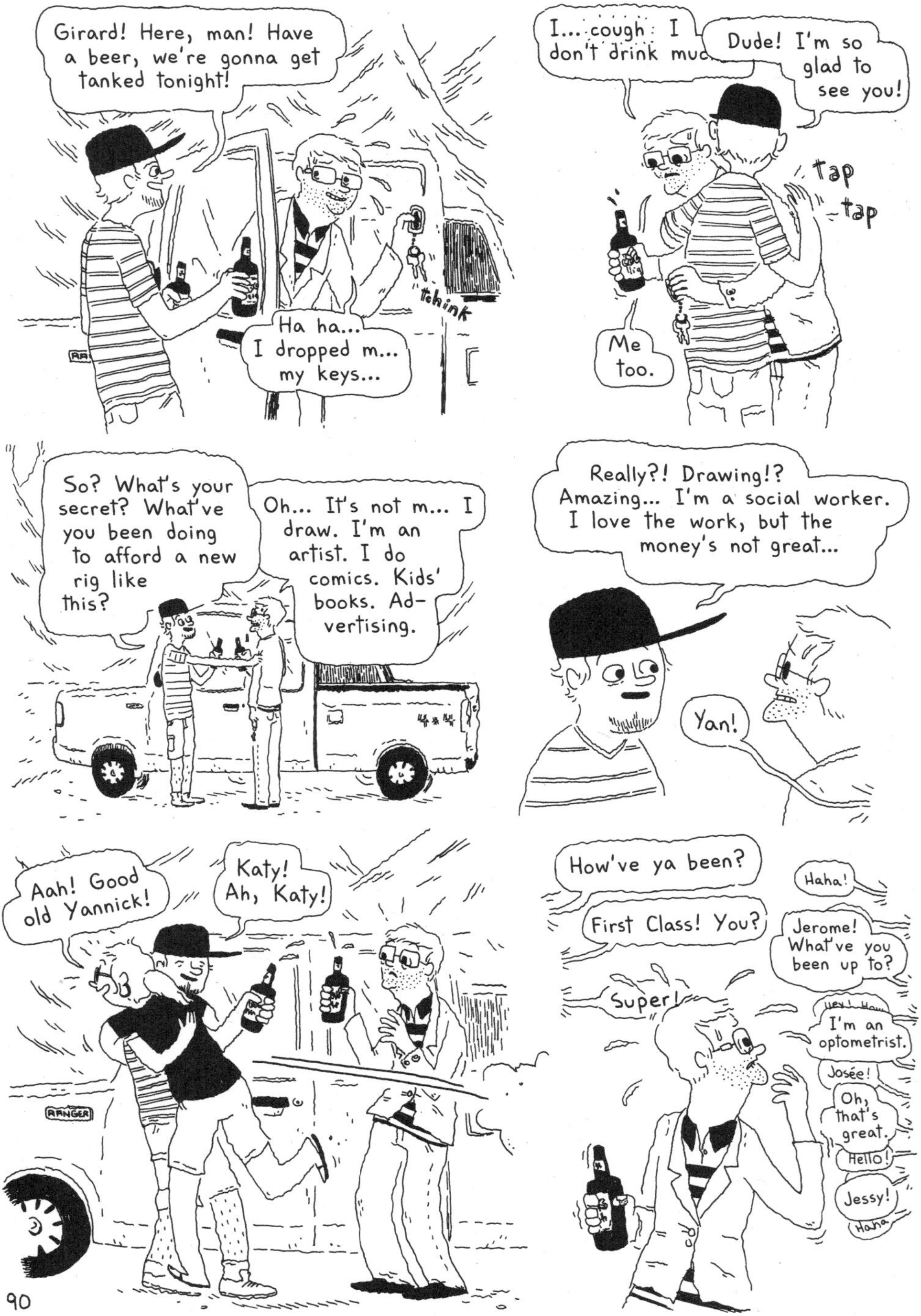

Girard! Here, man! Have a beer, we're gonna get tanked tonight!
Ha ha... I dropped m... my keys...
tchink
I... cough I don't drink muc
Dude! I'm so glad to see you!
tap
tap
Me too.
So? What's your secret? What've you been doing to afford a new rig like this?
Oh... It's not m... I draw. I'm an artist. I do comics. Kids' books. Advertising.
Really?! Drawing!? Amazing... I'm a social worker. I love the work, but the money's not great...
Yan!
Aah! Good old Yannick!
Katy! Ah, Katy!
RANGER
How've ya been?
First Class! You?
Super!
Haha!
Jerome! What've you been up to?
I'm an optometrist.
Josée!
Oh, that's great.
Hello!
Jessy!
Haha

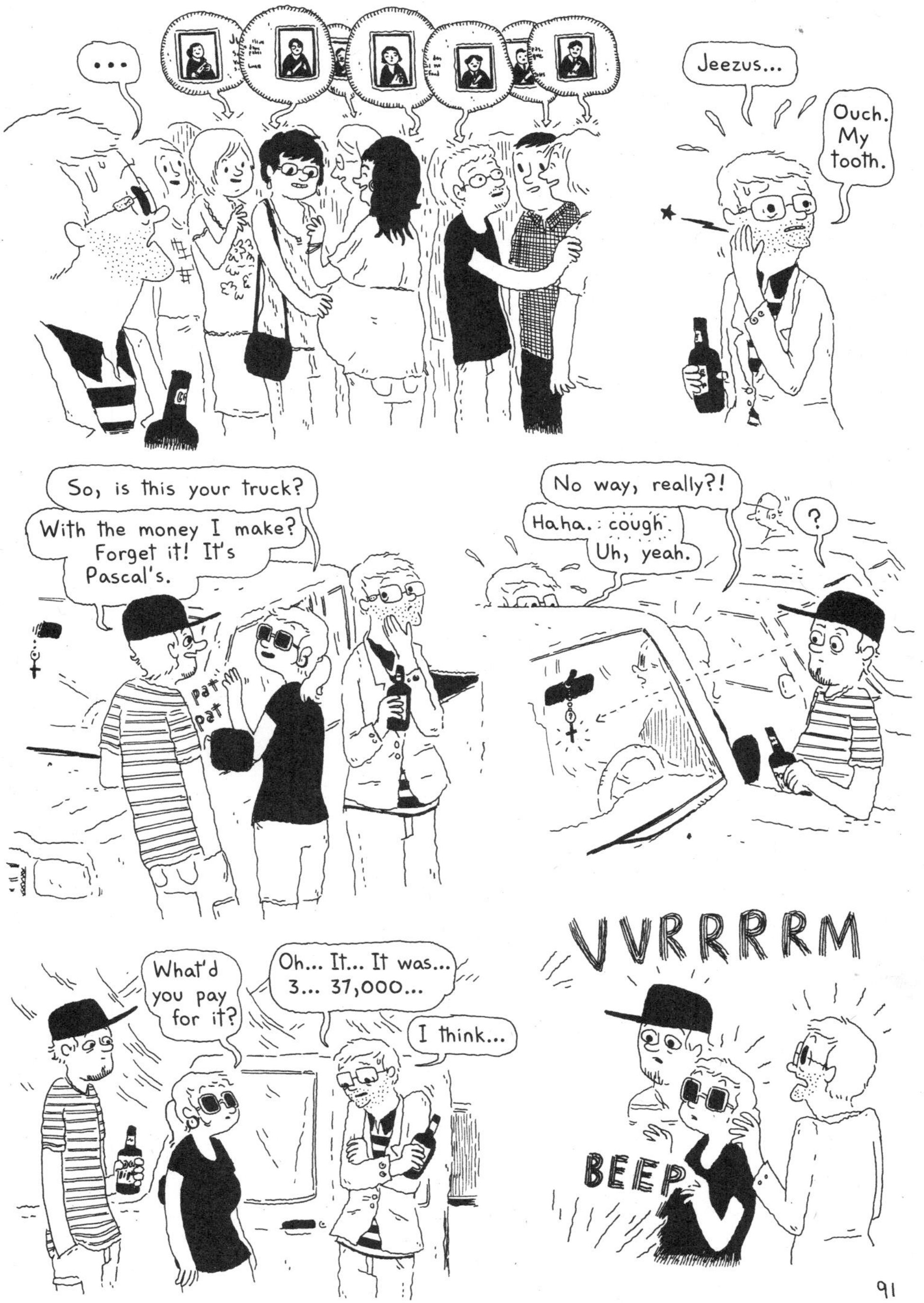
...
Jeezus...
Ouch. My tooth.
So, is this your truck?
With the money I make? Forget it! It's Pascal's.
pat pat
No way, really?!
Haha. cough
Uh, yeah.
?
What'd you pay for it?
Oh... It... It was... 3... 37,000...
I think...
VVRRRRM
BEEP

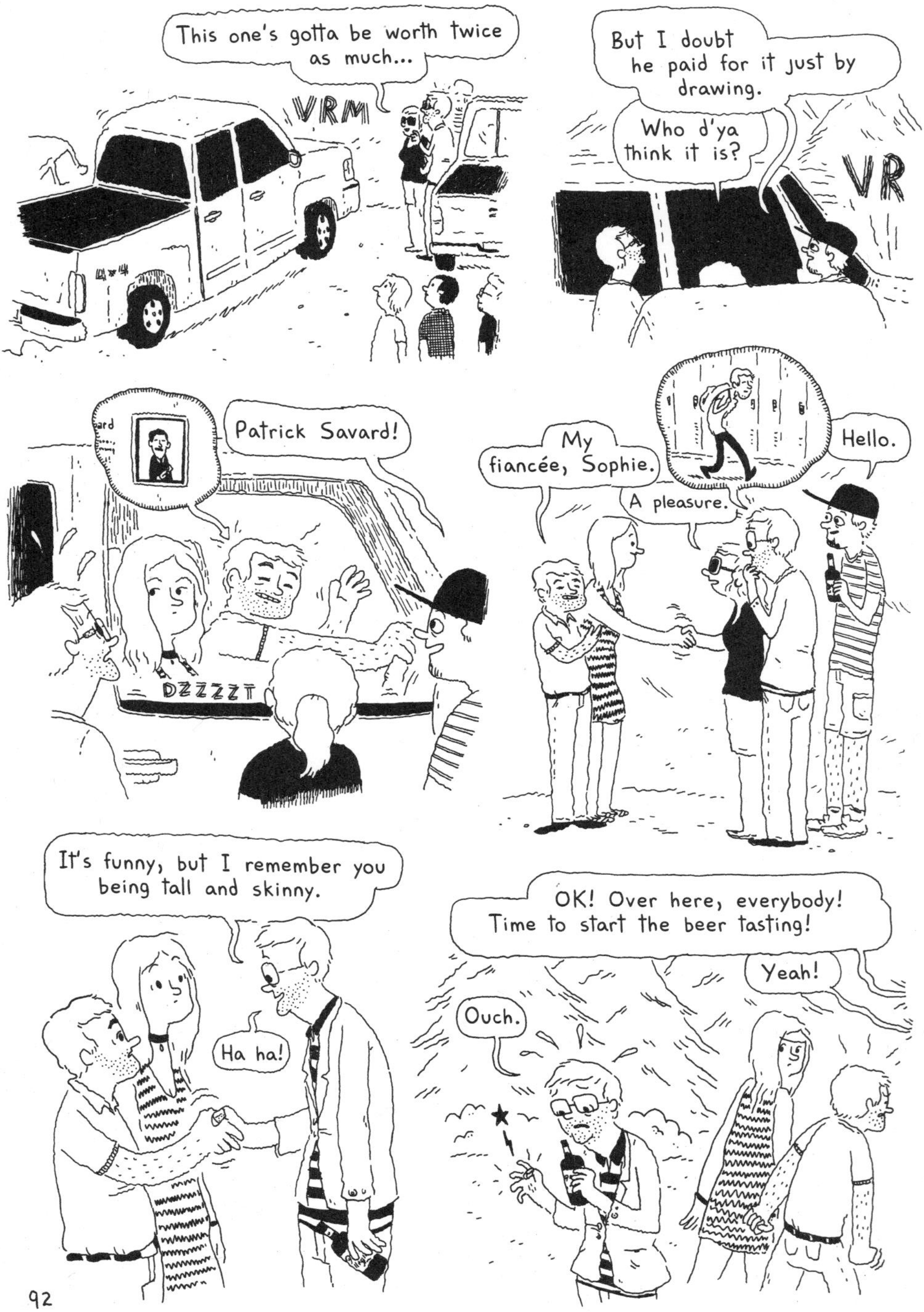

This one's gotta be worth twice as much...
VRM
But I doubt he paid for it just by drawing.
Who d'ya think it is?
VR
Patrick Savard!
DZZZZT
My fiancée, Sophie.
Hello.
A pleasure.
It's funny, but I remember you being tall and skinny.
Ha ha!
OK! Over here, everybody! Time to start the beer tasting!
Yeah!
Ouch.

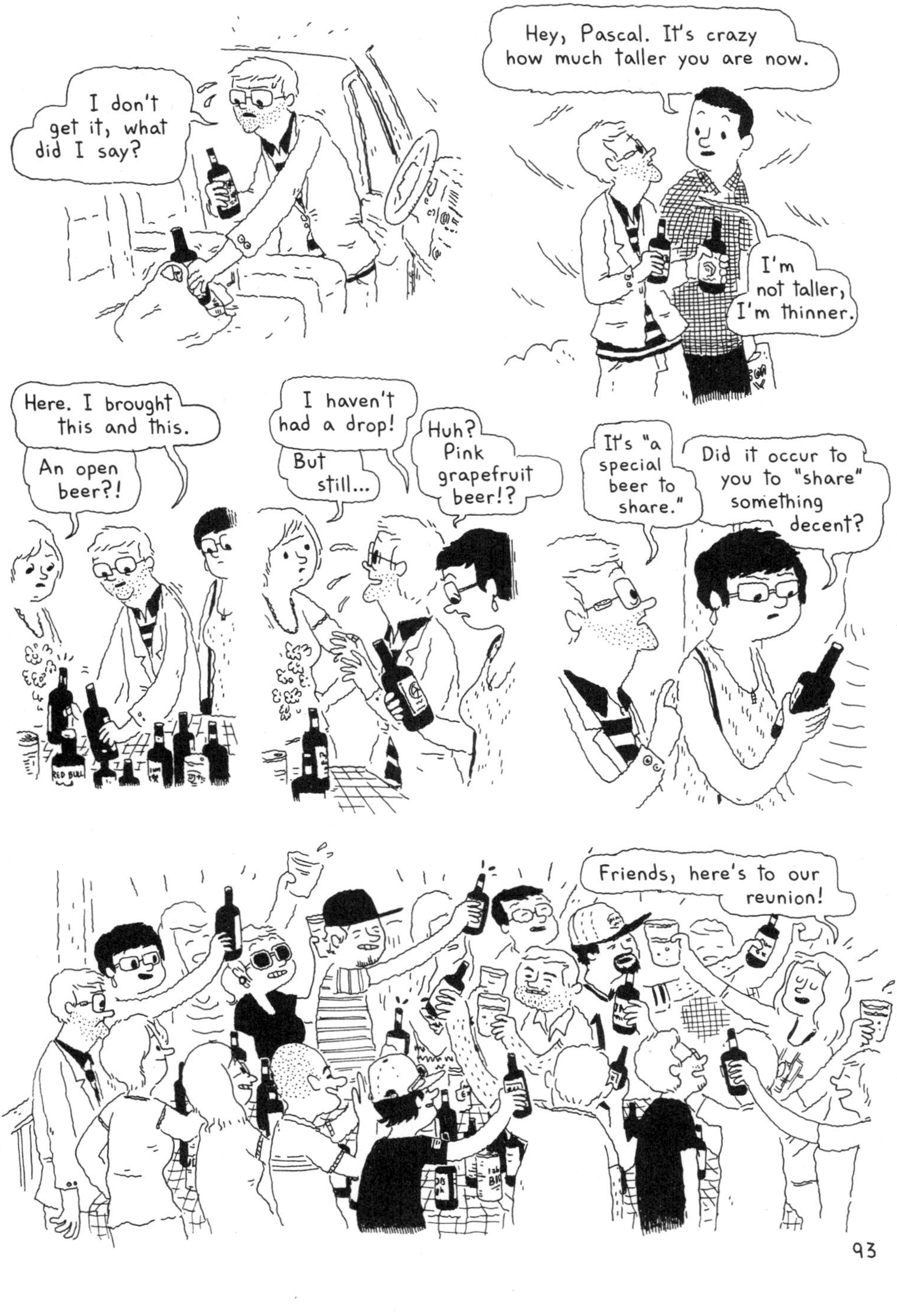
I don't get it, what did I say?
Hey, Pascal. It's crazy how much taller you are now.
I'm not taller, I'm thinner.
Here. I brought this and this.
An open beer?!
I haven't had a drop!
But still...
Huh? Pink grapefruit beer!?
It's "a special beer to share."
Did it occur to you to "share" something decent?
Friends, here's to our reunion!

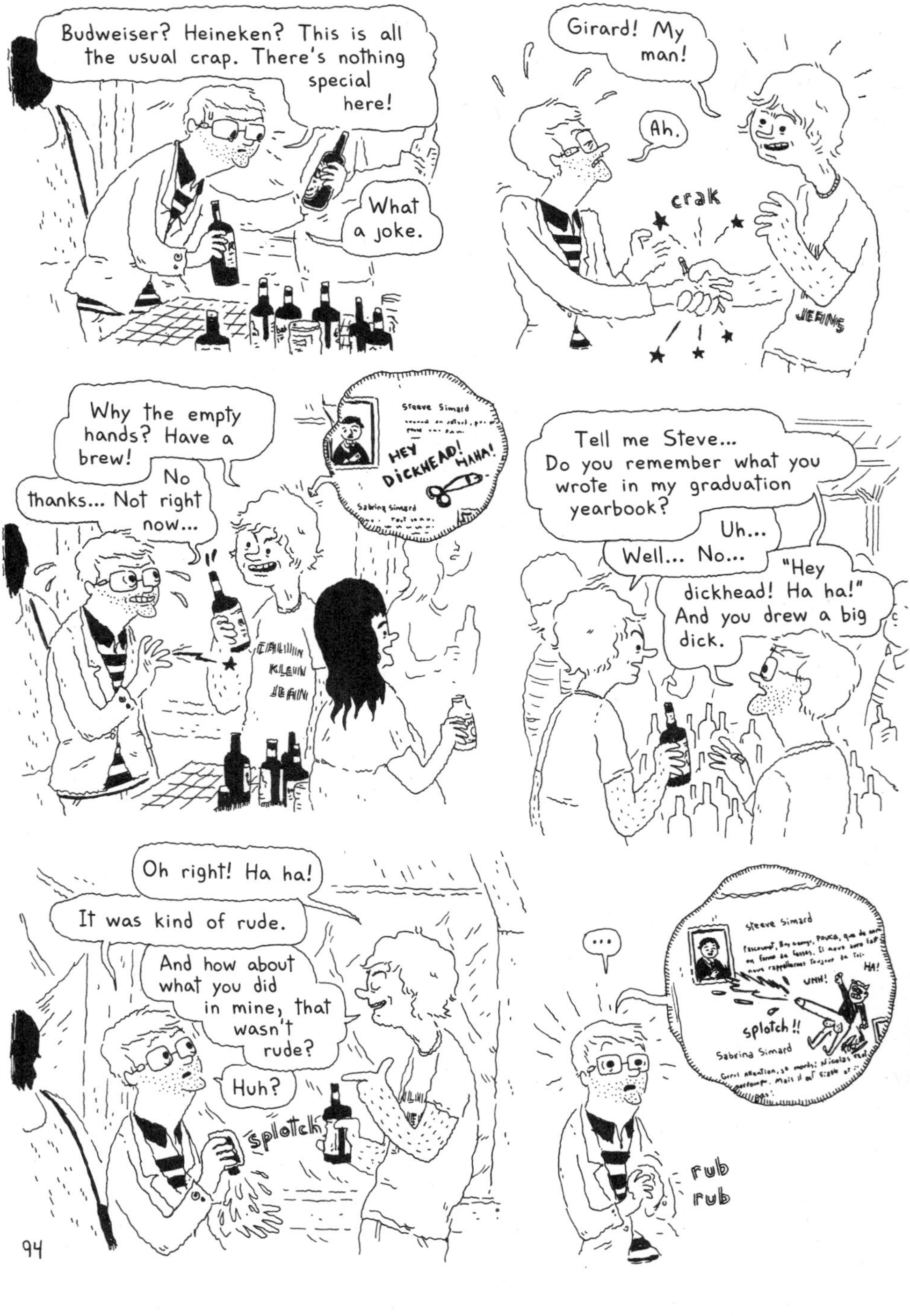
Budweiser? Heineken? This is all the usual crap. There's nothing special here!
What a joke.
Girard! My man!
Ah.
crak
JEANS
Why the empty hands? Have a brew!
No thanks... Not right now...
Steeve Simard
HEY DICKHEAD! HAHA!
Sabrina Simard
Tell me Steve... Do you remember what you wrote in my graduation yearbook?
Uh...
Well... No...
"Hey dickhead! Ha ha!" And you drew a big dick.
Oh right! Ha ha!
It was kind of rude.
And how about what you did in mine, that wasn't rude?
Huh?
splotch
...
Steeve Simard
HA!
UNH!
splotch!!
Sabrina Simard
rub rub

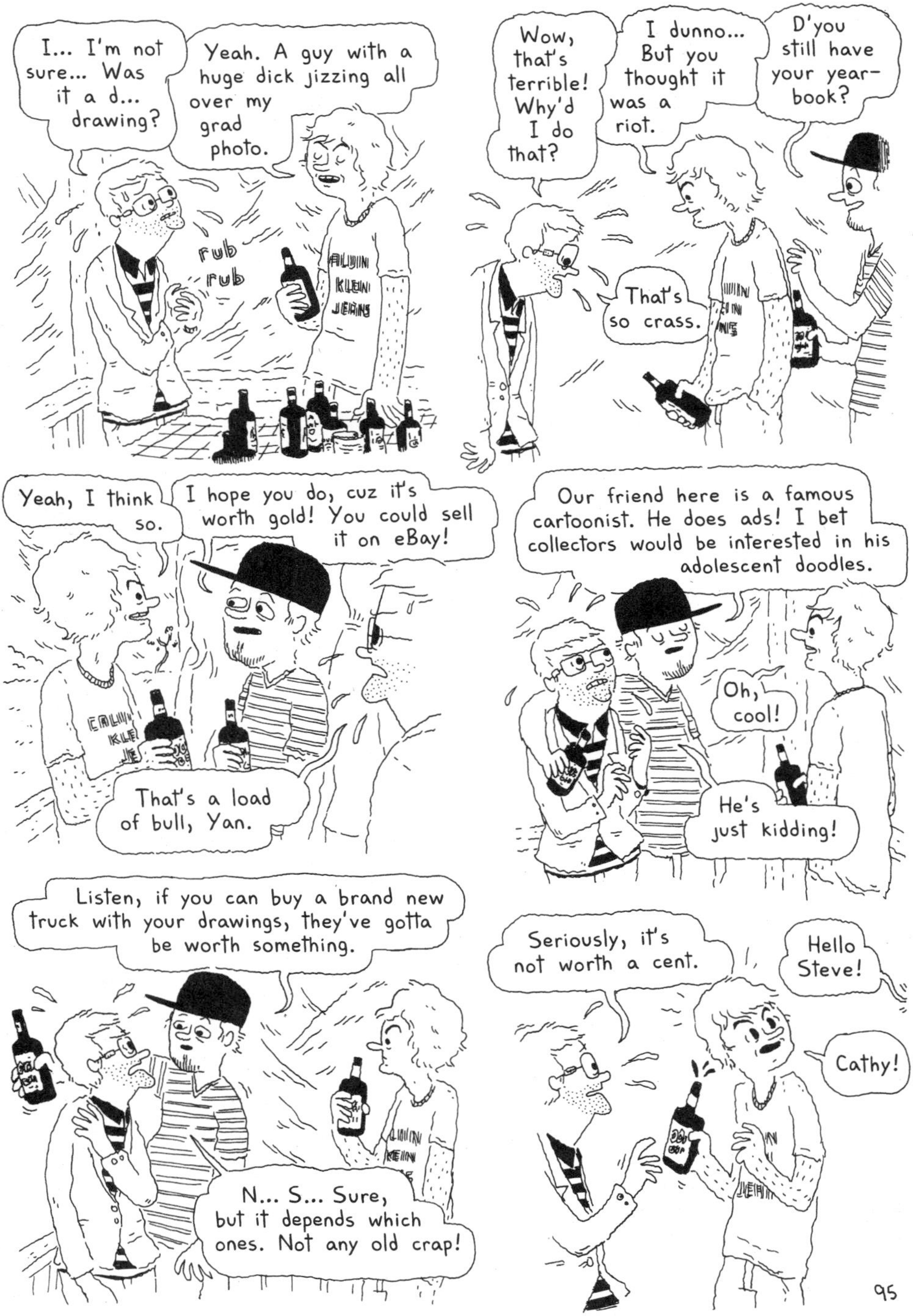

I... I'm not sure... Was it a d... drawing?
Yeah. A guy with a huge dick jizzing all over my grad photo.
rub rub
ALVIN KLEIN JEANS
Wow, that's terrible! Why'd I do that?
I dunno... But you thought it was a riot.
D'you still have your year-book?
That's so crass.
Yeah, I think so.
I hope you do, cuz it's worth gold! You could sell it on eBay!
That's a load of bull, Yan.
Our friend here is a famous cartoonist. He does ads! I bet collectors would be interested in his adolescent doodles.
Oh, cool!
He's just kidding!
Listen, if you can buy a brand new truck with your drawings, they've gotta be worth something.
N... S... Sure, but it depends which ones. Not any old crap!
Seriously, it's not worth a cent.
Hello Steve!
Cathy!

Cathy! God, y...you look fantastic! Cathy, baby! How are things? You're gorgeous! Want a beer?
She does look great...
In high school, she was covered in acne. Remember? We used to call her "pizza face"...
C'mon, let's go where we can talk.
You and Steve did. I never called her that.
She was crazy about him.
Well, here's her chance to get even.
Doesn't look like it...
Hey, Anne-Marie! I am so glad you came!
Want a beer?

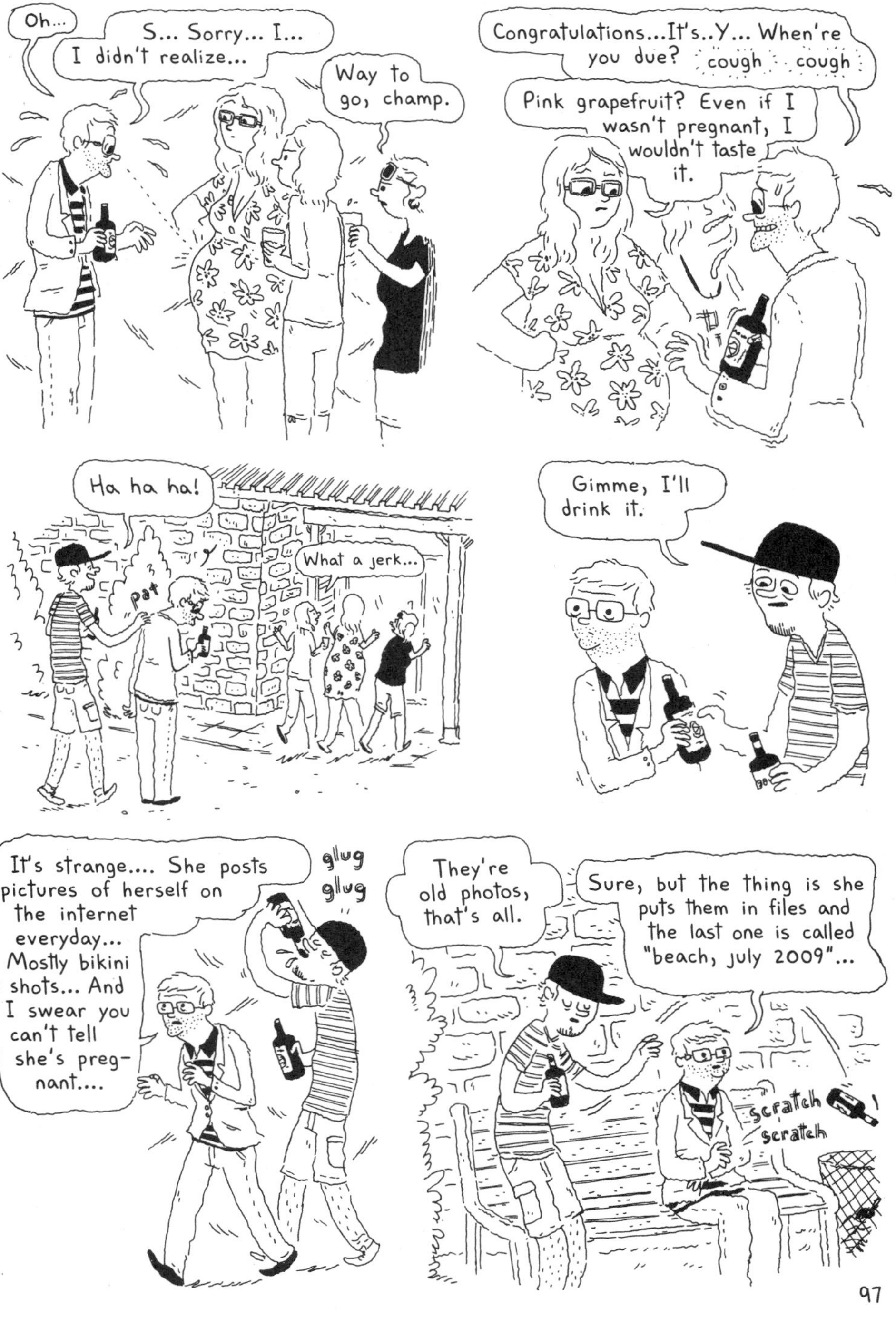
Oh...
S... Sorry... I... I didn't realize...
Way to go, champ.
Congratulations...It's..Y... When're you due? cough cough
Pink grapefruit? Even if I wasn't pregnant, I wouldn't taste it.
Ha ha ha!
pat
What a jerk...
Gimme, I'll drink it.
It's strange.... She posts pictures of herself on the internet everyday... Mostly bikini shots... And I swear you can't tell she's preg-nant....
glug glug
They're old photos, that's all.
Sure, but the thing is she puts them in files and the last one is called "beach, july 2009"...
scratch scratch

So she made a mis-take. Who cares...
The person I want to see is Lucie Côté. She was the love of my life in high school.
scratch scratch
pshhh
H... Huh?! "The love of your life"? Lucie Côté?! You never told me!
glug glug
Yeachh... This shit is vile!
Y... You know... I was... I was i..in love with her too...
Course I know, we talked about it all the time...
...But only when we were totally wasted.
Yannick! My man!
Hey Ouellet!
Huh?
clak
Oh...
You're such a great guy, man. You deserve her way more than me!

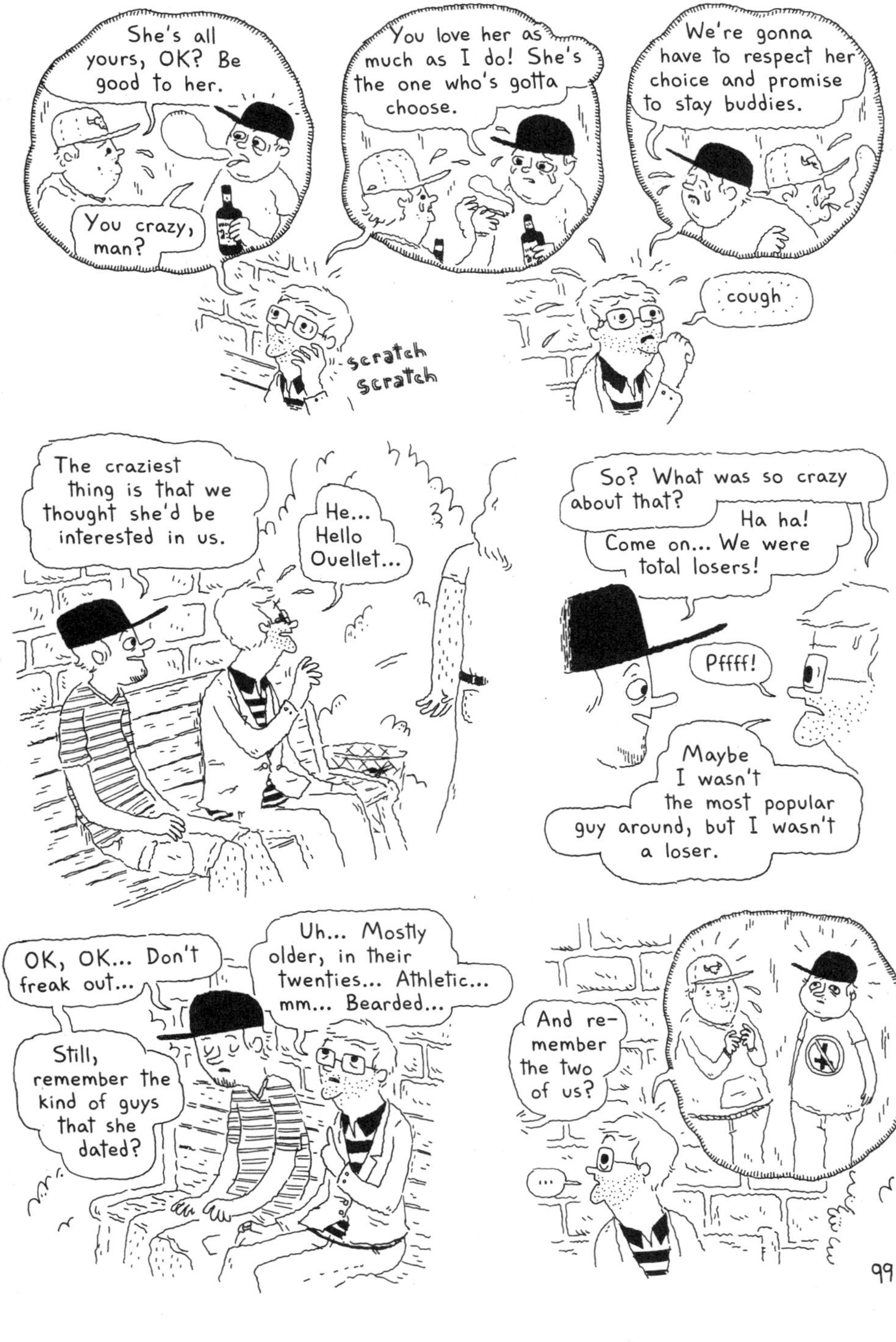
She's all yours, OK? Be good to her.
You crazy, man?
You love her as much as I do! She's the one who's gotta choose.
We're gonna have to respect her choice and promise to stay buddies.
scratch scratch
cough
The craziest thing is that we thought she'd be interested in us.
He... Hello Ouellet...
So? What was so crazy about that?
Ha ha! Come on... We were total losers!
Pffff!
Maybe I wasn't the most popular guy around, but I wasn't a loser.
OK, OK... Don't freak out...
Still, remember the kind of guys that she dated?
Uh... Mostly older, in their twenties... Athletic... mm... Bearded...
And re-member the two of us?
...

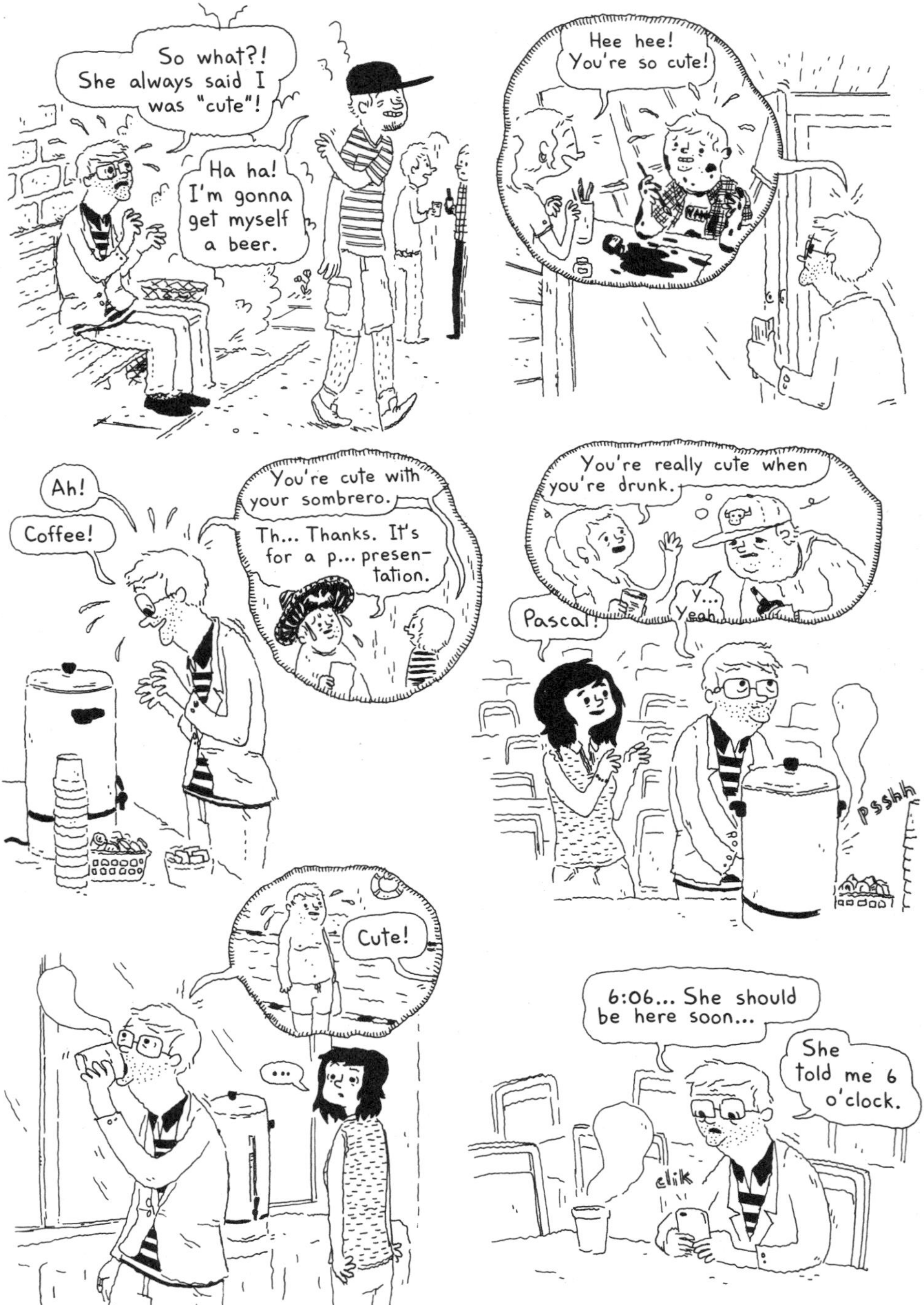
So what?! She always said I was "cute"!
Ha ha! I'm gonna get myself a beer.
Hee hee! You're so cute!
Ah!
Coffee!
You're cute with your sombrero.
Th... Thanks. It's for a p... presentation.
You're really cute when you're drunk.
Y... Yeah.
Pascal!
psshh
Cute!
...
6:06... She should be here soon...
She told me 6 o'clock.
clik

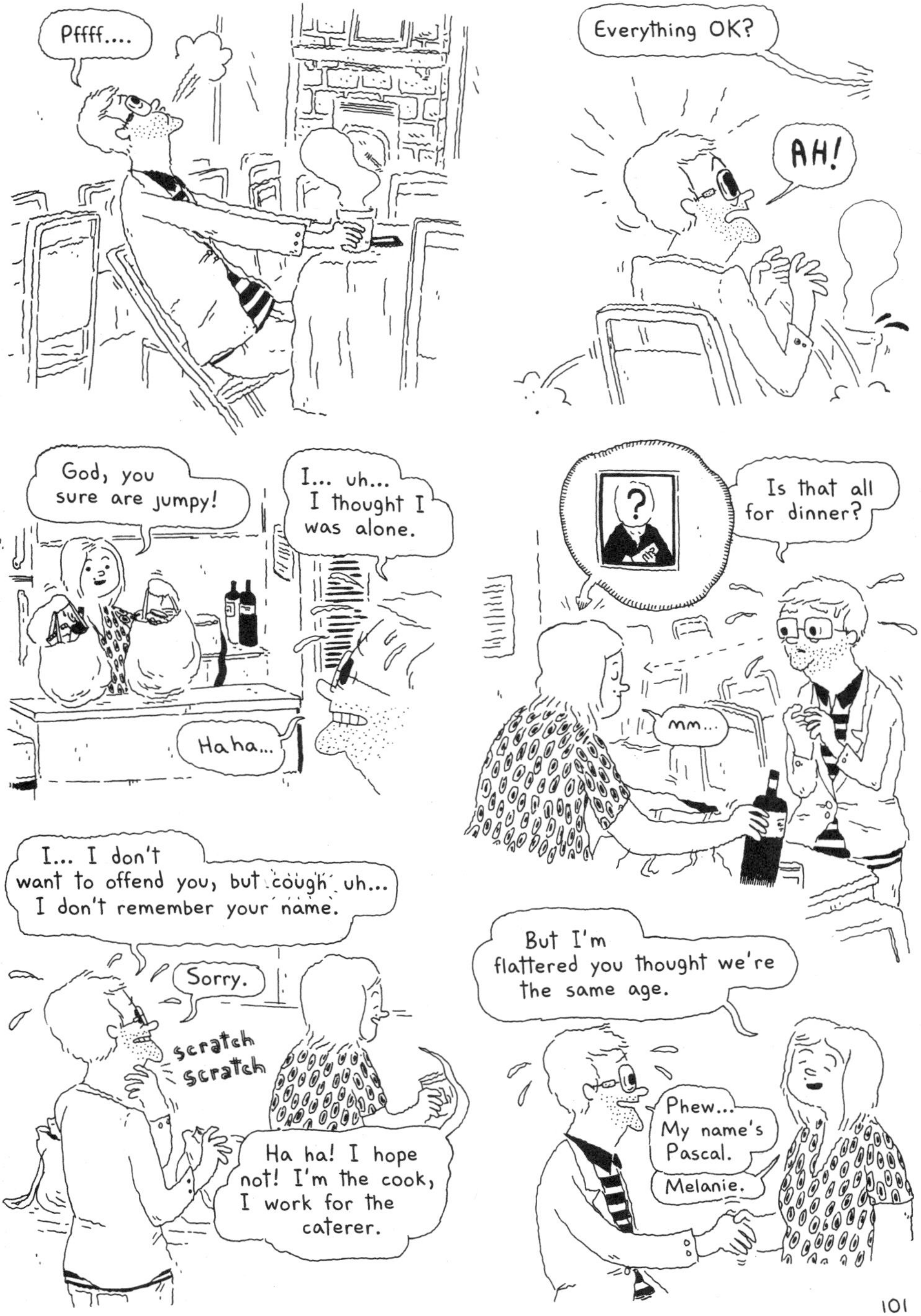
Pffff....
Everything OK?
AH!
God, you sure are jumpy!
I... uh... I thought I was alone.
Haha...
Is that all for dinner?
mm...
I... I don't want to offend you, but cough uh... I don't remember your name.
Sorry.
scratch scratch
Ha ha! I hope not! I'm the cook, I work for the caterer.
But I'm flattered you thought we're the same age.
Phew... My name's Pascal.
Melanie.

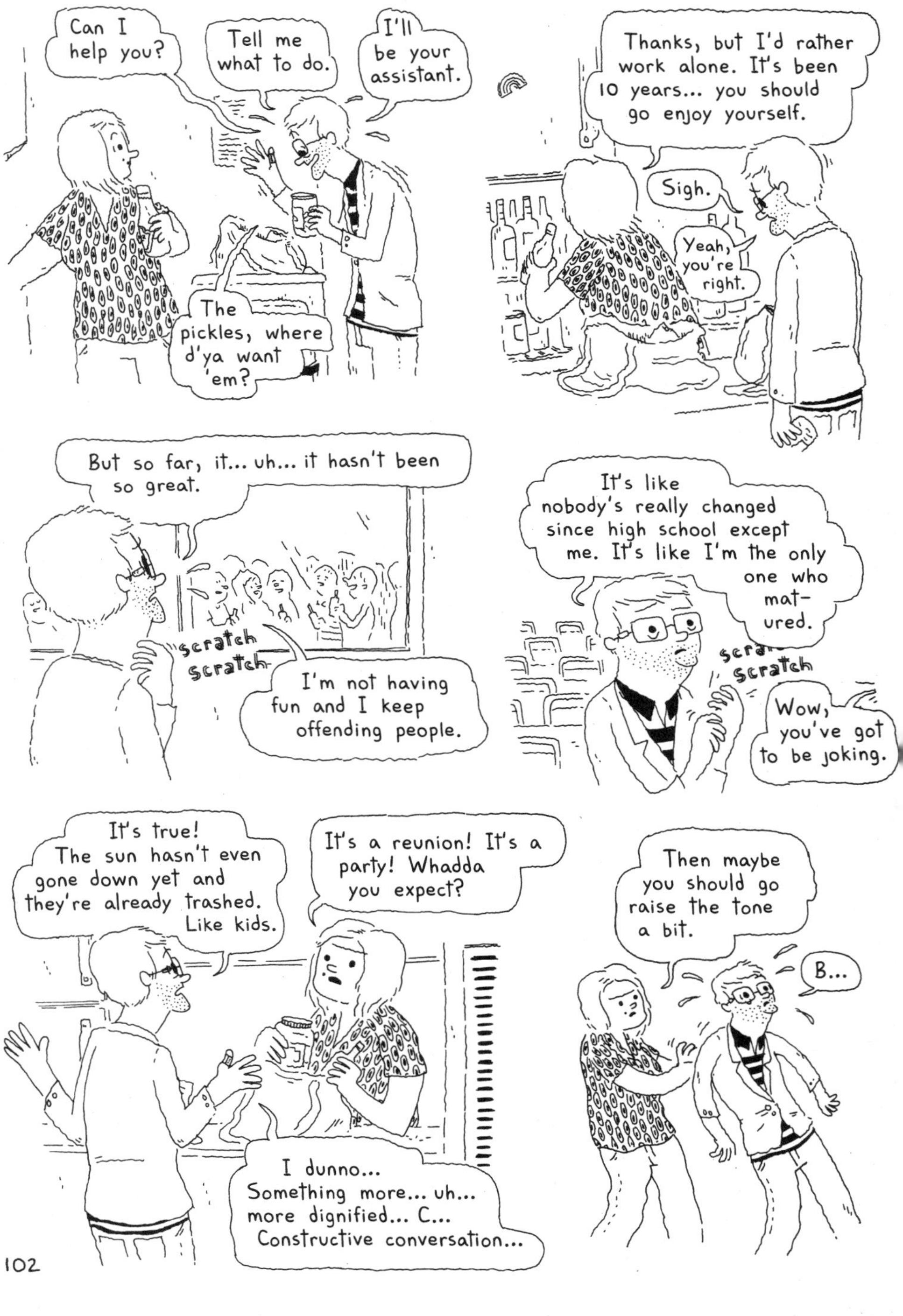

Can I help you?
Tell me what to do.
I'll be your assistant.
The pickles, where d'ya want 'em?
Thanks, but I'd rather work alone. It's been 10 years... you should go enjoy yourself.
Sigh.
Yeah, you're right.
But so far, it... uh... it hasn't been so great.
scratch scratch
I'm not having fun and I keep offending people.
It's like nobody's really changed since high school except me. It's like I'm the only one who mat-ured.
scratch
Wow, you've got to be joking.
It's true! The sun hasn't even gone down yet and they're already trashed. Like kids.
It's a reunion! It's a party! Whadda you expect?
I dunno... Something more... uh... more dignified... C... Constructive conversation...
Then maybe you should go raise the tone a bit.
B...

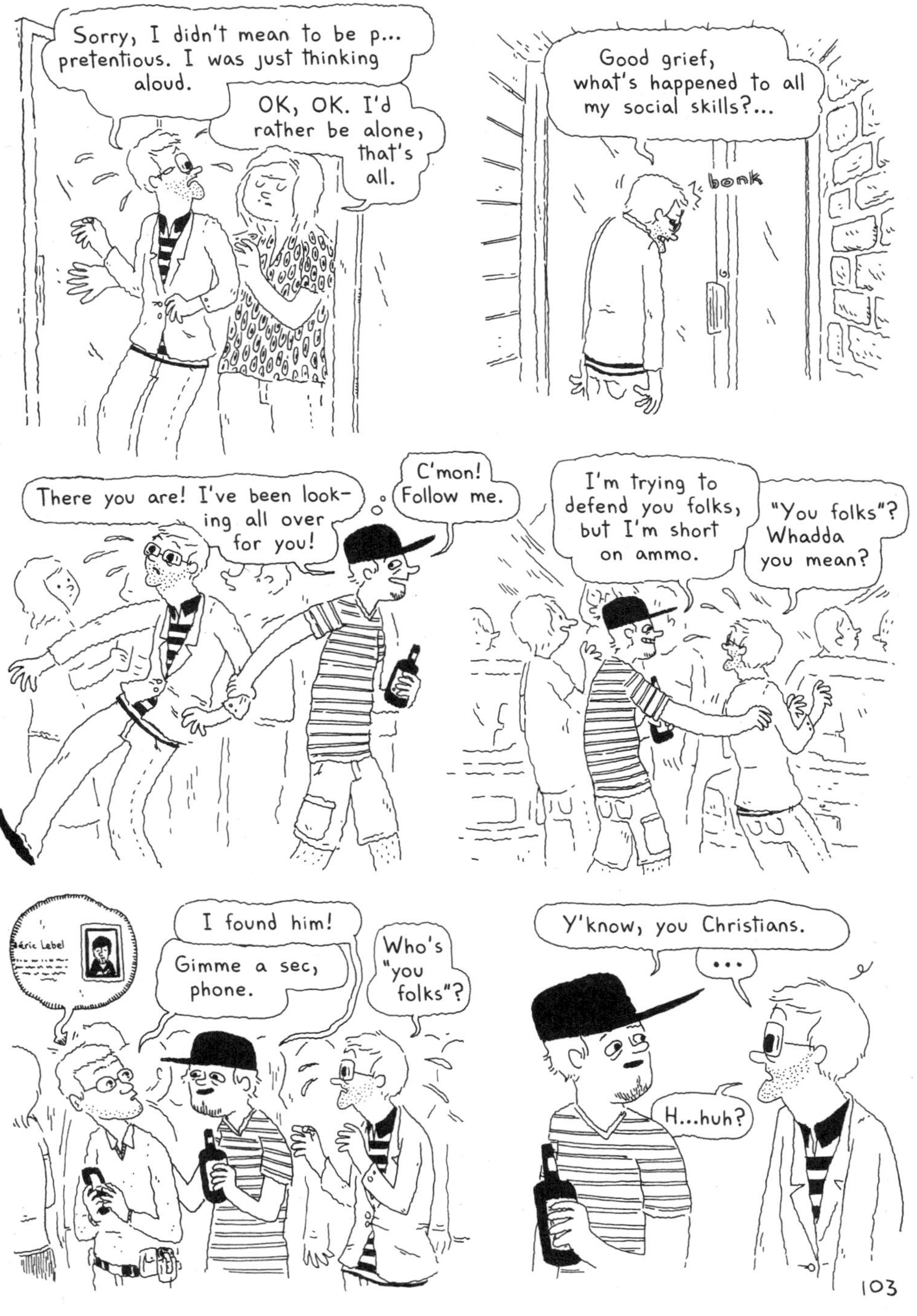

Sorry, I didn't mean to be p... pretentious. I was just thinking aloud.
OK, OK. I'd rather be alone, that's all.
Good grief, what's happened to all my social skills?...
bonk
There you are! I've been looking all over for you!
C'mon! Follow me.
I'm trying to defend you folks, but I'm short on ammo.
"You folks"? Whadda you mean?
I found him!
Gimme a sec, phone.
Who's "you folks"?
Y'know, you Christians.
...
H...huh?

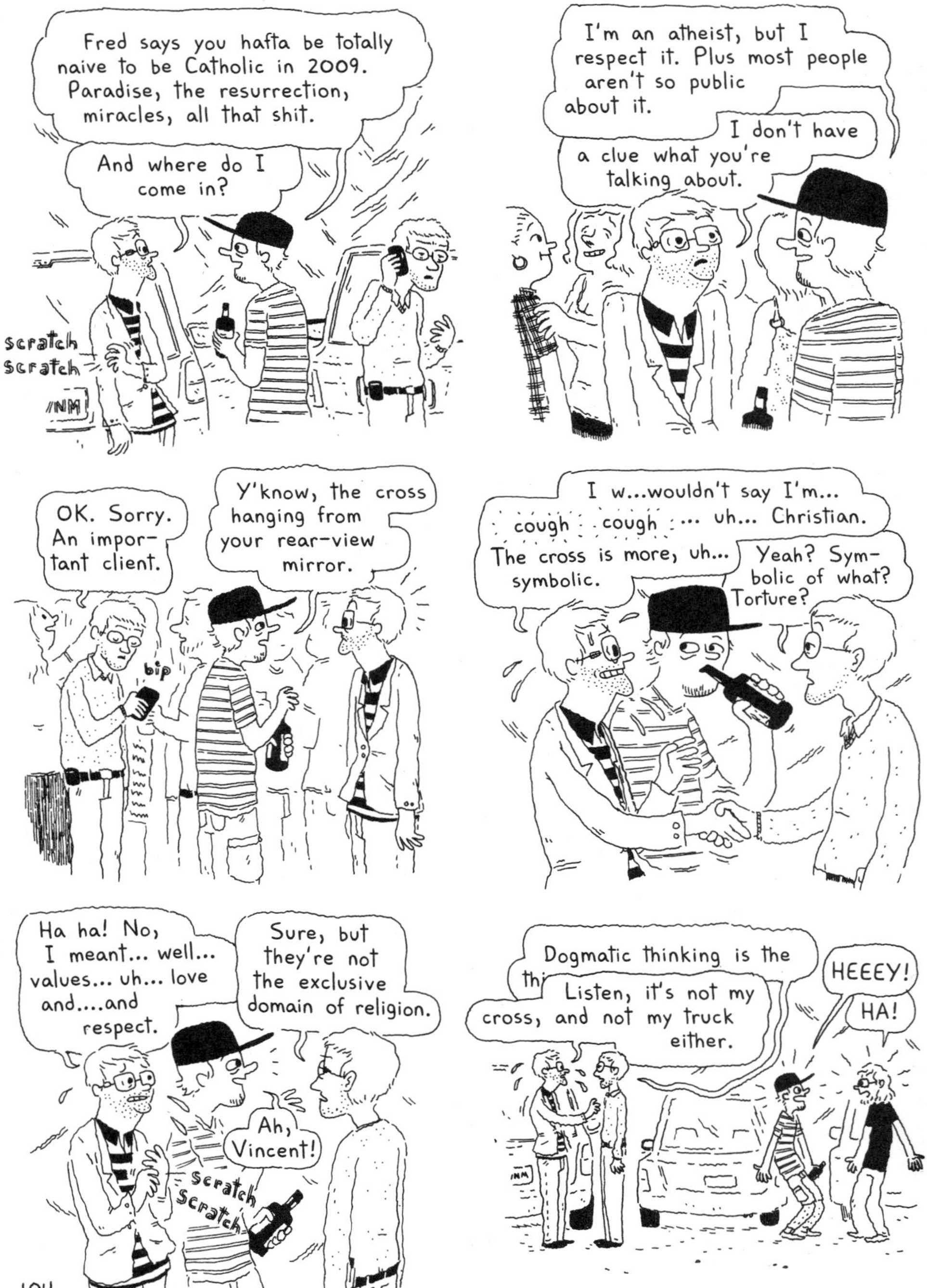
Fred says you hafta be totally naive to be Catholic in 2009. Paradise, the resurrection, miracles, all that shit.
And where do I come in?
scratch scratch
I'm an atheist, but I respect it. Plus most people aren't so public about it.
I don't have a clue what you're talking about.
OK. Sorry. An important client.
Y'know, the cross hanging from your rear-view mirror.
bip
I w...wouldn't say I'm... cough cough ... uh... Christian.
The cross is more, uh... symbolic.
Yeah? Symbolic of what? Torture?
Ha ha! No, I meant... well... values... uh... love and....and respect.
Sure, but they're not the exclusive domain of religion.
Ah, Vincent!
scratch scratch
Dogmatic thinking is the thi
Listen, it's not my cross, and not my truck either.
HEEEY!
HA!

It's my father's, but I let Yannick think it's mine.
How come?
Ah, long story...
Nothing interesting, really. Ha ha!
Oh, by the way, is it true that you only invited me to your parties because I always brought pot?
Trying to change the topic now, huh?...
Not at all!
You're the one who doesn't want to answer my question.
C'mon, let's go set Yannick straight.
No, no, we don't need to.
Admit it, you're hiding something!
riiing
Uh... Isn't that one of your phones?
riiinng
riiing
riiing
Yes... Yes... Hold on, I'll check. I've got the file in my car.
Aaaah...
4x4

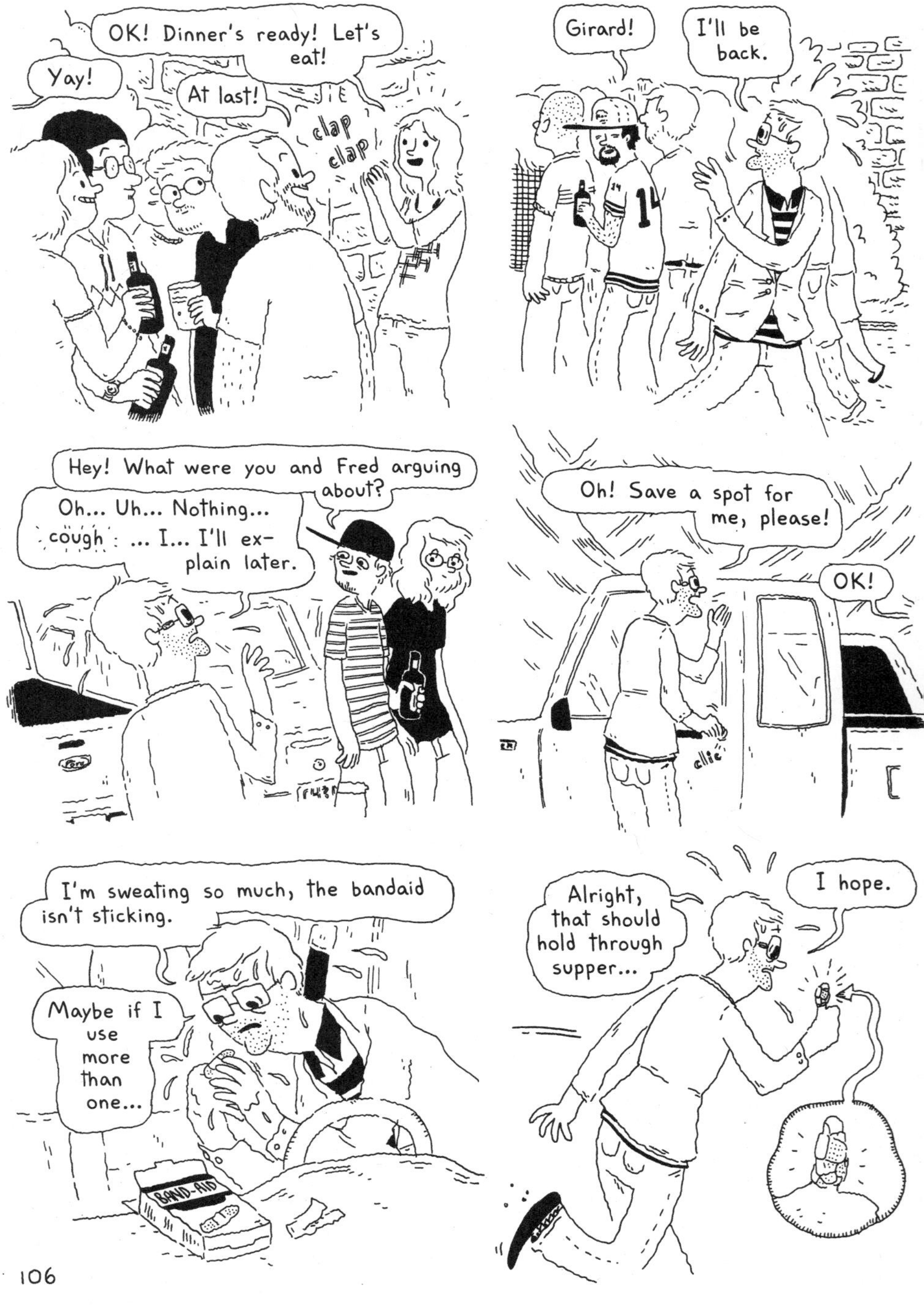
OK! Dinner's ready! Let's eat!
Yay!
At last!
clap clap
Girard!
I'll be back.
Hey! What were you and Fred arguing about?
Oh... Uh... Nothing... cough ... I... I'll explain later.
Oh! Save a spot for me, please!
OK!
I'm sweating so much, the bandaid isn't sticking.
Maybe if I use more than one...
BAND-AID
Alright, that should hold through supper...
I hope.

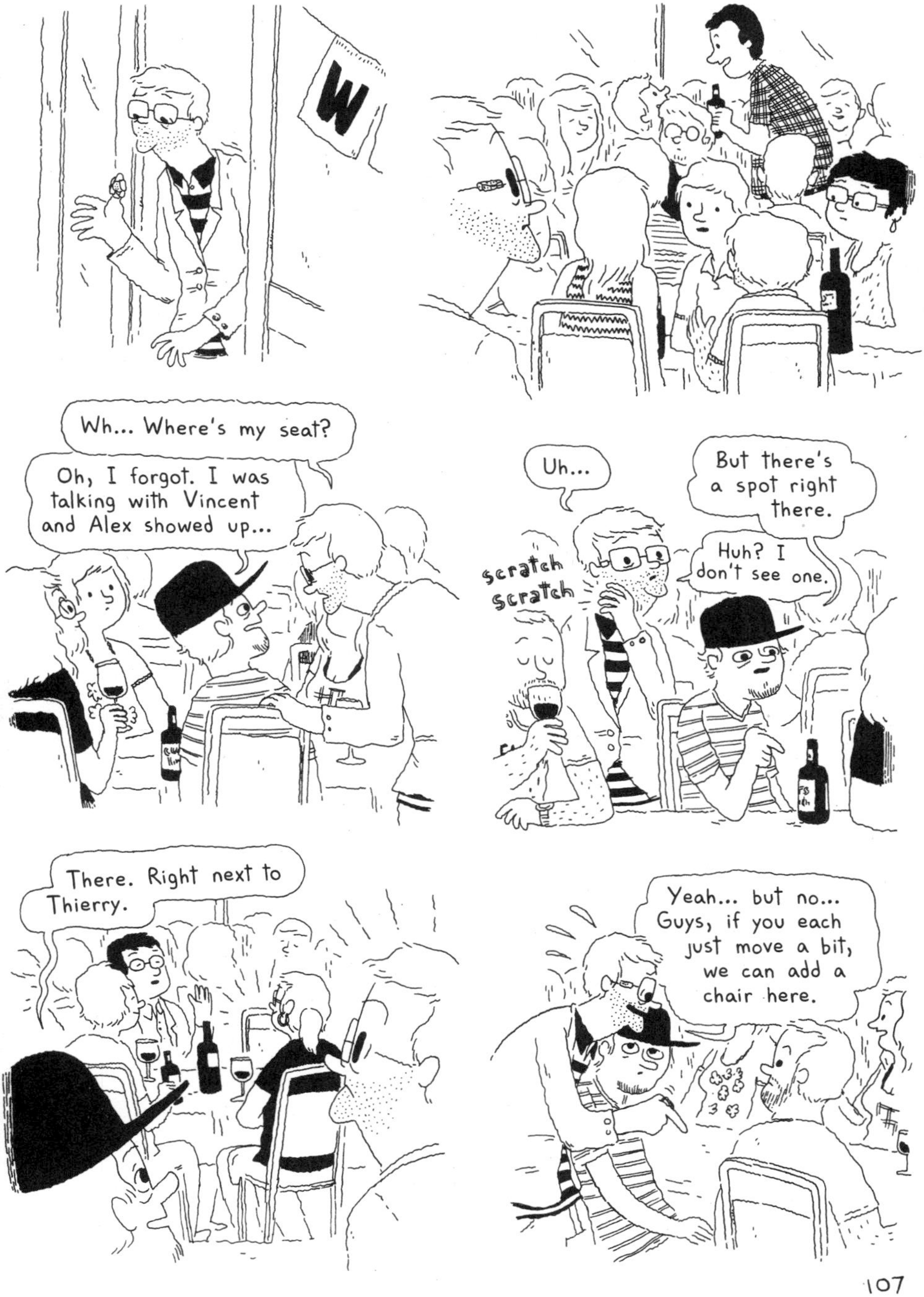
Wh... Where's my seat?
Oh, I forgot. I was talking with Vincent and Alex showed up...
Uh...
But there's a spot right there.
Huh? I don't see one.
scratch scratch
There. Right next to Thierry.
Yeah... but no... Guys, if you each just move a bit, we can add a chair here.

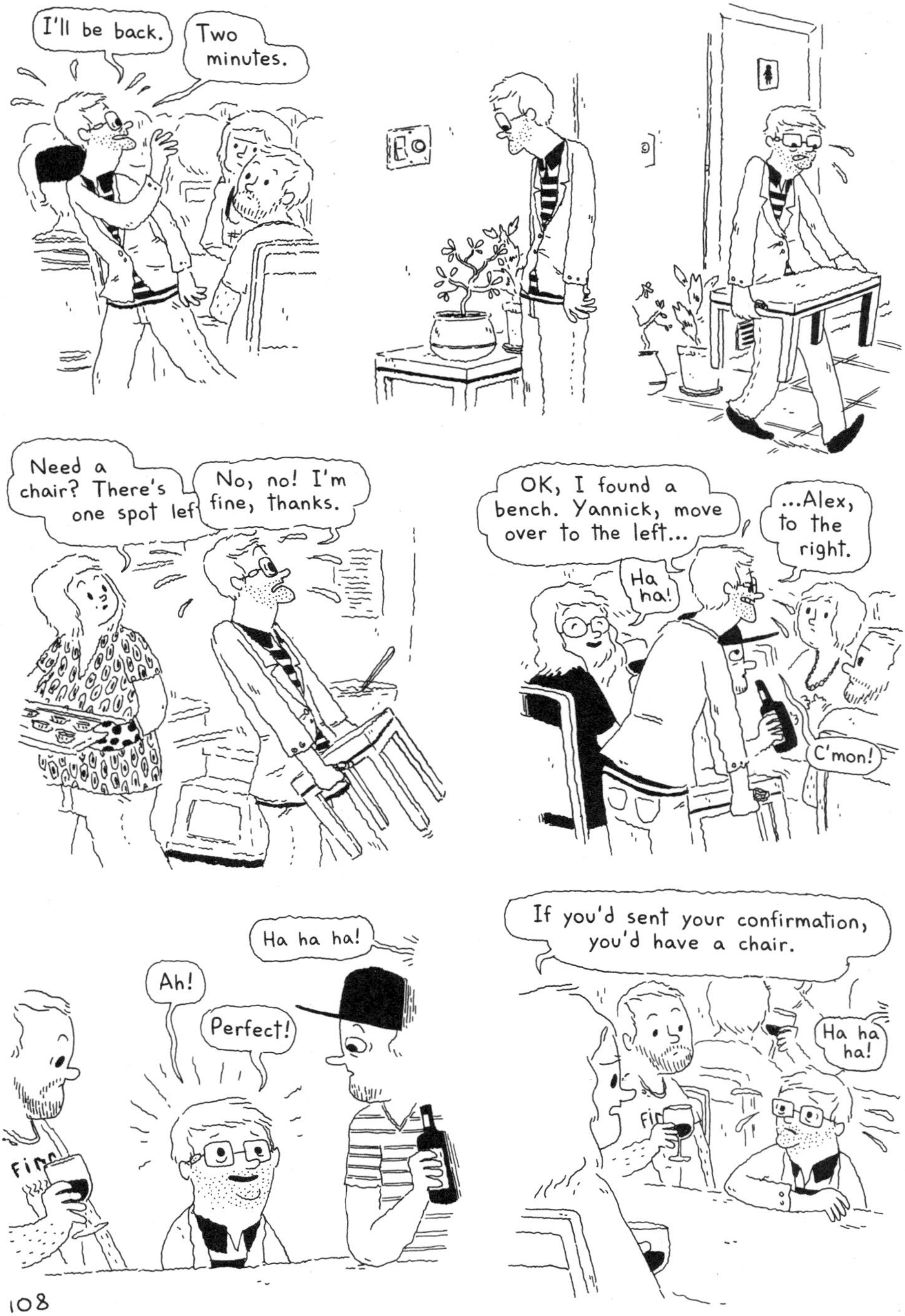
I'll be back.
Two minutes.
Need a chair? There's one spot lef
No, no! I'm fine, thanks.
OK, I found a bench. Yannick, move over to the left...
Ha ha!
...Alex, to the right.
C'mon!
Ah!
Perfect!
Ha ha ha!
If you'd sent your confirmation, you'd have a chair.
Ha ha ha!

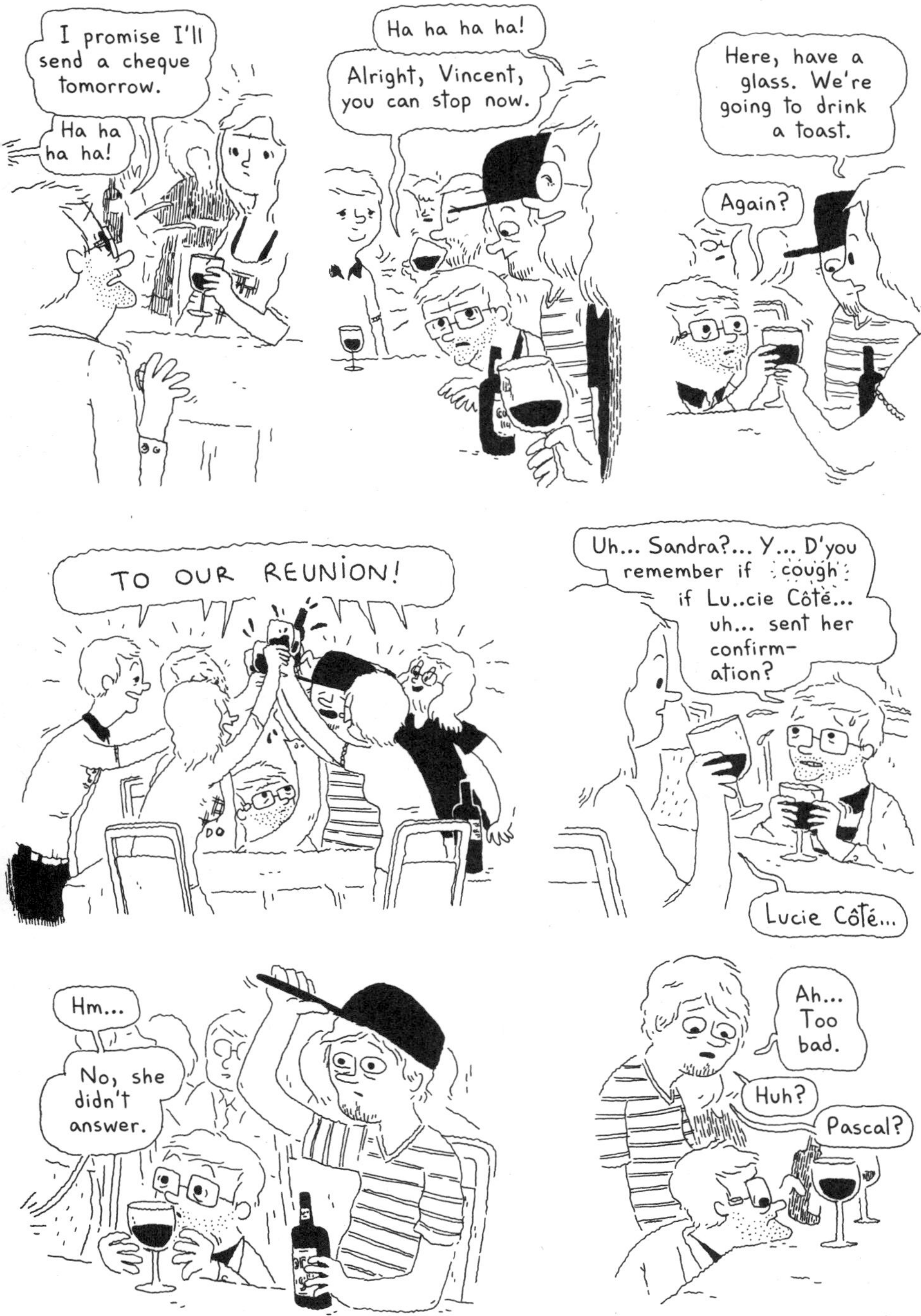
I promise I'll send a cheque tomorrow.
Ha ha ha ha!
Ha ha ha ha!
Alright, Vincent, you can stop now.
Here, have a glass. We're going to drink a toast.
Again?
TO OUR REUNION!
Uh... Sandra?... Y... D'you remember if cough if Lu..cie Côté... uh... sent her confirmation?
Lucie Côté...
Hm...
No, she didn't answer.
Ah... Too bad.
Huh?
Pascal?

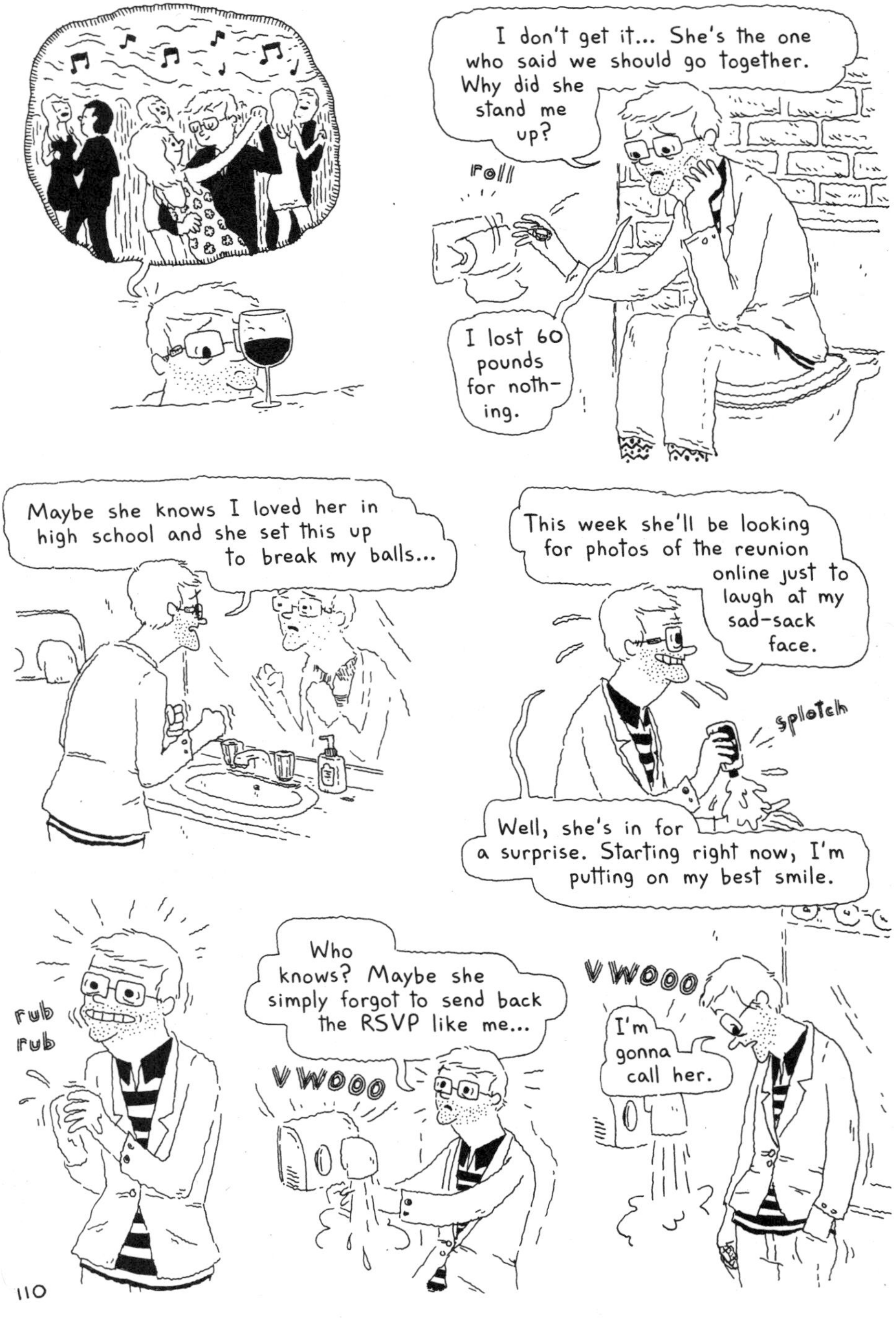
I don't get it... She's the one who said we should go together.
Why did she stand me up?
roll
I lost 60 pounds for noth-ing.
Maybe she knows I loved her in high school and she set this up to break my balls...
This week she'll be looking for photos of the reunion online just to laugh at my sad-sack face.
splotch
Well, she's in for a surprise. Starting right now, I'm putting on my best smile.
rub rub
Who knows? Maybe she simply forgot to send back the RSVP like me...
VWOOO
VWOOO
I'm gonna call her.

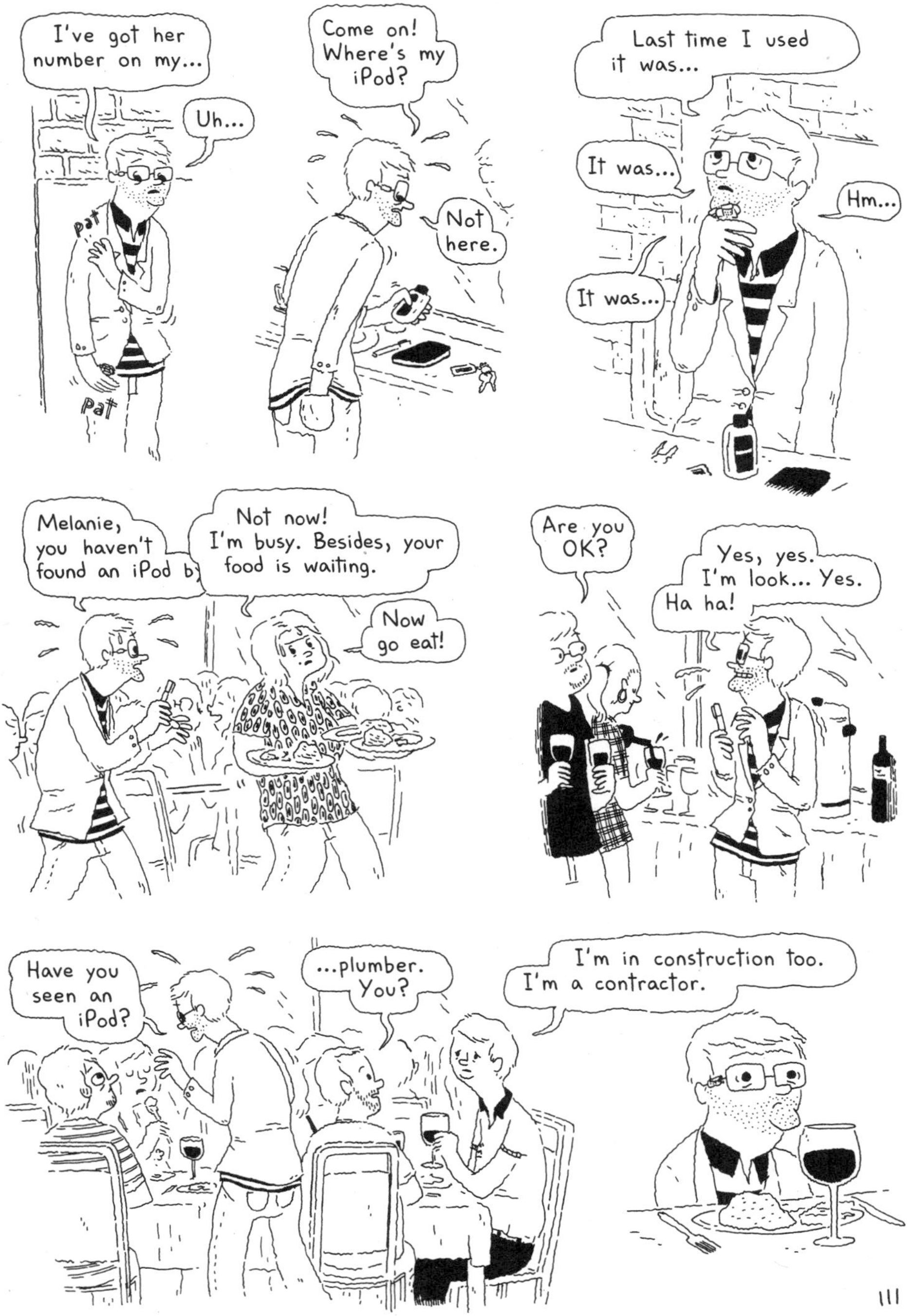
I've got her number on my...
pat
pat
Uh...
Come on! Where's my iPod?
Not here.
Last time I used it was...
It was...
It was...
Hm...
Melanie, you haven't found an iPod b
Not now! I'm busy. Besides, your food is waiting.
Now go eat!
Are you OK?
Yes, yes. I'm look... Yes. Ha ha!
Have you seen an iPod?
...plumber. You?
I'm in construction too. I'm a contractor.

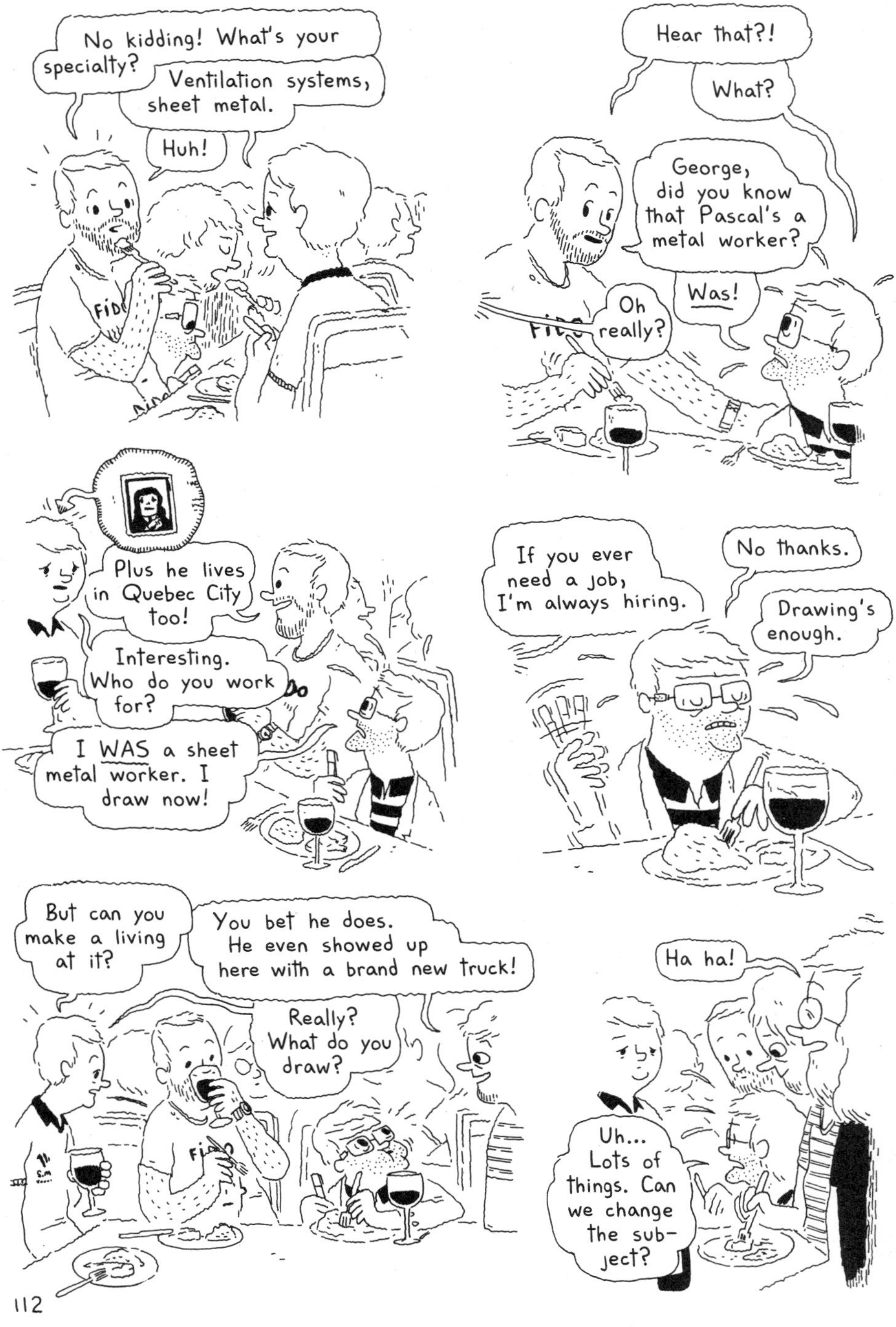
No kidding! What's your specialty?
Ventilation systems, sheet metal.
Huh!
FIDO
Hear that?!
What?
George, did you know that Pascal's a metal worker?
Was!
Oh really?
Plus he lives in Quebec City too!
Interesting. Who do you work for?
I WAS a sheet metal worker. I draw now!
If you ever need a job, I'm always hiring.
No thanks.
Drawing's enough.
But can you make a living at it?
You bet he does. He even showed up here with a brand new truck!
Really? What do you draw?
Ha ha!
Uh... Lots of things. Can we change the sub-ject?

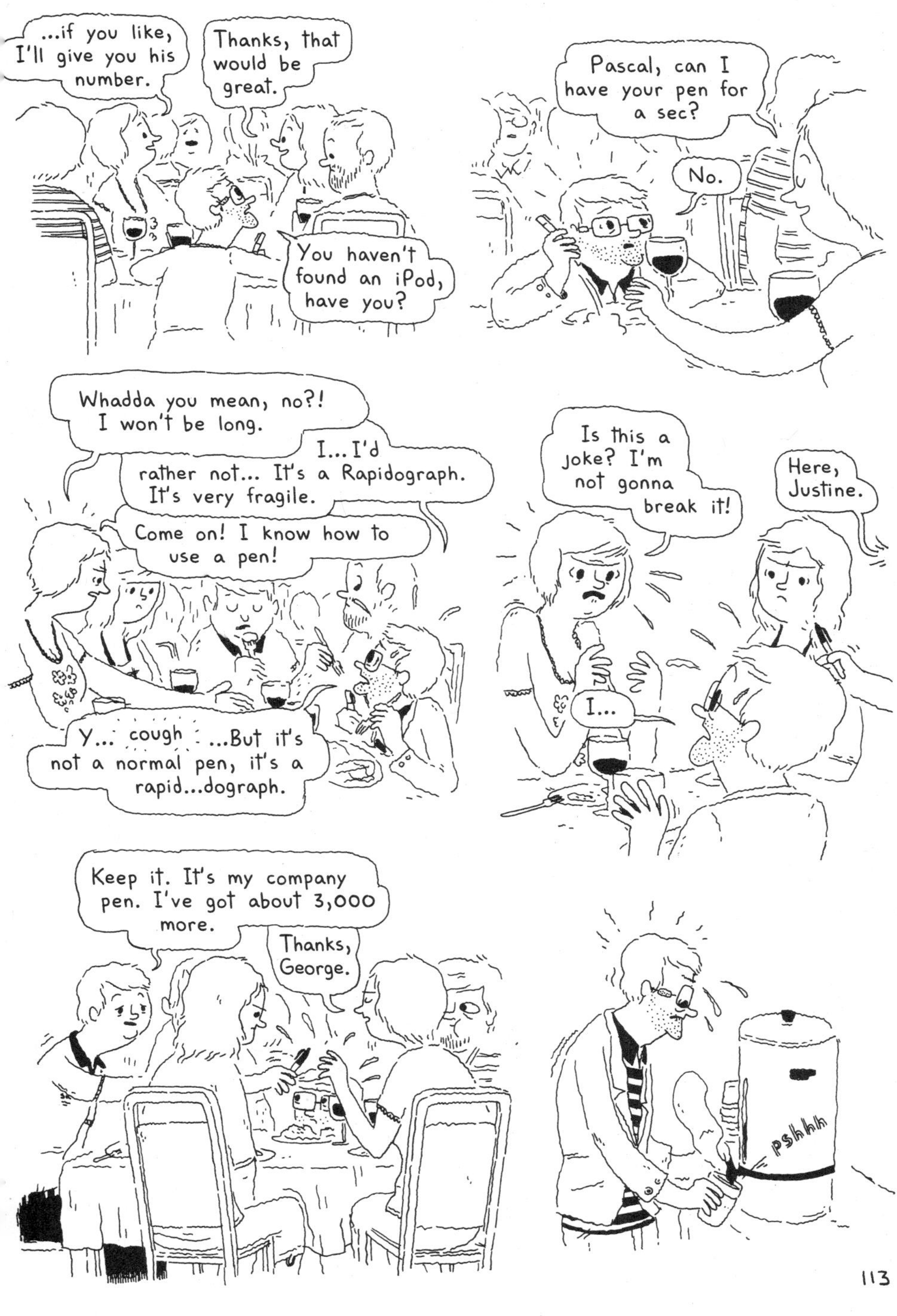
...if you like, I'll give you his number.
Thanks, that would be great.
You haven't found an iPod, have you?
Pascal, can I have your pen for a sec?
No.
Whadda you mean, no?! I won't be long.
I... I'd rather not... It's a Rapidograph. It's very fragile.
Come on! I know how to use a pen!
Y... cough ...But it's not a normal pen, it's a rapid...dograph.
Is this a joke? I'm not gonna break it!
I...
Here, Justine.
Keep it. It's my company pen. I've got about 3,000 more.
Thanks, George.
pshhh

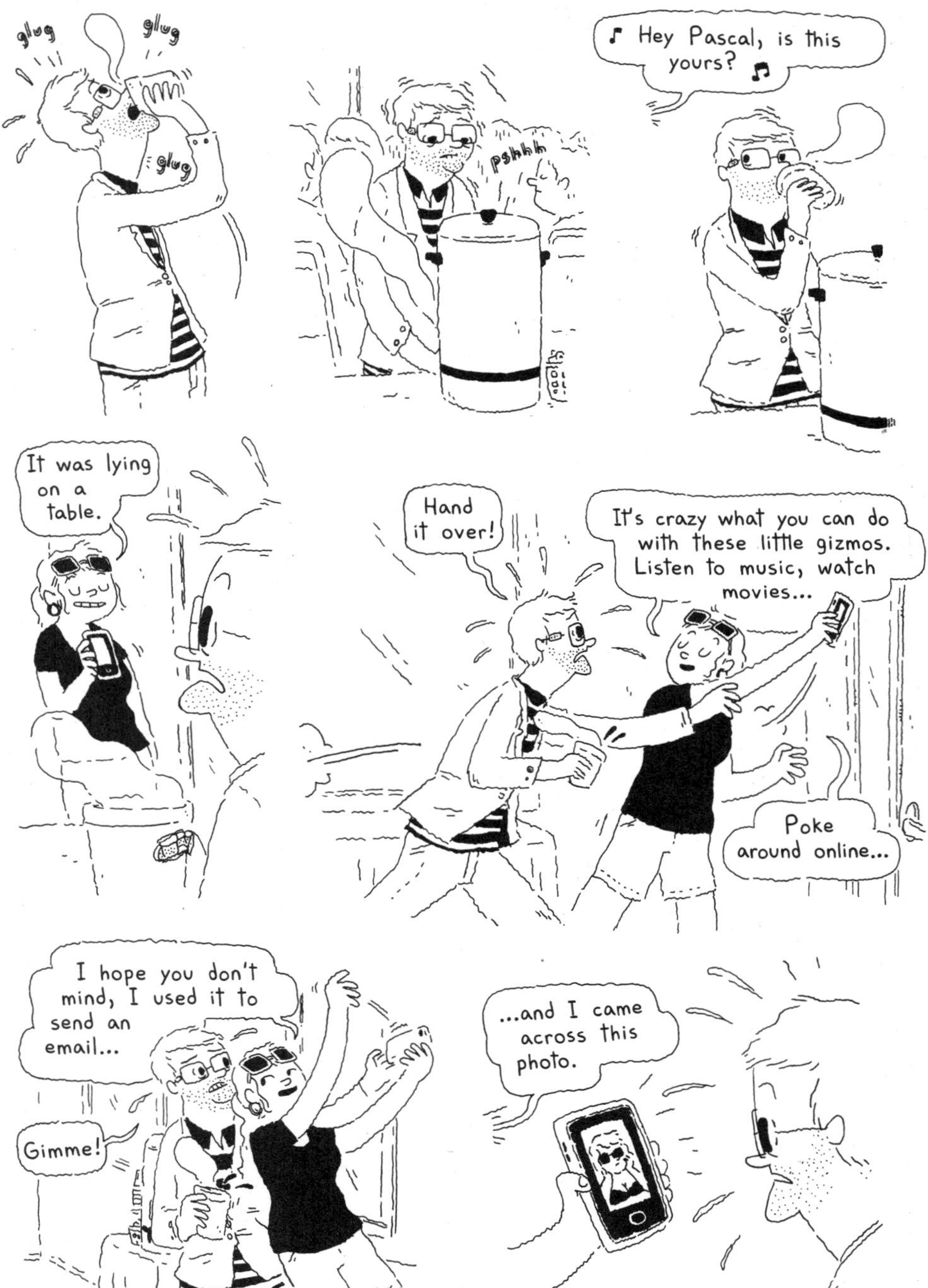
glug
glug
glug
pshhh
♪ Hey Pascal, is this yours? ♫
It was lying on a table.
Hand it over!
It's crazy what you can do with these little gizmos. Listen to music, watch movies...
Poke around online...
I hope you don't mind, I used it to send an email...
Gimme!
...and I came across this photo.

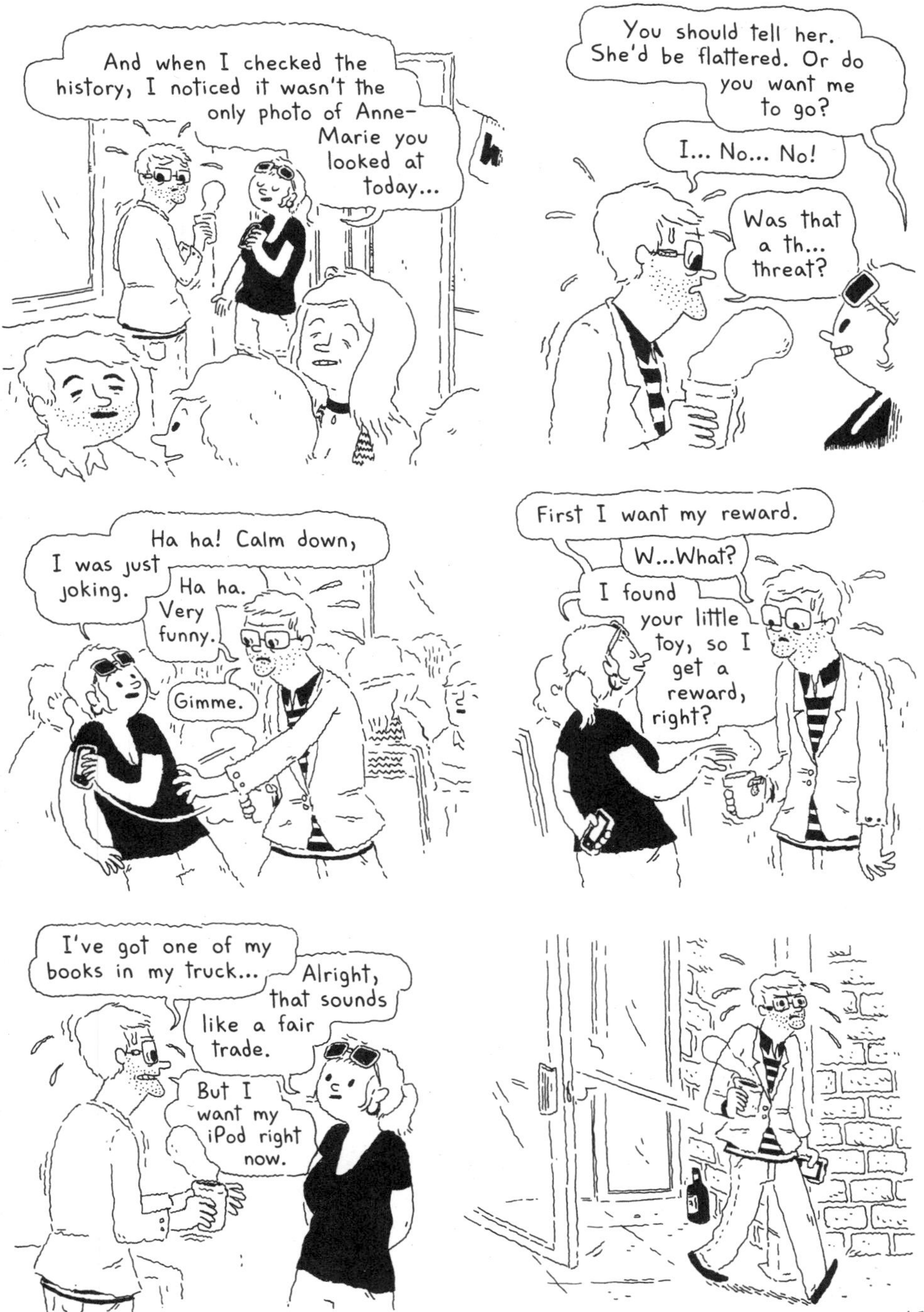
And when I checked the history, I noticed it wasn't the only photo of Anne-Marie you looked at today...
You should tell her. She'd be flattered. Or do you want me to go?
I... No... No!
Was that a th... threat?
Ha ha! Calm down, I was just joking.
Ha ha. Very funny.
Gimme.
First I want my reward.
W...What?
I found your little toy, so I get a reward, right?
I've got one of my books in my truck...
Alright, that sounds like a fair trade.
But I want my iPod right now.

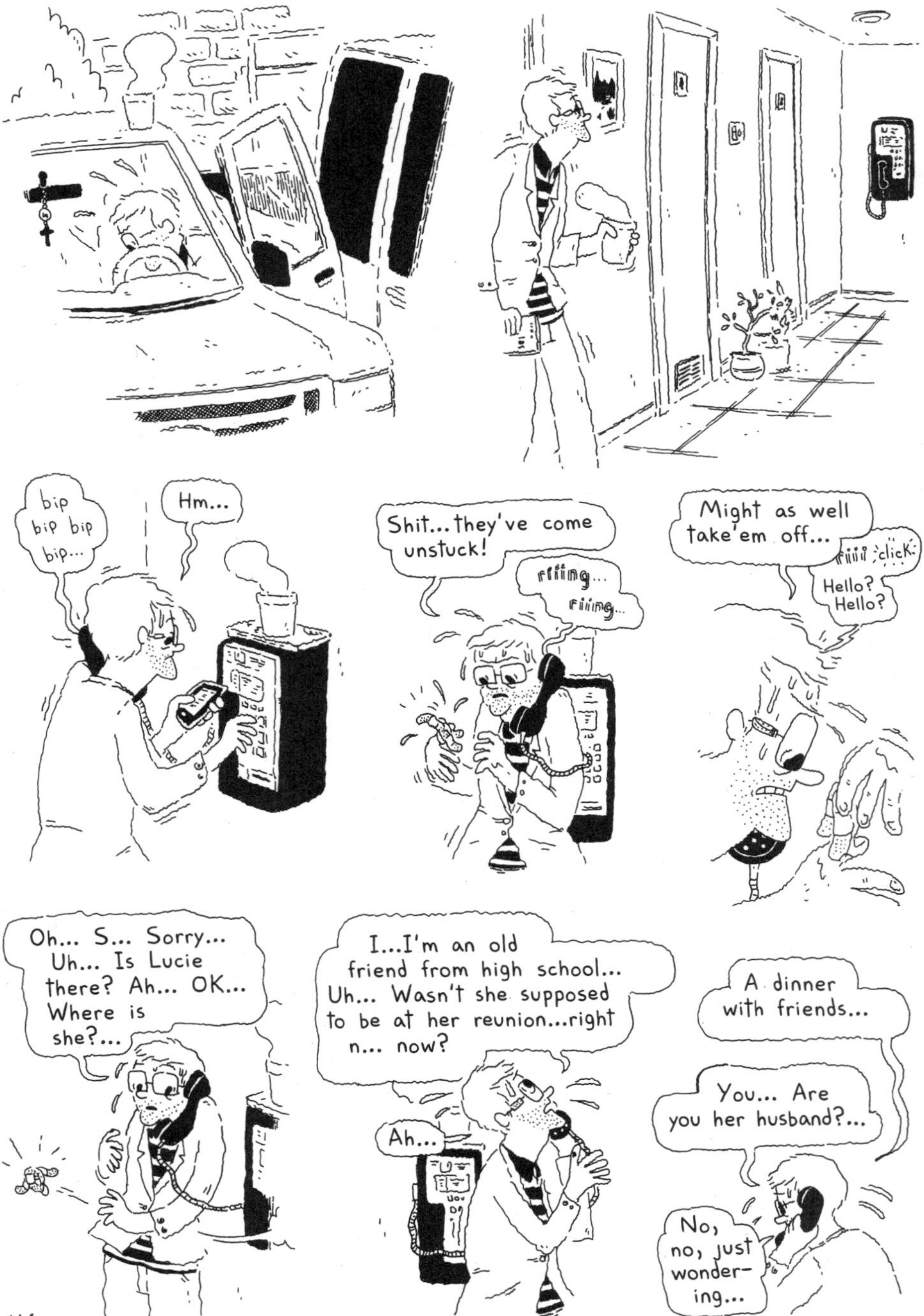

bip bip bip bip...
Hm...
Shit... they've come unstuck!
riiing... riiing...
Might as well take'em off...
riiii click
Hello? Hello?
Oh... S... Sorry... Uh... Is Lucie there? Ah... OK... Where is she?...
I...I'm an old friend from high school... Uh... Wasn't she supposed to be at her reunion...right n... now?
Ah...
A dinner with friends...
You... Are you her husband?...
No, no, just wondering...

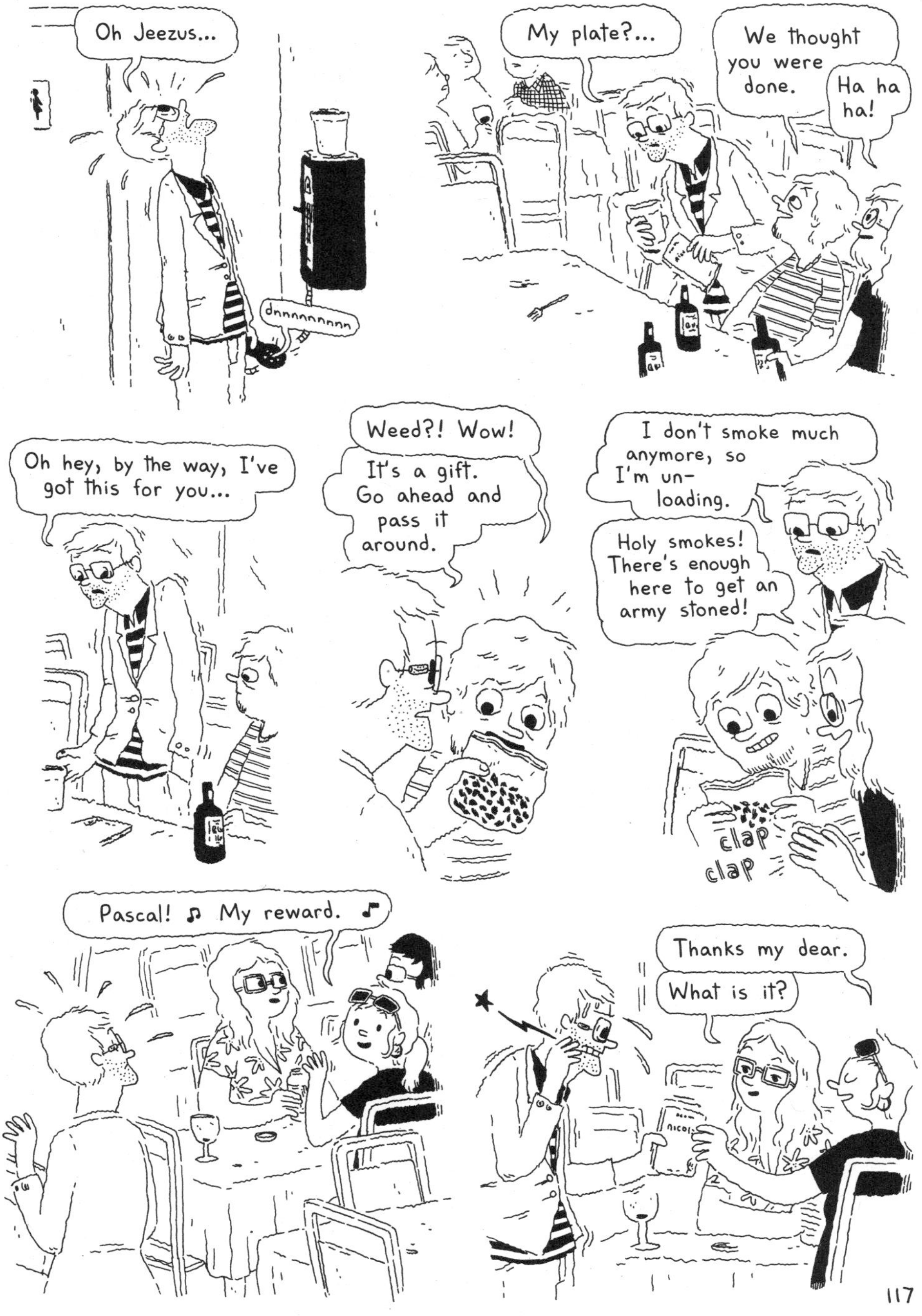
Oh Jeezus...
dnnnnnnnnn
My plate?...
We thought you were done.
Ha ha ha!
Oh hey, by the way, I've got this for you...
Weed?! Wow!
It's a gift. Go ahead and pass it around.
I don't smoke much anymore, so I'm un-loading.
Holy smokes! There's enough here to get an army stoned!
clap
clap
Pascal! ♫ My reward. ♪
Thanks my dear.
What is it?

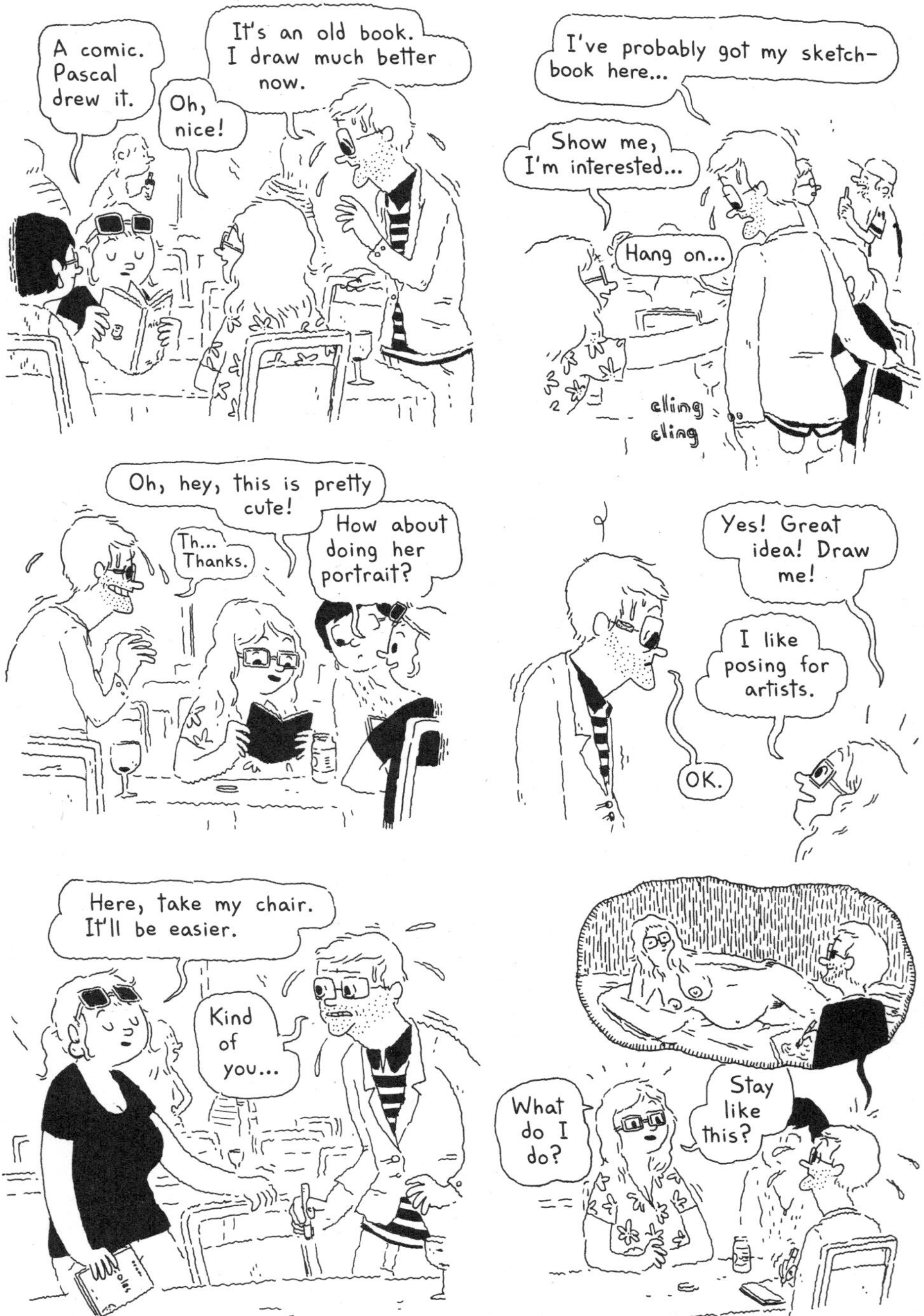
A comic. Pascal drew it.
It's an old book. I draw much better now.
Oh, nice!
I've probably got my sketch-book here...
Show me, I'm interested...
Hang on...
cling cling
Oh, hey, this is pretty cute!
Th... Thanks.
How about doing her portrait?
Yes! Great idea! Draw me!
I like posing for artists.
OK.
Here, take my chair. It'll be easier.
Kind of you...
What do I do?
Stay like this?

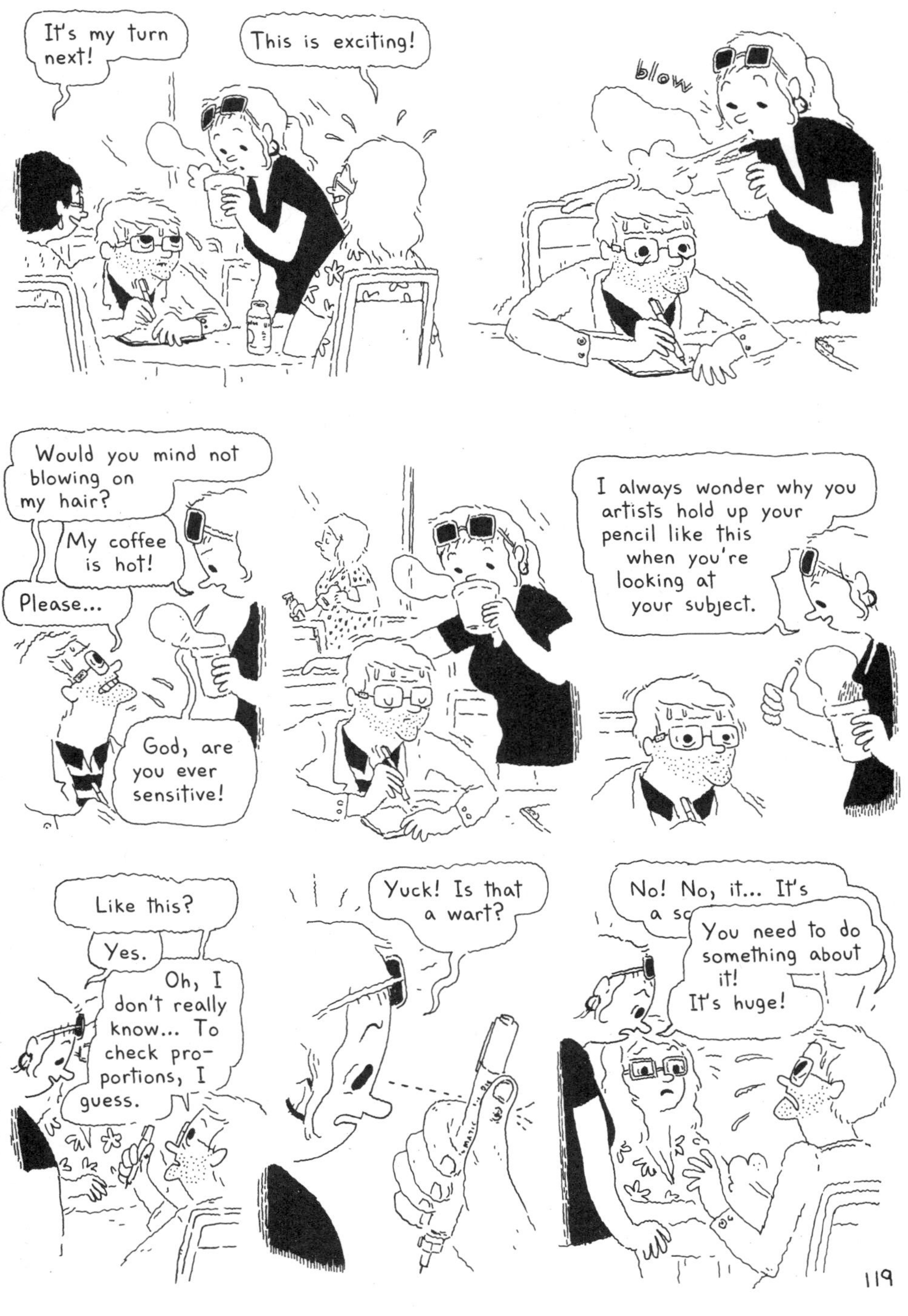

It's my turn next!
This is exciting!
blow
Would you mind not blowing on my hair?
My coffee is hot!
Please...
God, are you ever sensitive!
I always wonder why you artists hold up your pencil like this when you're looking at your subject.
Like this?
Yes.
Oh, I don't really know... To check proportions, I guess.
Yuck! Is that a wart?
No! No, it... It's a sc
You need to do something about it! It's huge!

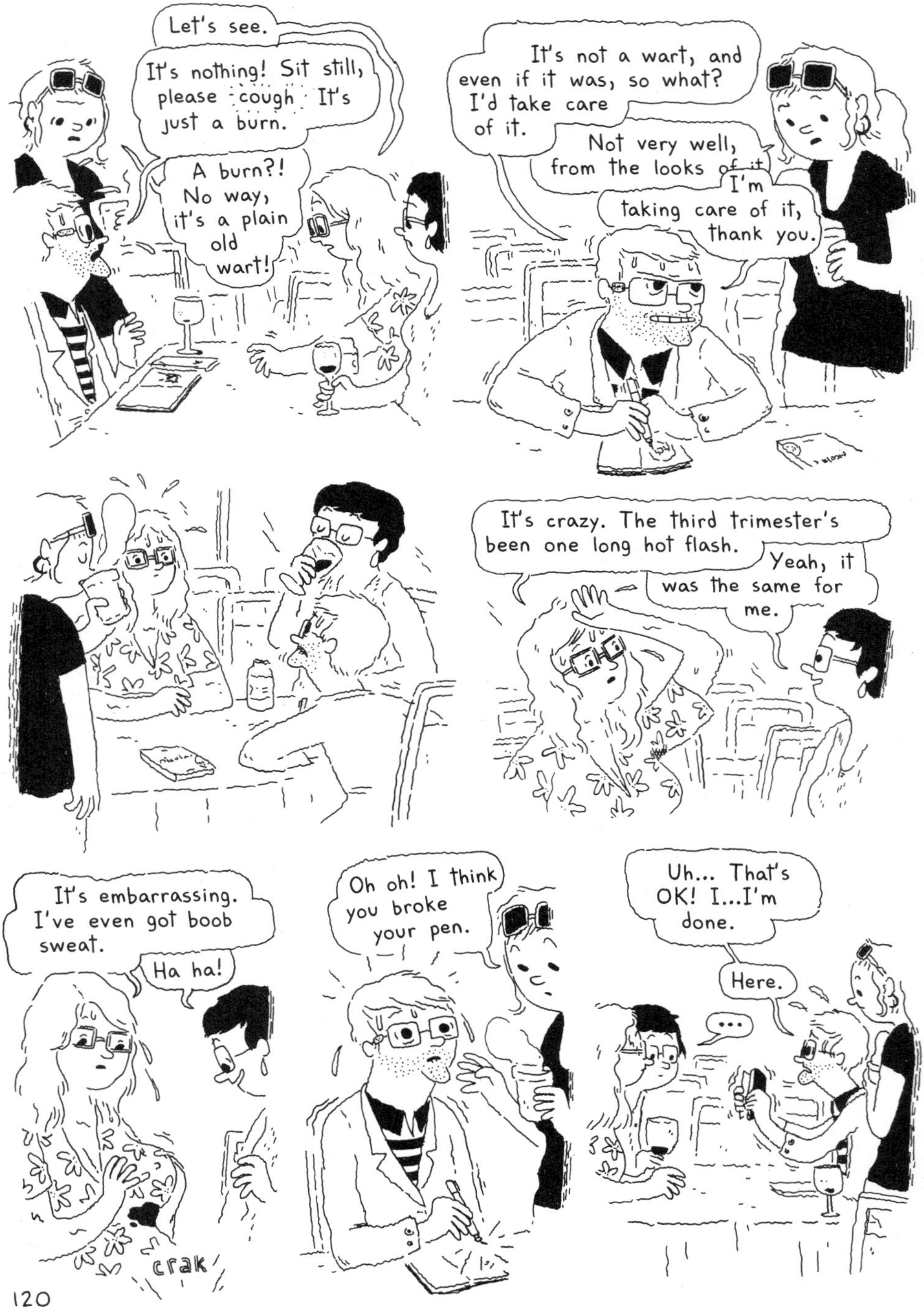
Let's see.
It's nothing! Sit still, please cough It's just a burn.
A burn?! No way, it's a plain old wart!
It's not a wart, and even if it was, so what? I'd take care of it.
Not very well, from the looks of it
I'm taking care of it, thank you.
It's crazy. The third trimester's been one long hot flash.
Yeah, it was the same for me.
It's embarrassing. I've even got boob sweat.
Ha ha!
crak
Oh oh! I think you broke your pen.
Uh... That's OK! I...I'm done.
Here.
...

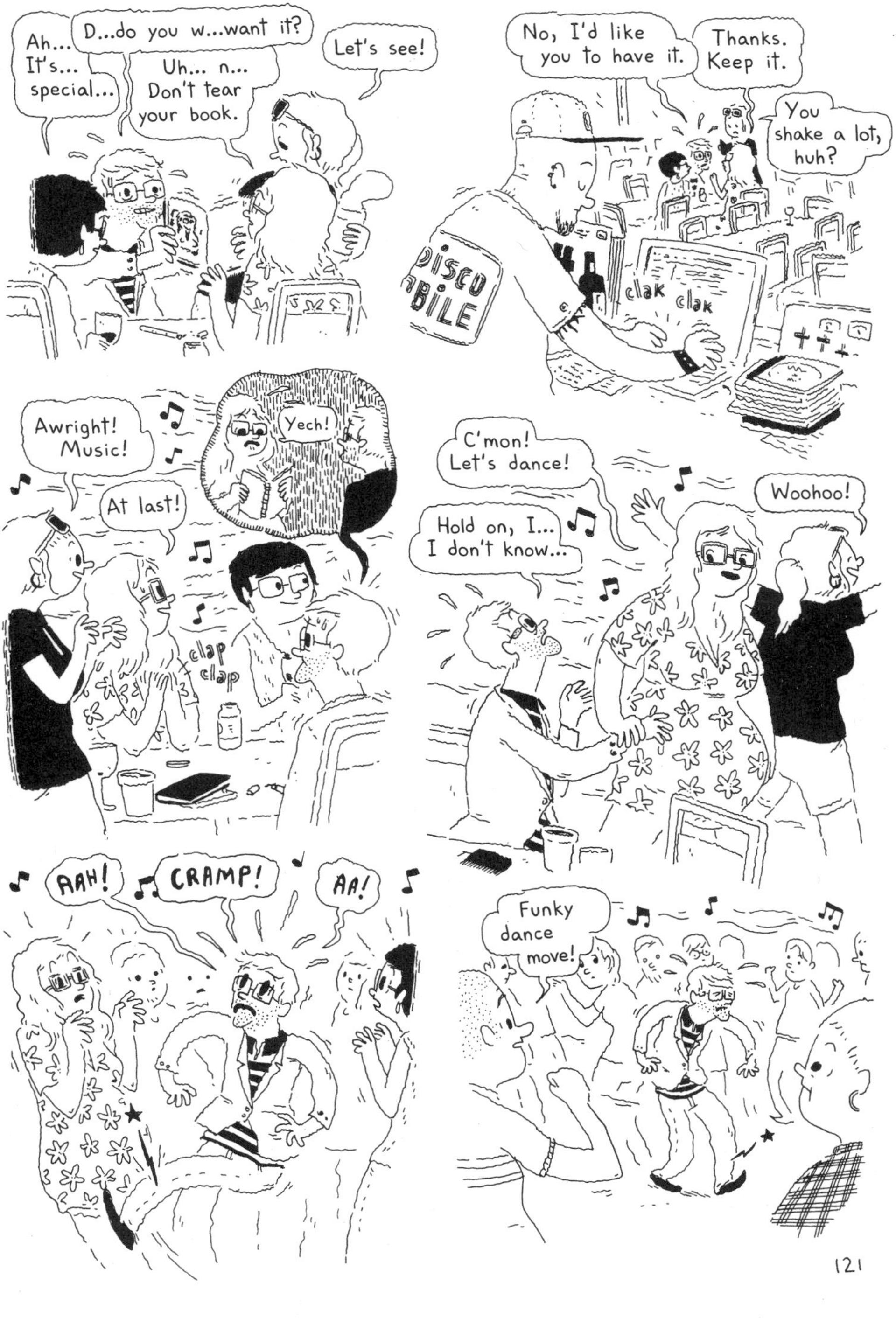

Ah... It's... special...
D...do you w...want it?
Uh... n... Don't tear your book.
Let's see!
No, I'd like you to have it.
Thanks. Keep it.
You shake a lot, huh?
DISCO
BILE
clak clak
Awright! Music!
At last!
Yech!
clap clap
C'mon! Let's dance!
Hold on, I... I don't know...
Woohoo!
AAH!
CRAMP!
AA!
Funky dance move!

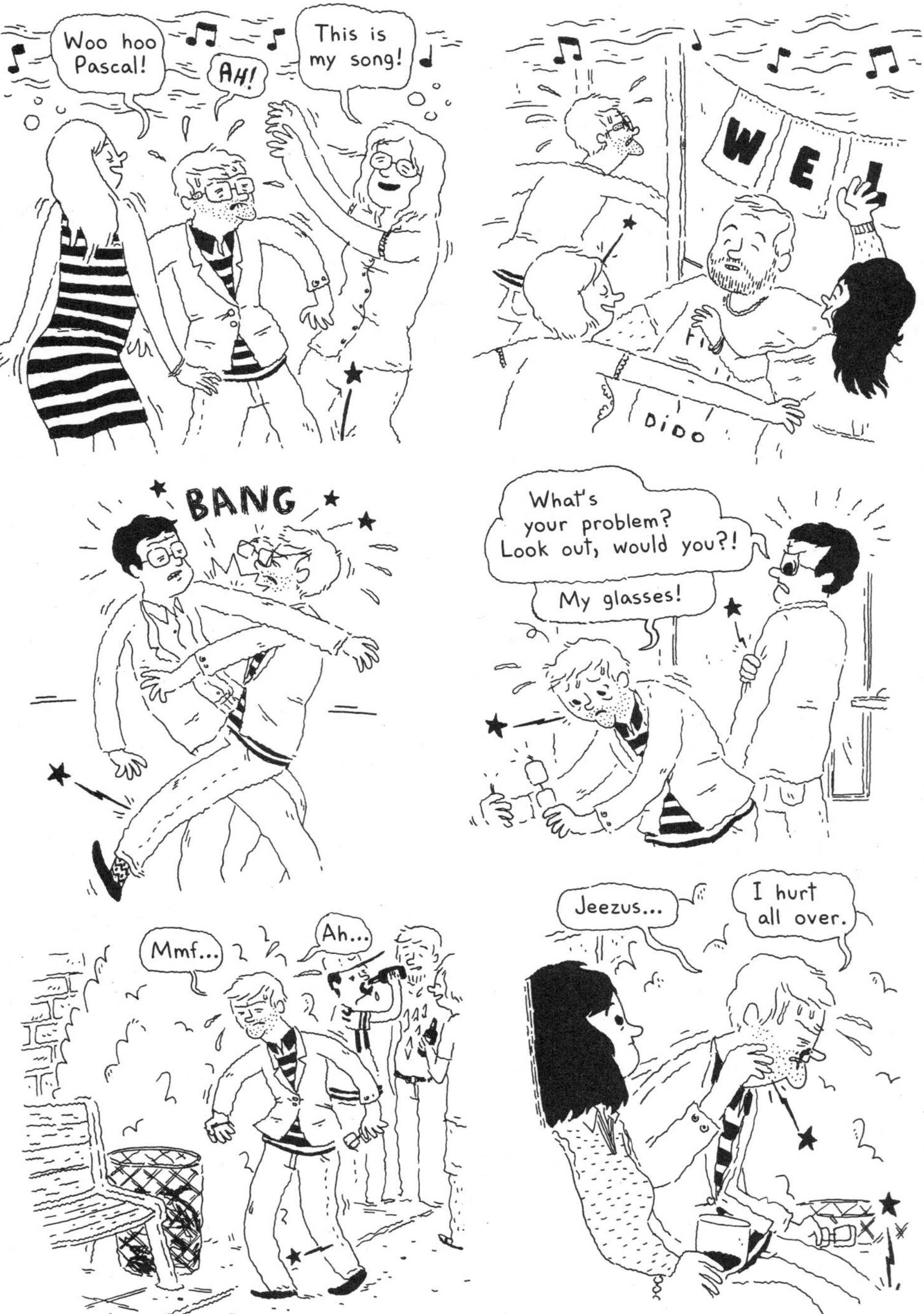

Woo hoo Pascal!
AH!
This is my song!
WEL
DIDO
BANG
What's your problem? Look out, would you?!
My glasses!
Mmf...
Ah...
Jeezus...
I hurt all over.

Don't move. You're bleeding.
Oh!
wipe wipe
Yeah, I lost the right pad on my glasses and... with the impact...
What's wrong with your leg?
I get cramps.
Ah! Camille! Camille Perron!
Did you just get here?
Are you kidding?
I said hello earlier.
You did?
Sure, before dinner. I spoke to you and you ignored me.
R... Really? cough I... Sorry... I must've... Uh...
No big deal.
Oh dear!
AAH!

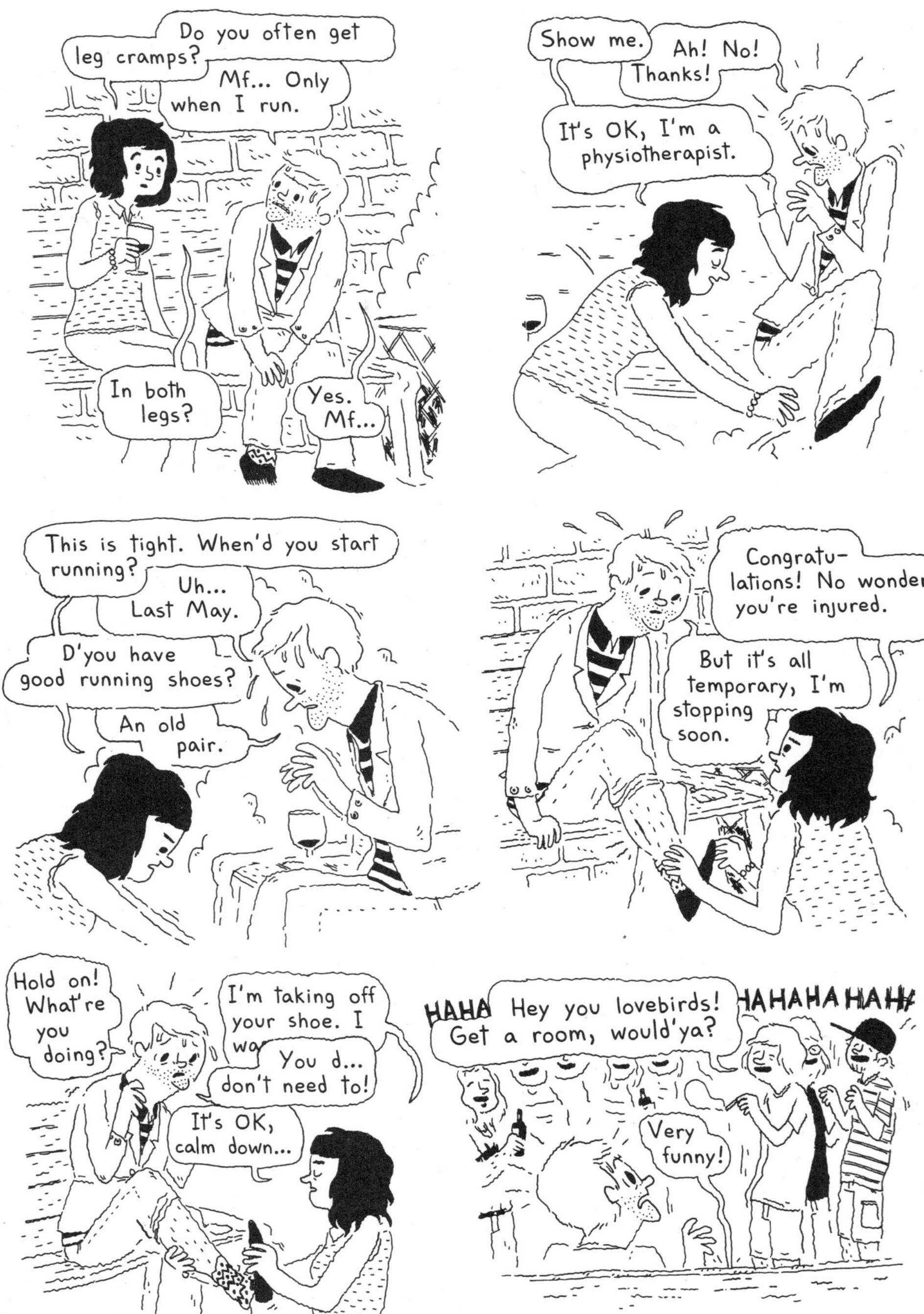

Do you often get leg cramps?
Mf... Only when I run.
In both legs?
Yes. Mf...
Show me.
Ah! No! Thanks!
It's OK, I'm a physiotherapist.
This is tight. When'd you start running?
Uh... Last May.
D'you have good running shoes?
An old pair.
Congratu-lations! No wonder you're injured.
But it's all temporary, I'm stopping soon.
Hold on! What're you doing?
I'm taking off your shoe. I wa
You d... don't need to!
It's OK, calm down...
HAHA
Hey you lovebirds! Get a room, would'ya?
HAHAHAHAH
Very funny!

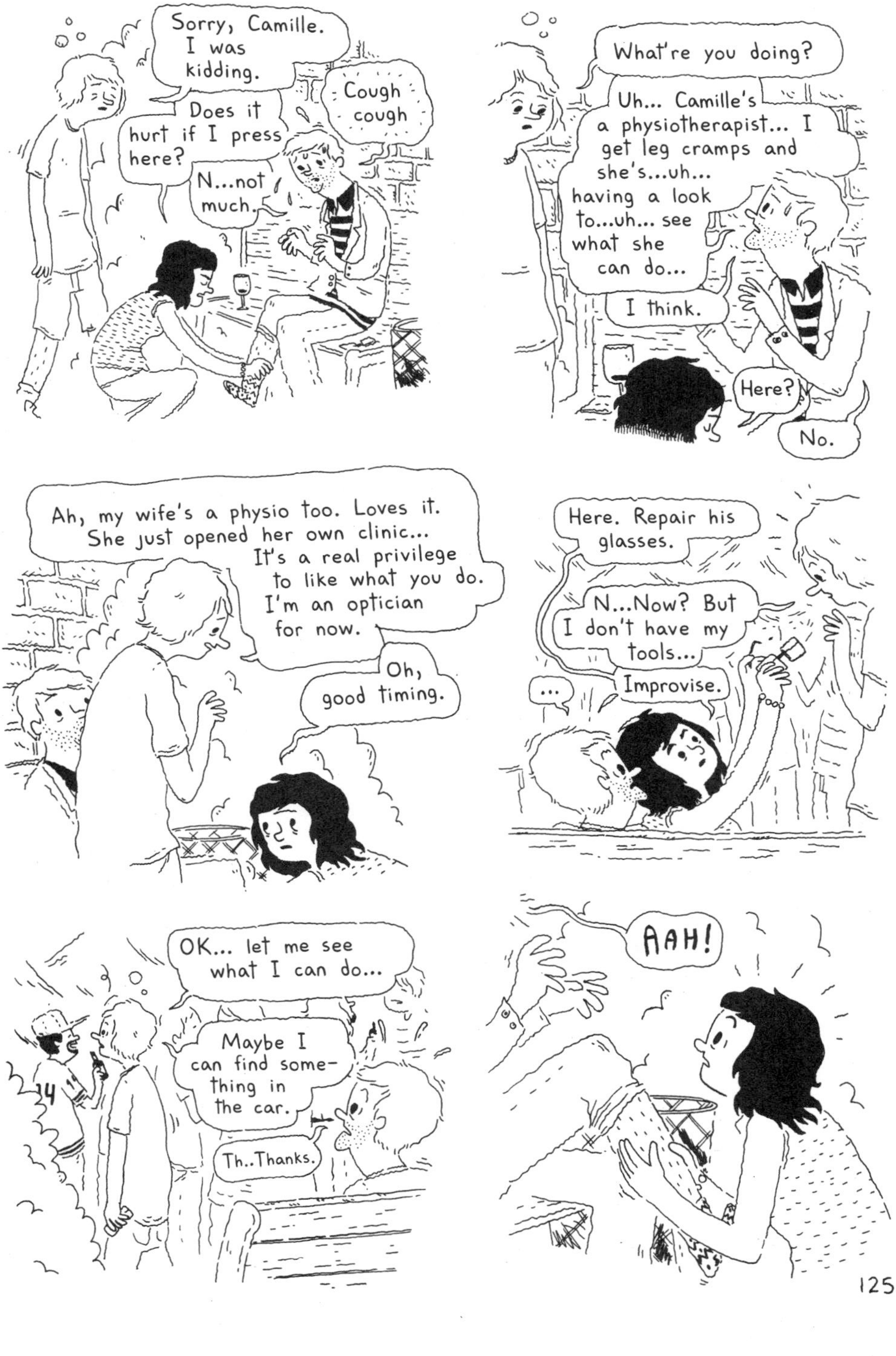
Sorry, Camille. I was kidding.
Does it hurt if I press here?
Cough cough
N...not much.
What're you doing?
Uh... Camille's a physiotherapist... I get leg cramps and she's...uh... having a look to...uh... see what she can do...
I think.
Here?
No.
Ah, my wife's a physio too. Loves it. She just opened her own clinic... It's a real privilege to like what you do. I'm an optician for now.
Oh, good timing.
Here. Repair his glasses.
N...Now? But I don't have my tools...
...
Improvise.
OK... let me see what I can do...
Maybe I can find something in the car.
Th..Thanks.
AAH!

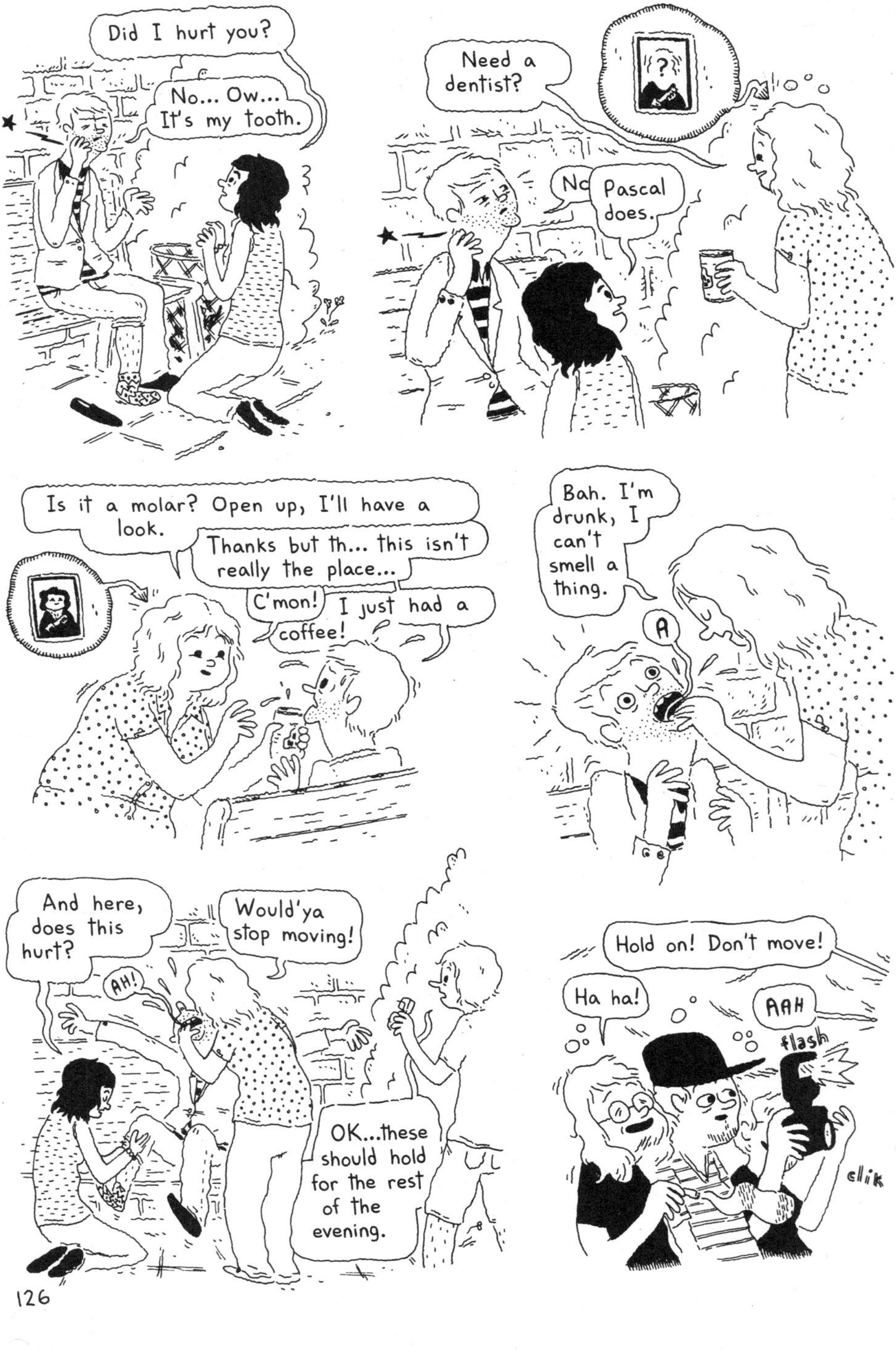
Did I hurt you?
No... Ow... It's my tooth.
Need a dentist?
No
Pascal does.
?
Is it a molar? Open up, I'll have a look.
Thanks but th... this isn't really the place...
C'mon!
I just had a coffee!
Bah. I'm drunk, I can't smell a thing.
A
And here, does this hurt?
Would'ya stop moving!
AH!
OK...these should hold for the rest of the evening.
Hold on! Don't move!
Ha ha!
AAH
flash
clik

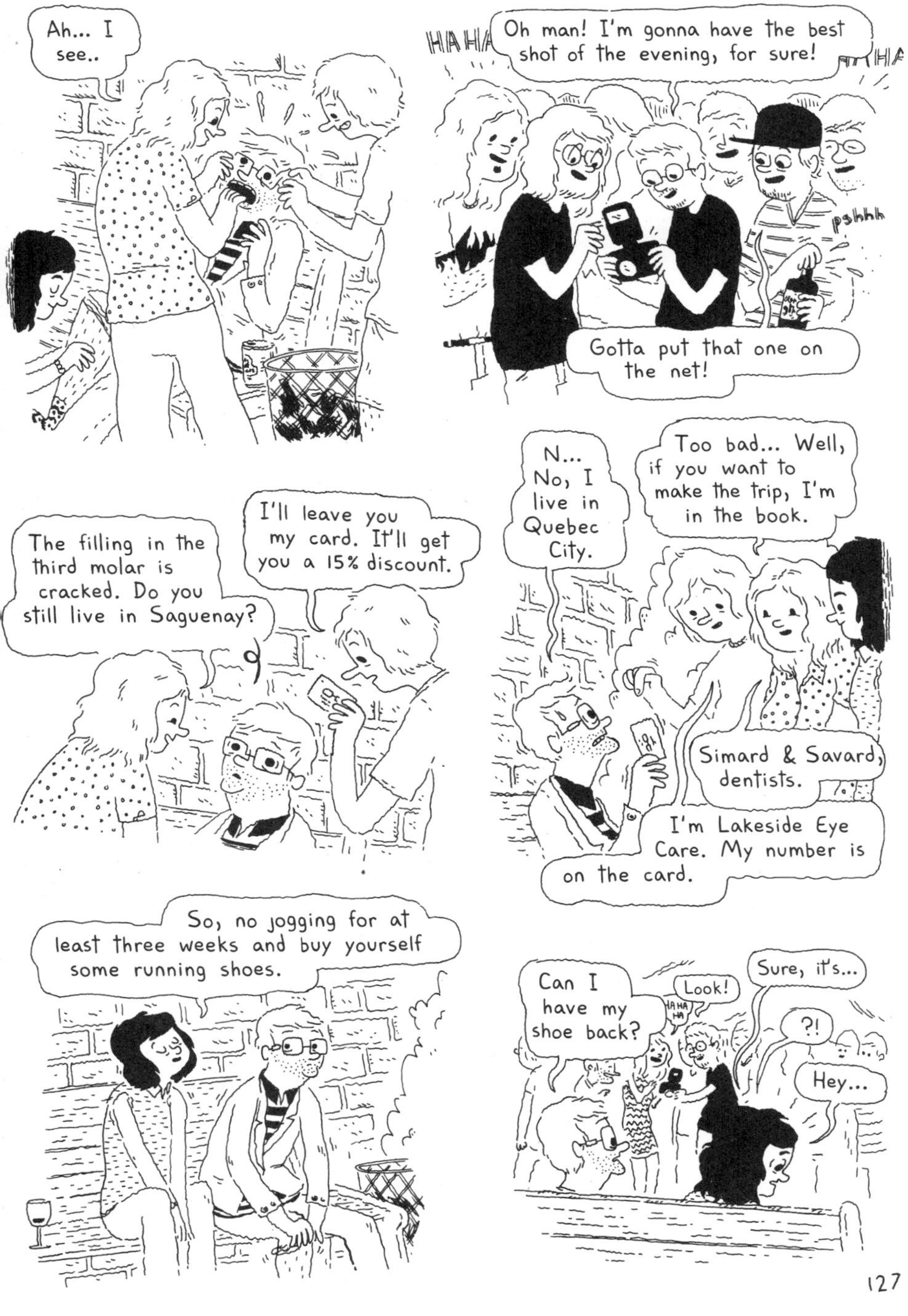
Ah... I see..
HAHA
Oh man! I'm gonna have the best shot of the evening, for sure!
HAHA
pshhh
Gotta put that one on the net!
The filling in the third molar is cracked. Do you still live in Saguenay?
I'll leave you my card. It'll get you a 15% discount.
N... No, I live in Quebec City.
Too bad... Well, if you want to make the trip, I'm in the book.
Simard & Savard, dentists.
I'm Lakeside Eye Care. My number is on the card.
So, no jogging for at least three weeks and buy yourself some running shoes.
Can I have my shoe back?
HA HA HA
Look!
Sure, it's...
?!
Hey...

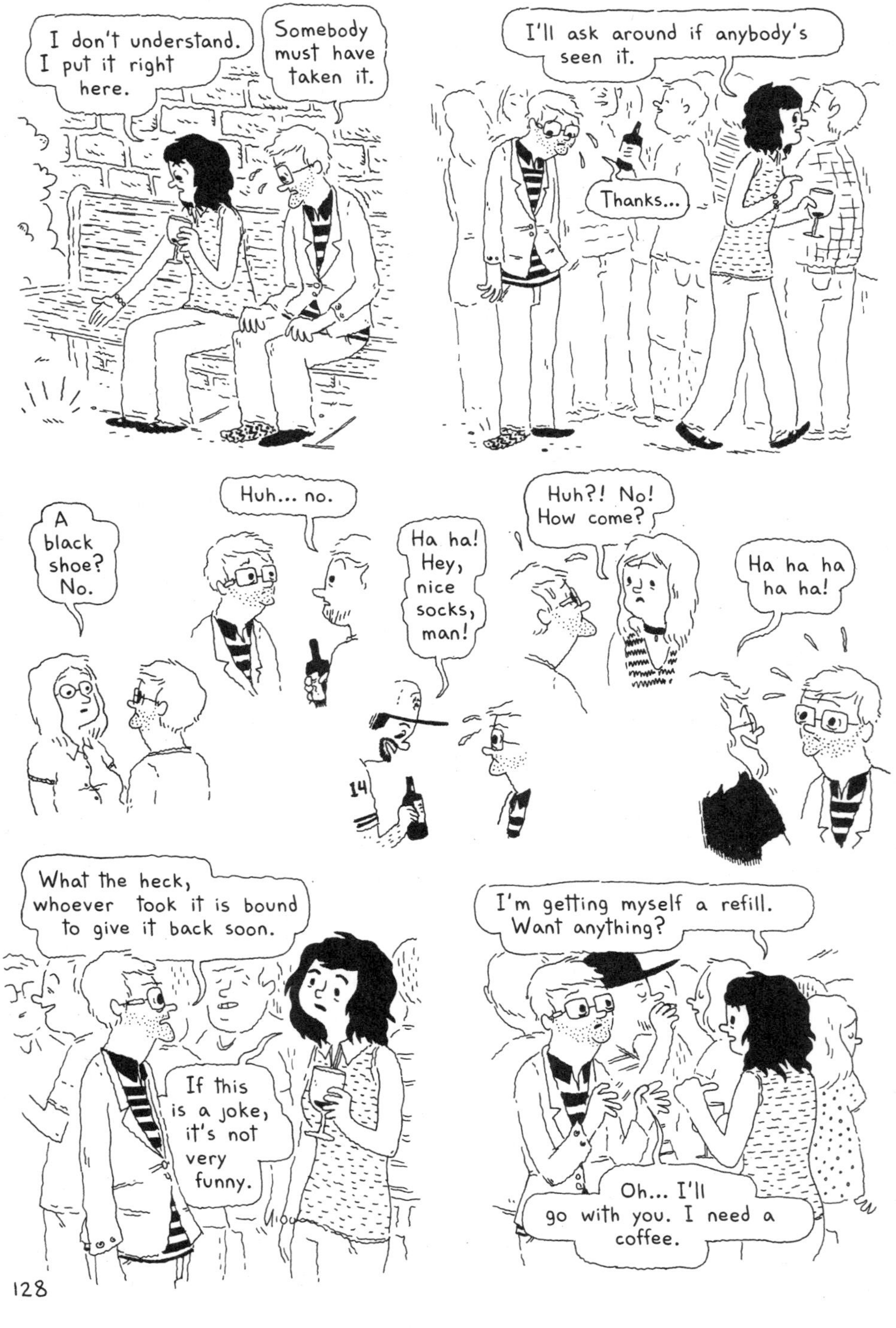
I don't understand. I put it right here.
Somebody must have taken it.
I'll ask around if anybody's seen it.
Thanks...
A black shoe? No.
Huh... no.
Ha ha! Hey, nice socks, man!
14
Huh?! No! How come?
Ha ha ha ha ha!
What the heck, whoever took it is bound to give it back soon.
If this is a joke, it's not very funny.
I'm getting myself a refill. Want anything?
Oh... I'll go with you. I need a coffee.

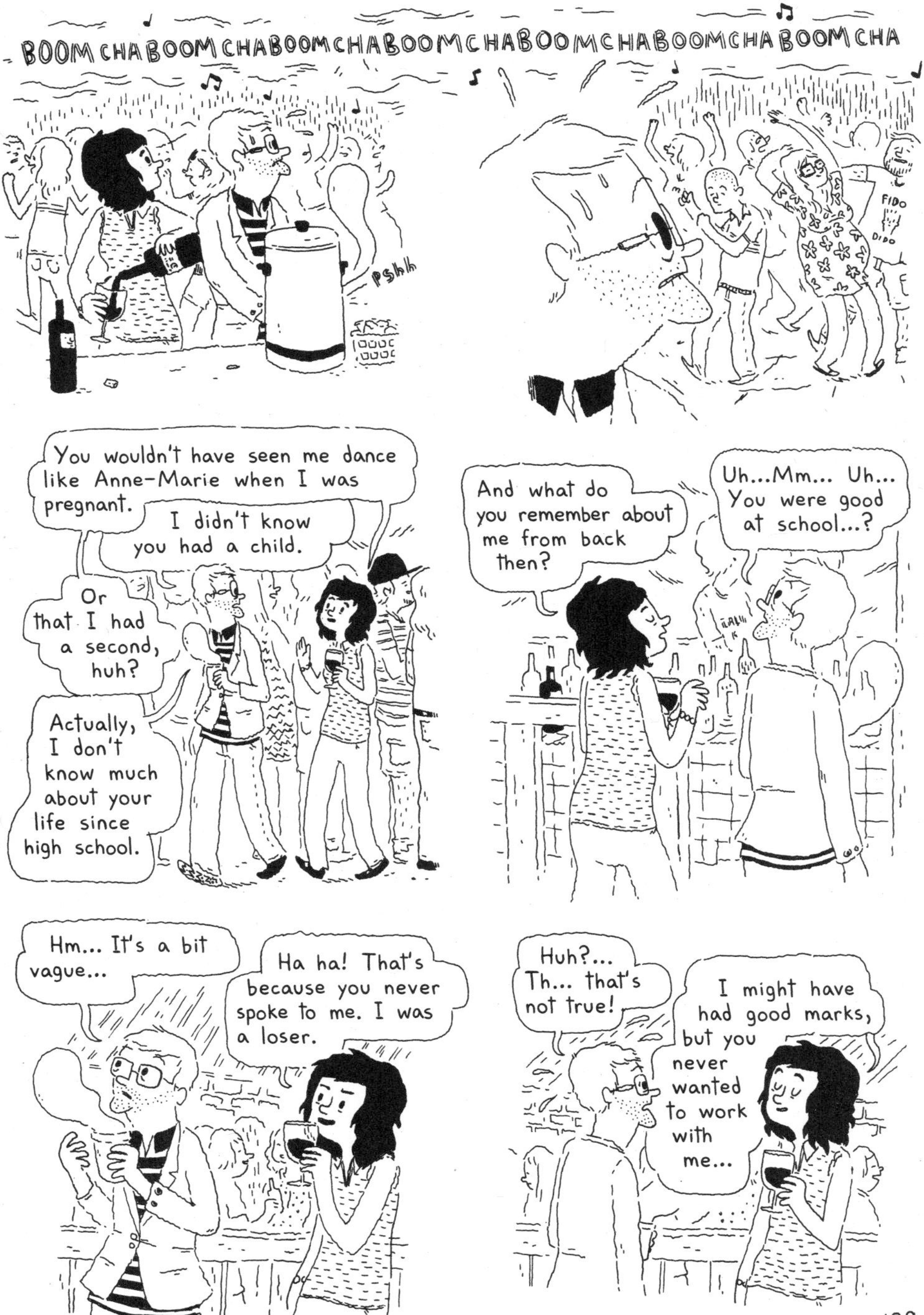
BOOM CHA BOOM CHA BOOM CHA BOOM CHA BOOM CHA BOOM CHA BOOM CHA
pshh
FIDO
DIDO
You wouldn't have seen me dance like Anne-Marie when I was pregnant.
I didn't know you had a child.
Or that I had a second, huh?
Actually, I don't know much about your life since high school.
And what do you remember about me from back then?
Uh...Mm... Uh... You were good at school...?
Hm... It's a bit vague...
Ha ha! That's because you never spoke to me. I was a loser.
Huh?... Th... that's not true!
I might have had good marks, but you never wanted to work with me...

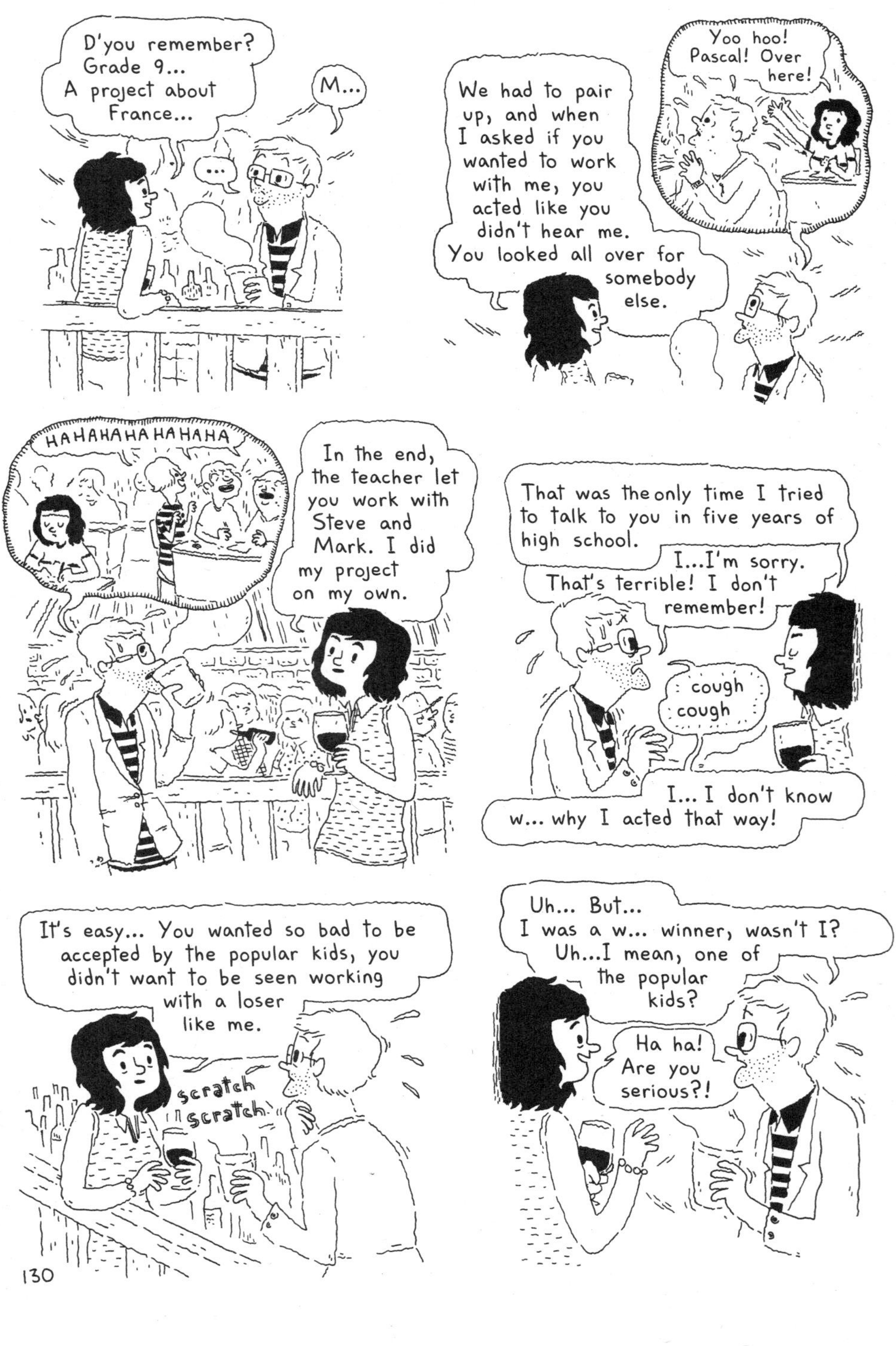

D'you remember? Grade 9... A project about France...
M...
...
We had to pair up, and when I asked if you wanted to work with me, you acted like you didn't hear me. You looked all over for somebody else.
Yoo hoo! Pascal! Over here!
HAHAHAHAHAHAHA
In the end, the teacher let you work with Steve and Mark. I did my project on my own.
That was the only time I tried to talk to you in five years of high school.
I...I'm sorry. That's terrible! I don't remember!
cough cough
I... I don't know w... why I acted that way!
It's easy... You wanted so bad to be accepted by the popular kids, you didn't want to be seen working with a loser like me.
scratch scratch
Uh... But... I was a w... winner, wasn't I? Uh...I mean, one of the popular kids?
Ha ha! Are you serious?!

No, not really. Ha ha! But if you thought so, that's great.
Just ask Steve, you'll see.
Ha ha ha!
You're the second person to tell me that today.
D'you want a nice answer or the truth?
Ha ha! Poor Pascal! You look like you just got handed a death sentence.
So if I was a loser back then and I haven't really changed, I'm still a loser.
If you label people as winners or losers, then yes, definitely.
I'm kidding... I... cough I'm not like that... now.
I hope not!
Camille!
Calm down.
Ah! Here's my husband with my daughter!
Coming!
You're married?

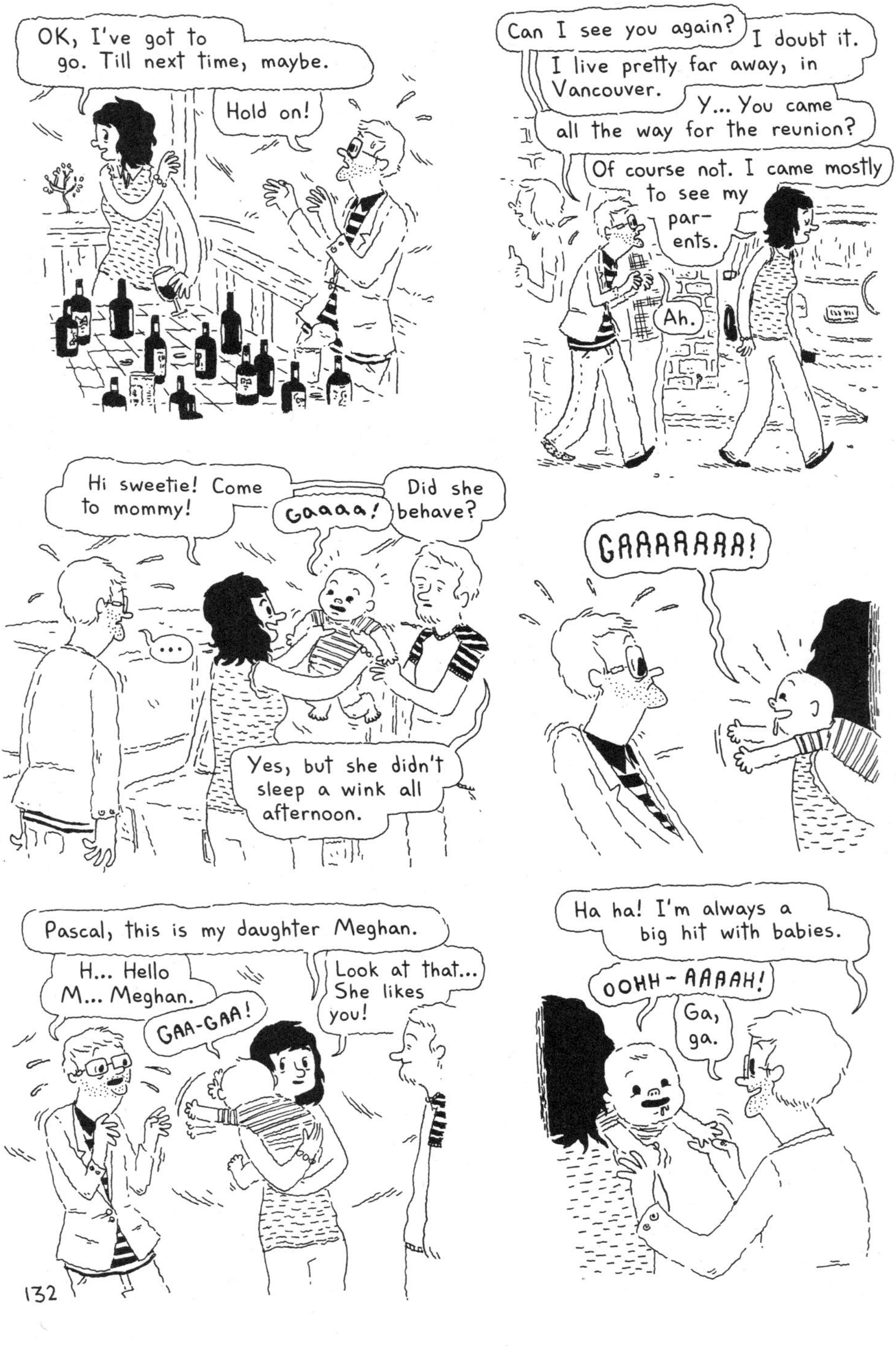
OK, I've got to go. Till next time, maybe.
Hold on!
Can I see you again?
I doubt it. I live pretty far away, in Vancouver.
Y... You came all the way for the reunion?
Of course not. I came mostly to see my par-ents.
Ah.
Hi sweetie! Come to mommy!
Gaaaa!
Did she behave?
...
Yes, but she didn't sleep a wink all afternoon.
GAAAAAAA!
Pascal, this is my daughter Meghan.
H... Hello M... Meghan.
GAA-GAA!
Look at that... She likes you!
Ha ha! I'm always a big hit with babies.
OOHH-AAAAH!
Ga, ga.

Here... I think she wants you to take her!
Uh...I'd rather not...
BWAAAAA!
Ha ha!
Ho ho ho!
Do you have kids?
Me? No, no.
C...can I have my hands back, Meghan?
It's OK, baby. You can let go now.
Here, Simon, you hold her.
OK. I'm gonna go.
A...Ah... OK.
D'you have an email address?
You can just google my name.
Oh... Thanks.
I... It was a pleasure.
VR
...
WAAAAAH!
VRRRM

Who just snuck out without saying good bye?
Uh... Camille Perron.
Oh yeah...
I don't think I ever talked to her.
glug glug
Hey, Alex... That t-shirt... You had it back then, right?
W... I... What a weird question! No, I don't think so...
In fact, weren't you even wearing it in one of the grad yearbook photos?
H... Huh?!
No, I bought it last year.
A Fido Dido t-shirt? Last year? That's strange.
I dunno. Why do you even care?!
No reason. I just think it's... interesting to come to a re-union dressed in a shirt from your high school days.
Think you look so great, huh? A jacket here by the lake? Christ, we're out in the sticks, not at a 5-star joint!
I didn't m...mean to insult you!
Whoa. Hey guys, lighten up! Ha ha!

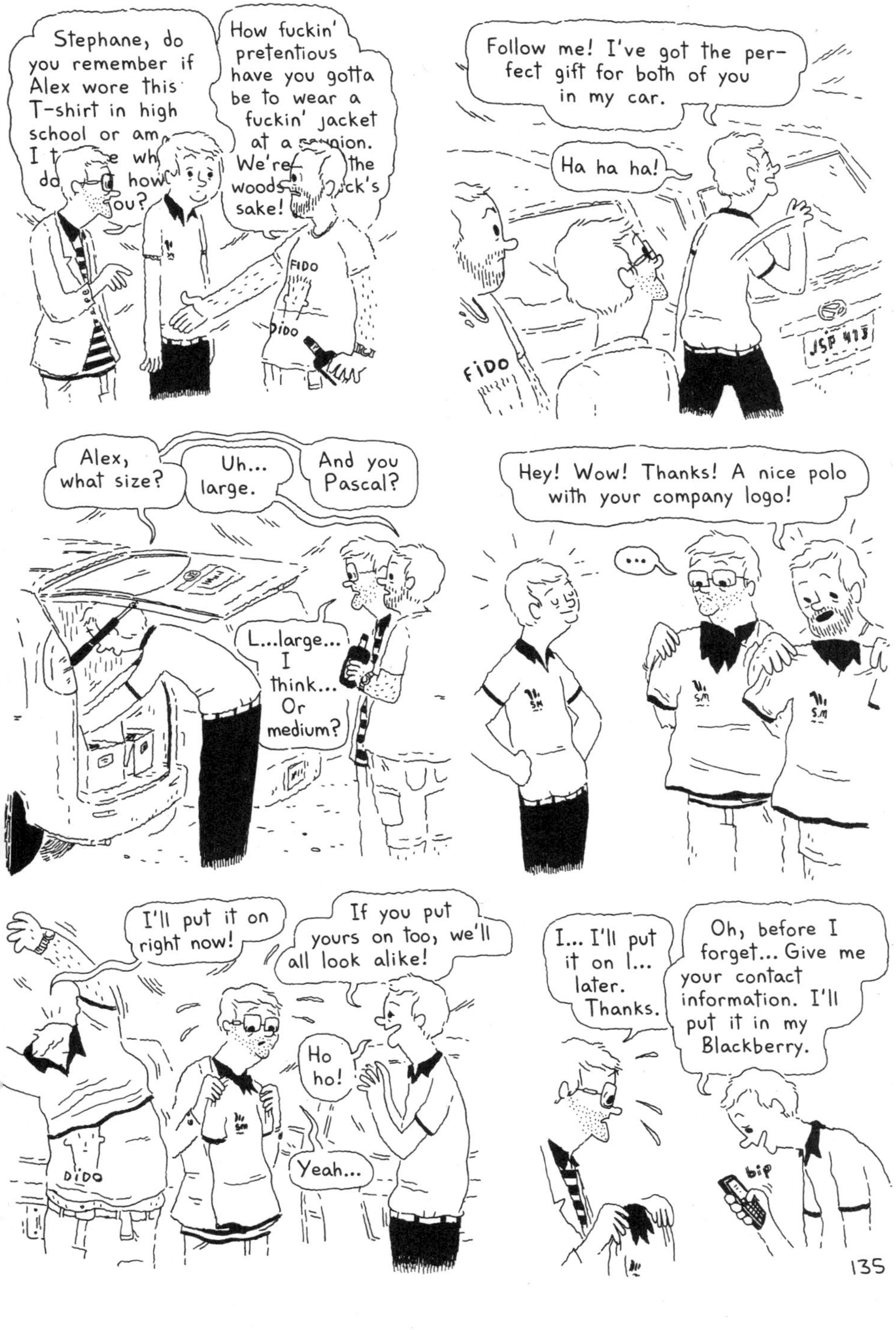
Stephane, do you remember if Alex wore this T-shirt in high school or am
How fuckin' pretentious have you gotta be to wear a fuckin' jacket at a
We're
the woods
ck's sake!
FIDO
DIDO
Follow me! I've got the perfect gift for both of you in my car.
Ha ha ha!
FIDO
JSP 413
Alex, what size?
Uh... large.
And you Pascal?
L...large... I think... Or medium?
Hey! Wow! Thanks! A nice polo with your company logo!
...
I'll put it on right now!
If you put yours on too, we'll all look alike!
Ho ho!
Yeah...
DIDO
I... I'll put it on I... later. Thanks.
Oh, before I forget... Give me your contact information. I'll put it in my Blackberry.
bip

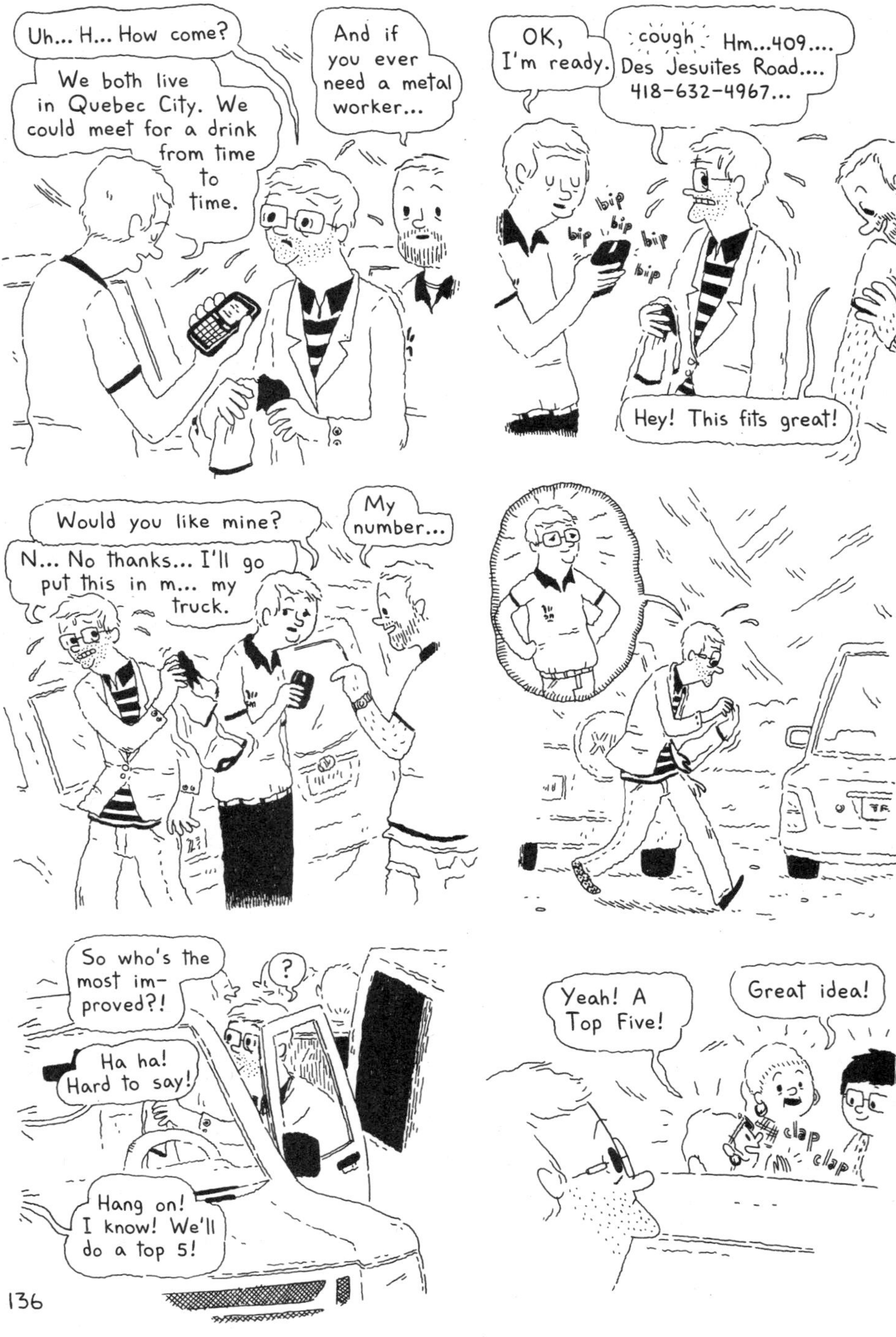
Uh... H... How come?
We both live in Quebec City. We could meet for a drink from time to time.
And if you ever need a metal worker...
OK, I'm ready.
cough Hm...409.... Des Jesuites Road.... 418-632-4967...
bip bip bip bip bip bip
Hey! This fits great!
Would you like mine?
My number...
N... No thanks... I'll go put this in m... my truck.
So who's the most im-proved?!
?
Ha ha! Hard to say!
Hang on! I know! We'll do a top 5!
Yeah! A Top Five!
Great idea!
clap clap

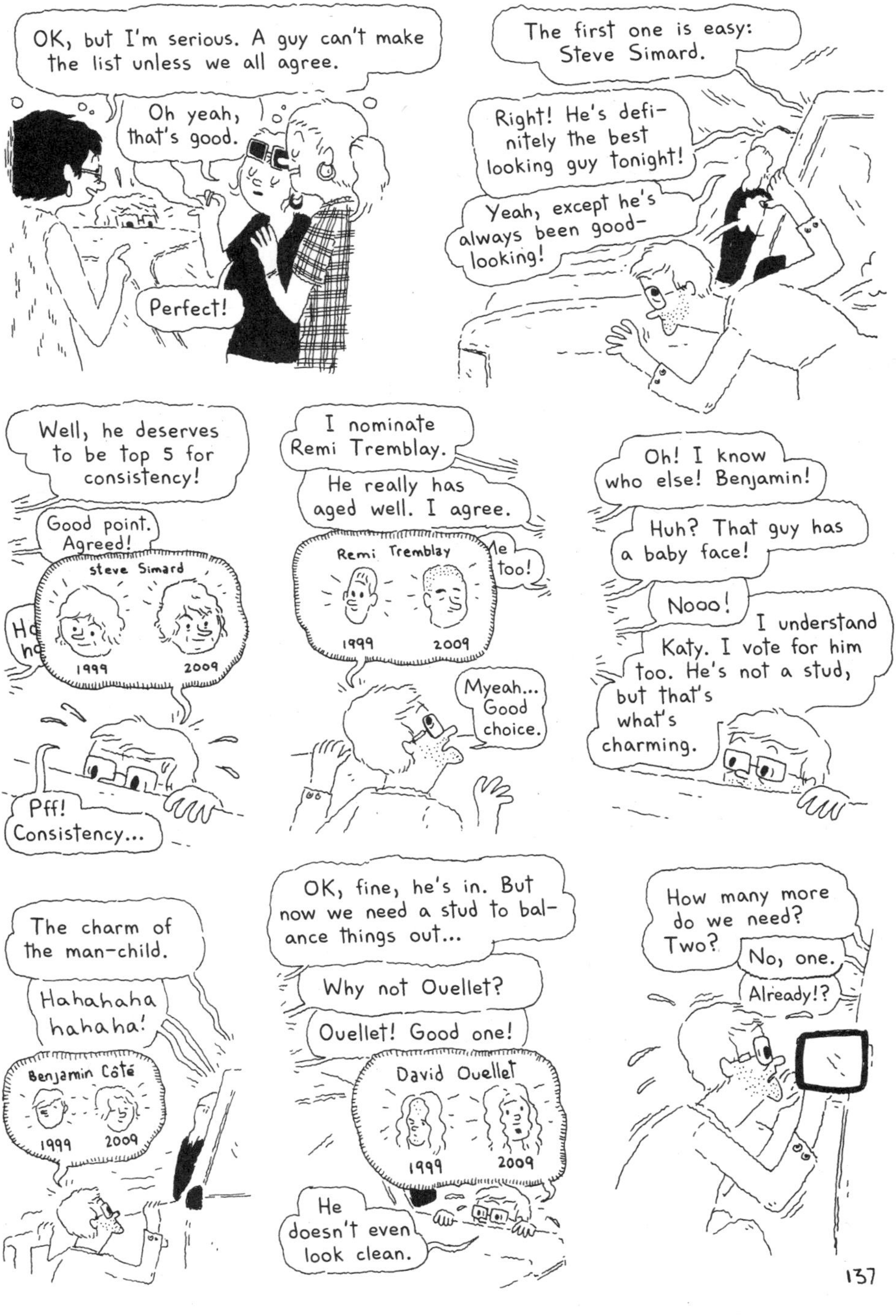

OK, but I'm serious. A guy can't make the list unless we all agree.
Oh yeah, that's good.
Perfect!
The first one is easy: Steve Simard.
Right! He's definitely the best looking guy tonight!
Yeah, except he's always been good-looking!
Well, he deserves to be top 5 for consistency!
Good point. Agreed!
Steve Simard
1999
2009
Pff! Consistency...
I nominate Remi Tremblay.
He really has aged well. I agree.
too!
Remi Tremblay
1999
2009
Myeah... Good choice.
Oh! I know who else! Benjamin!
Huh? That guy has a baby face!
Nooo!
I understand Katy. I vote for him too. He's not a stud, but that's what's charming.
The charm of the man-child.
Hahahaha hahaha!
Benjamin Côté
1999
2009
OK, fine, he's in. But now we need a stud to balance things out...
Why not Ouellet?
Ouellet! Good one!
David Ouellet
1999
2009
He doesn't even look clean.
How many more do we need? Two?
No, one.
Already!?

I think we should top the list with the guy who's lost the most weight.
Yes!
You're right, that deserves credit!
Yannick Bergeron!
Yannick Bergeron?!
Yannick Bergeron
1999
2009
Ha ha ha!
Let's go tell them!
Yeah... It's true, he's lost a lot of weight too...
Definitely not as much as me, though.
Whatever. They're too stoned to know what they're talking about.
And I'm not at my best. I haven't slept in two nights.
Is that why you're talking to yourself out loud? Cuz you haven't slept?
Let's go! Get up! Come chat a bit. It's been ten years. We need to make the most of this.
Congratulations. You made the top 5.

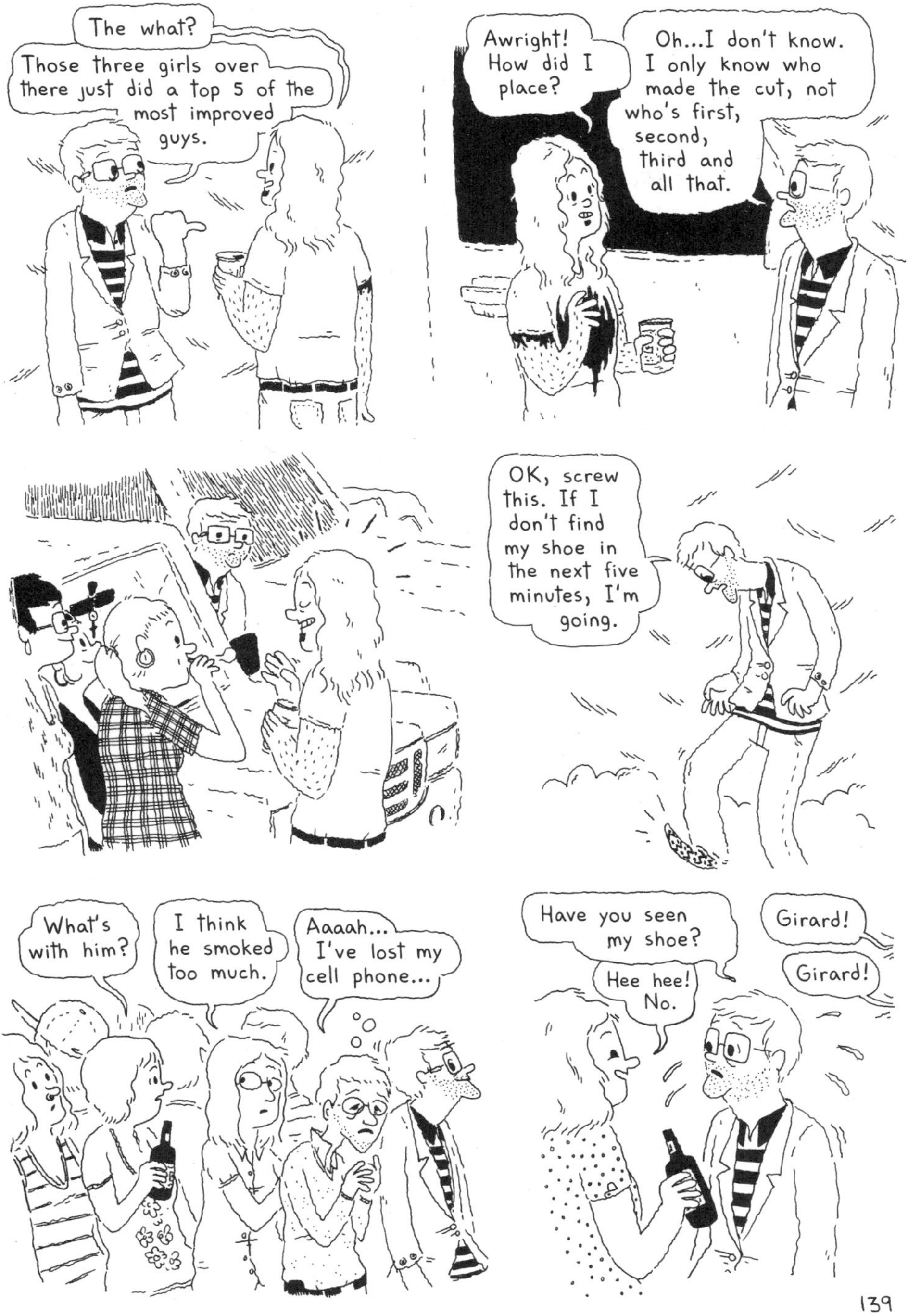
The what?
Those three girls over there just did a top 5 of the most improved guys.
Awright! How did I place?
Oh...I don't know. I only know who made the cut, not who's first, second, third and all that.
OK, screw this. If I don't find my shoe in the next five minutes, I'm going.
What's with him?
I think he smoked too much.
Aaaah... I've lost my cell phone...
Have you seen my shoe?
Hee hee! No.
Girard!
Girard!

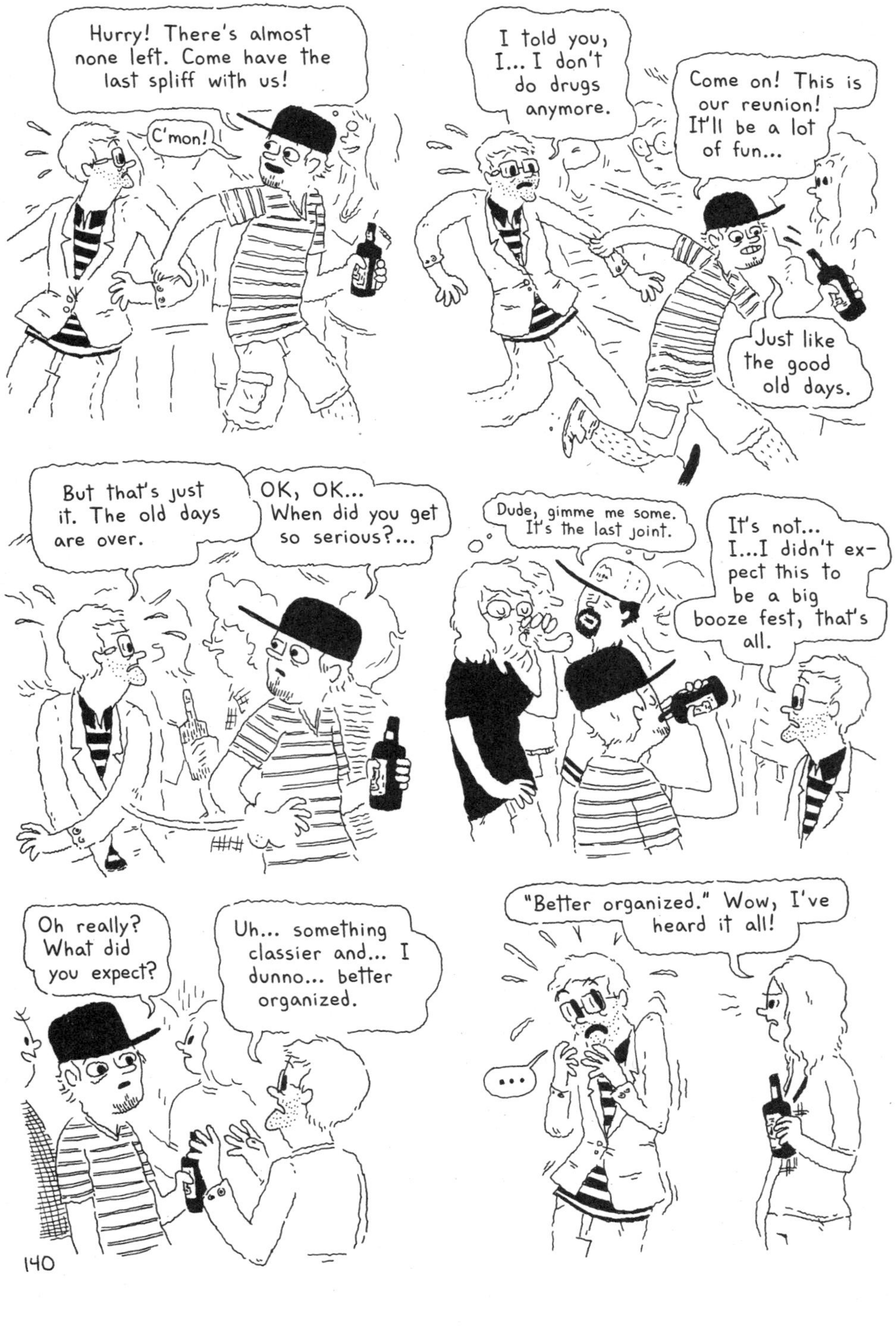
Hurry! There's almost none left. Come have the last spliff with us!
C'mon!
I told you, I... I don't do drugs anymore.
Come on! This is our reunion! It'll be a lot of fun...
Just like the good old days.
But that's just it. The old days are over.
OK, OK... When did you get so serious?...
Dude, gimme me some. It's the last joint.
It's not... I...I didn't expect this to be a big booze fest, that's all.
Oh really? What did you expect?
Uh... something classier and... I dunno... better organized.
"Better organized." Wow, I've heard it all!
...

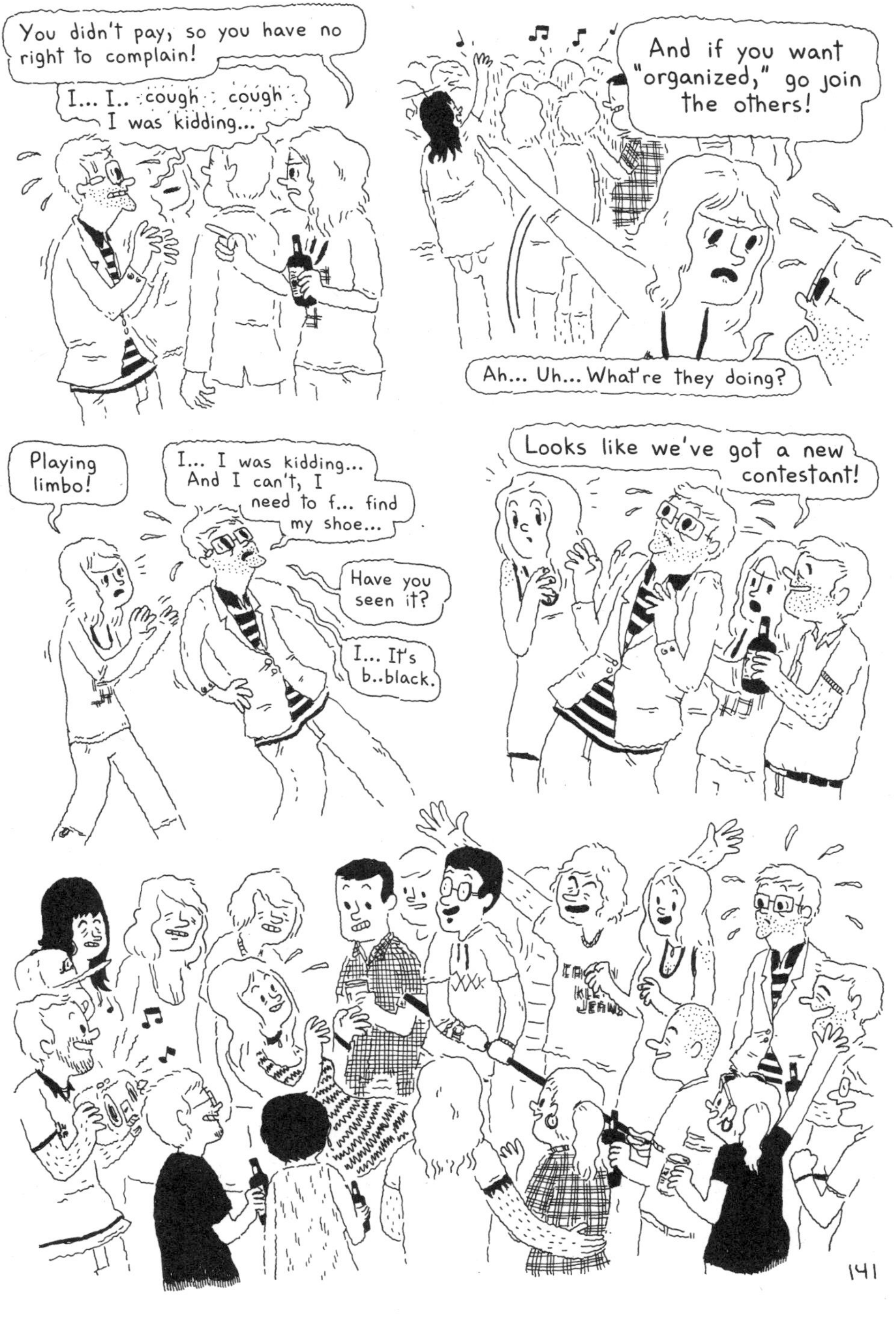

You didn't pay, so you have no right to complain!
I... I.. cough cough I was kidding...
And if you want "organized," go join the others!
Ah... Uh... What're they doing?
Playing limbo!
I... I was kidding... And I can't, I need to f... find my shoe...
Have you seen it?
I... It's b..black.
Looks like we've got a new contestant!

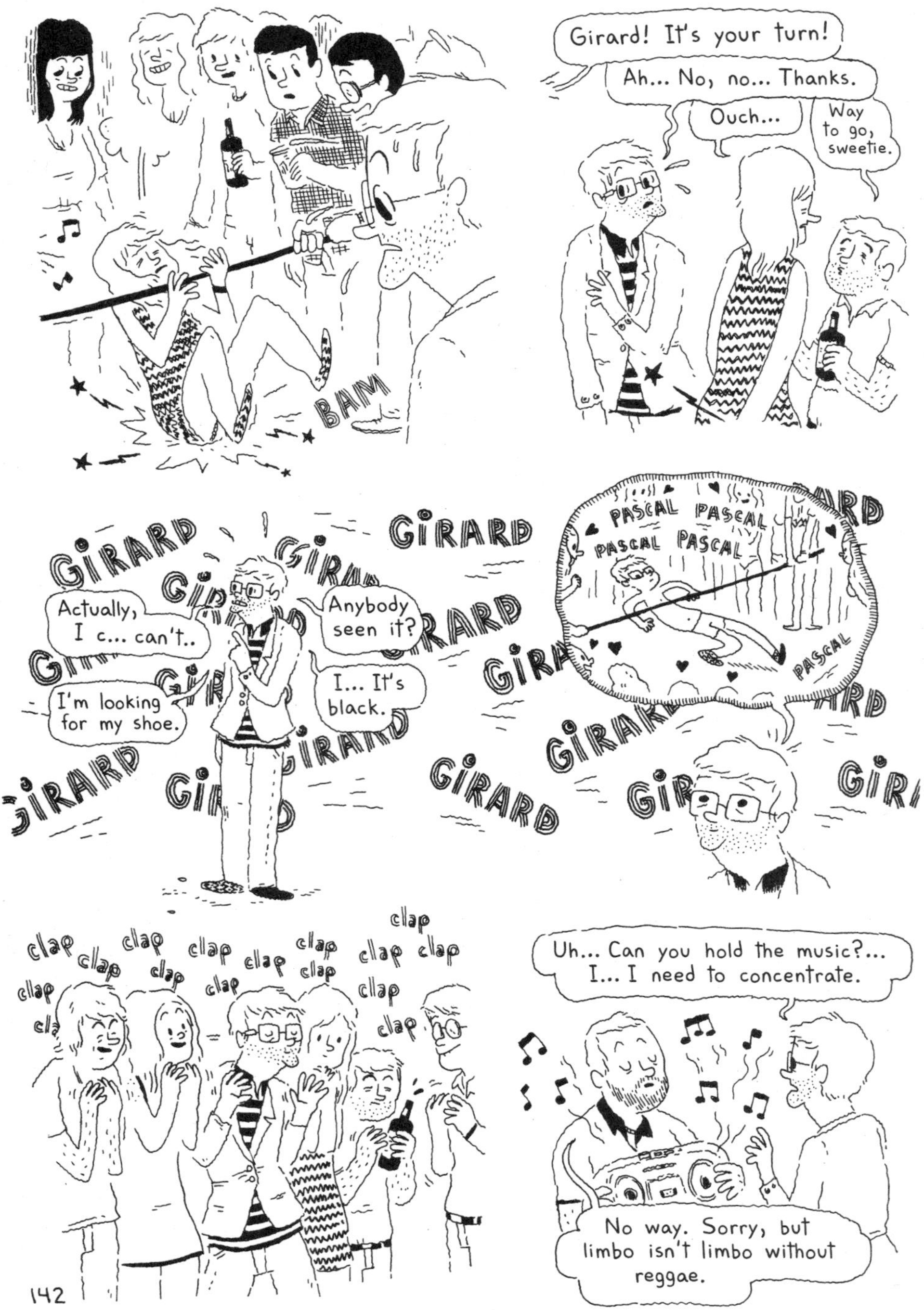
BAM
Girard! It's your turn!
Ah... No, no... Thanks.
Ouch...
Way to go, sweetie.
GIRARD GIRARD GIRARD GIRARD
Actually, I c... can't..
I'm looking for my shoe.
Anybody seen it?
I... It's black.
PASCAL PASCAL
PASCAL PASCAL
PASCAL
clap clap clap clap clap clap clap clap clap clap clap clap clap clap clap
Uh... Can you hold the music?... I... I need to concentrate.
No way. Sorry, but limbo isn't limbo without reggae.

OK... I haven't done this in ages...
clap
clap
clap
clap
clap
From what I can remember, I need to bend back and try to....
...keep my center of gravity right here...
BAAAM
HAHAHAHAHAHAHAHAHAHAHAHAHAHAHAHAH
Hey everybody! I just lit the campfire and Frankie's got his guitar! C'mon! We're gonna sing a coupla classics from way back!
Here. Give me your hand.
Thanks, I'm fine. I wanna stay here a moment...
OK. Have a nice nap.

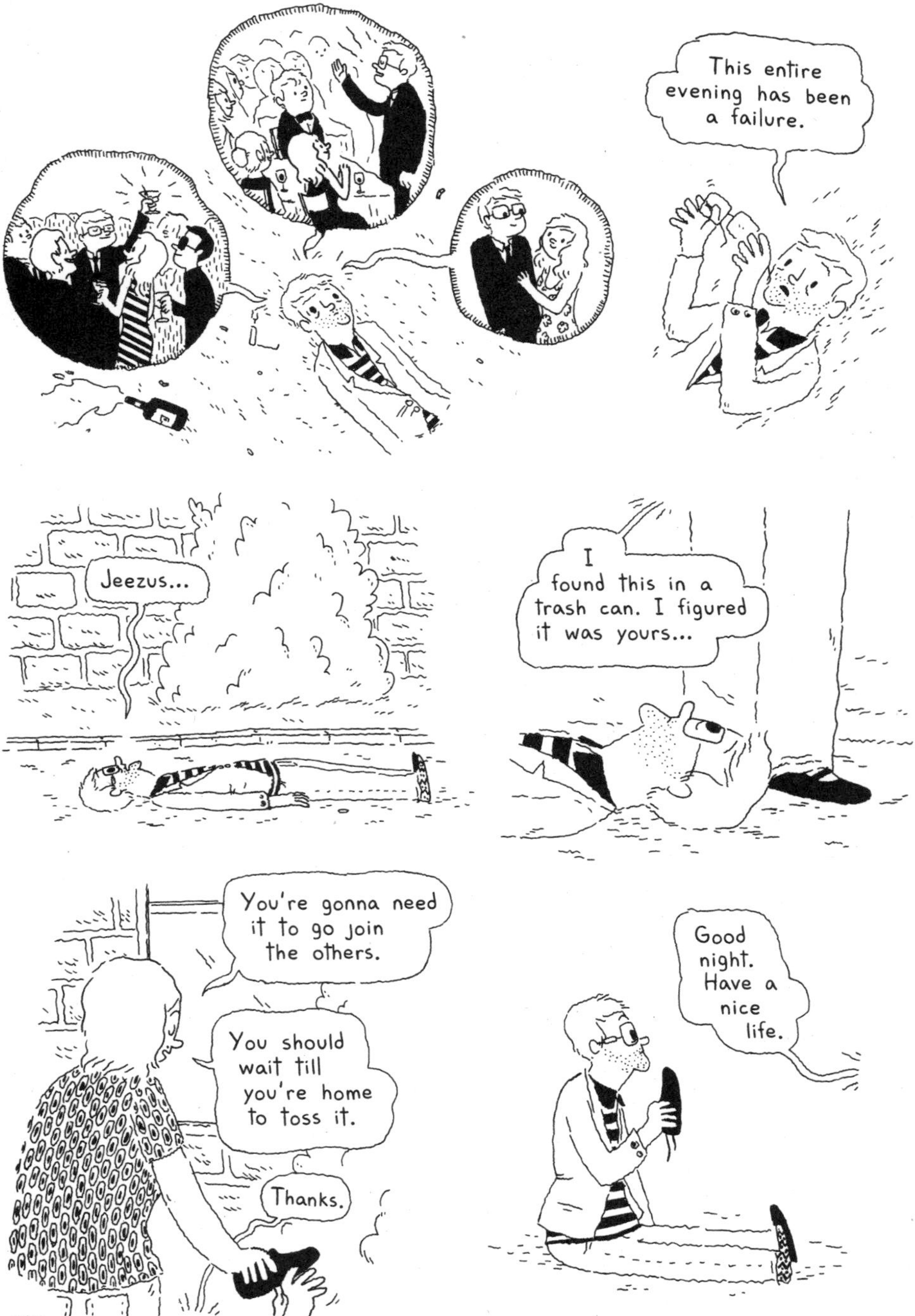
This entire evening has been a failure.
Jeezus...
I found this in a trash can. I figured it was yours...
You're gonna need it to go join the others.
You should wait till you're home to toss it.
Thanks.
Good night. Have a nice life.

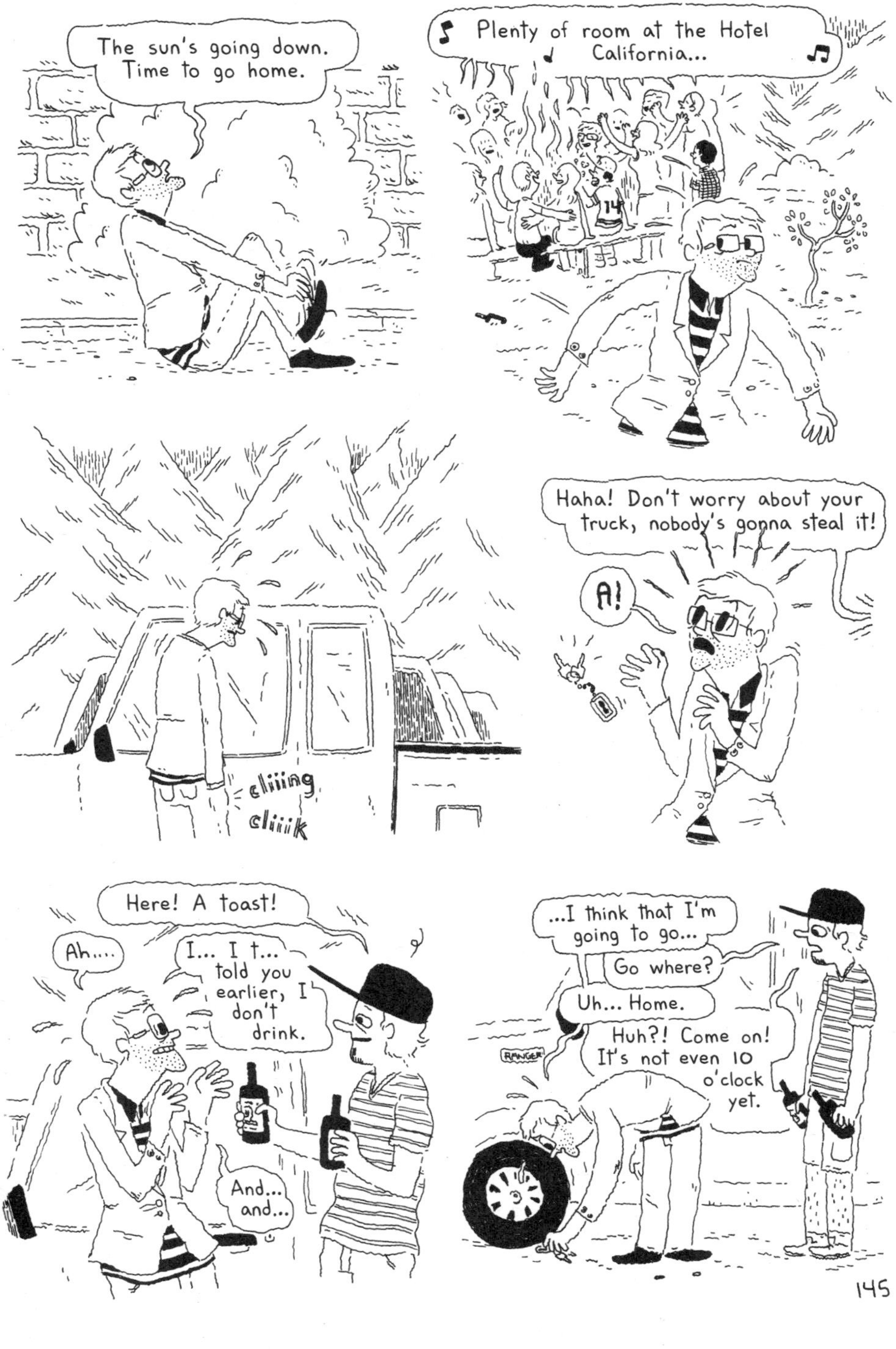
The sun's going down. Time to go home.
Plenty of room at the Hotel California...
14
Haha! Don't worry about your truck, nobody's gonna steal it!
A!
cliiing
cliiik
Here! A toast!
Ah....
I... I t... told you earlier, I don't drink.
And... and...
...I think that I'm going to go...
Go where?
Uh... Home.
Huh?! Come on! It's not even 10 o'clock yet.
RANGER

I haven't slept since Wednesday.
It's been ten years, buddy.
clik
So, are you a winner now?
Uh... What do you mean?
If you were a loser back then, what are you now?
I dunno, I don't care. I haven't thought of people that way in years.
How come?
Oh, nothing. It doesn't matter.
What do I say to the others when they ask why you snuck out?
I dunno... Say... Tell them I said good night and have a nice life.
Alright... OK... It was fun seeing you...

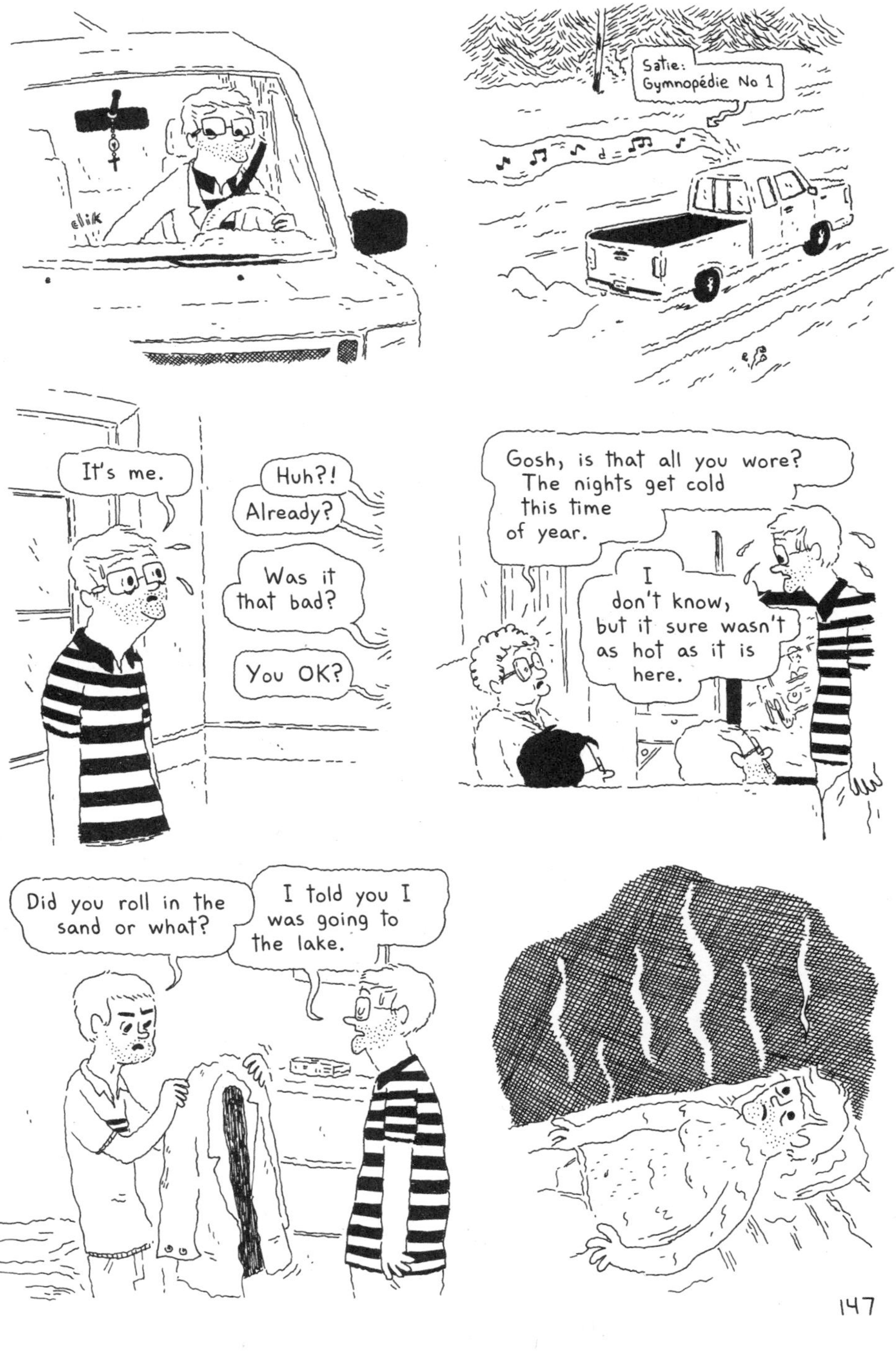
Satie:
Gymnopédie No 1
It's me.
Huh?!
Already?
Was it that bad?
You OK?
Gosh, is that all you wore? The nights get cold this time of year.
I don't know, but it sure wasn't as hot as it is here.
Did you roll in the sand or what?
I told you I was going to the lake.

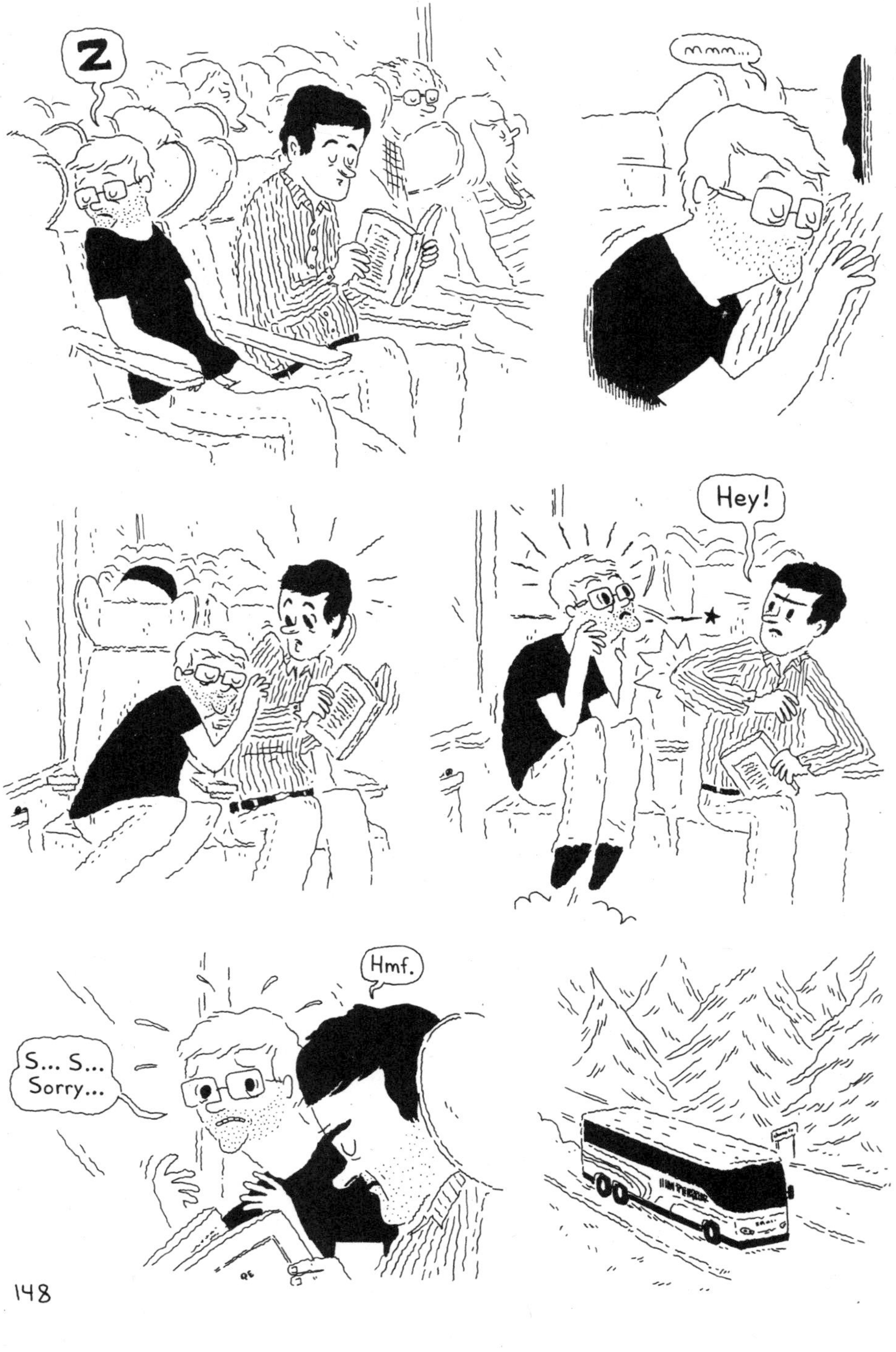
Z
mmm...
Hey!
S... S...
Sorry...
Hmf.

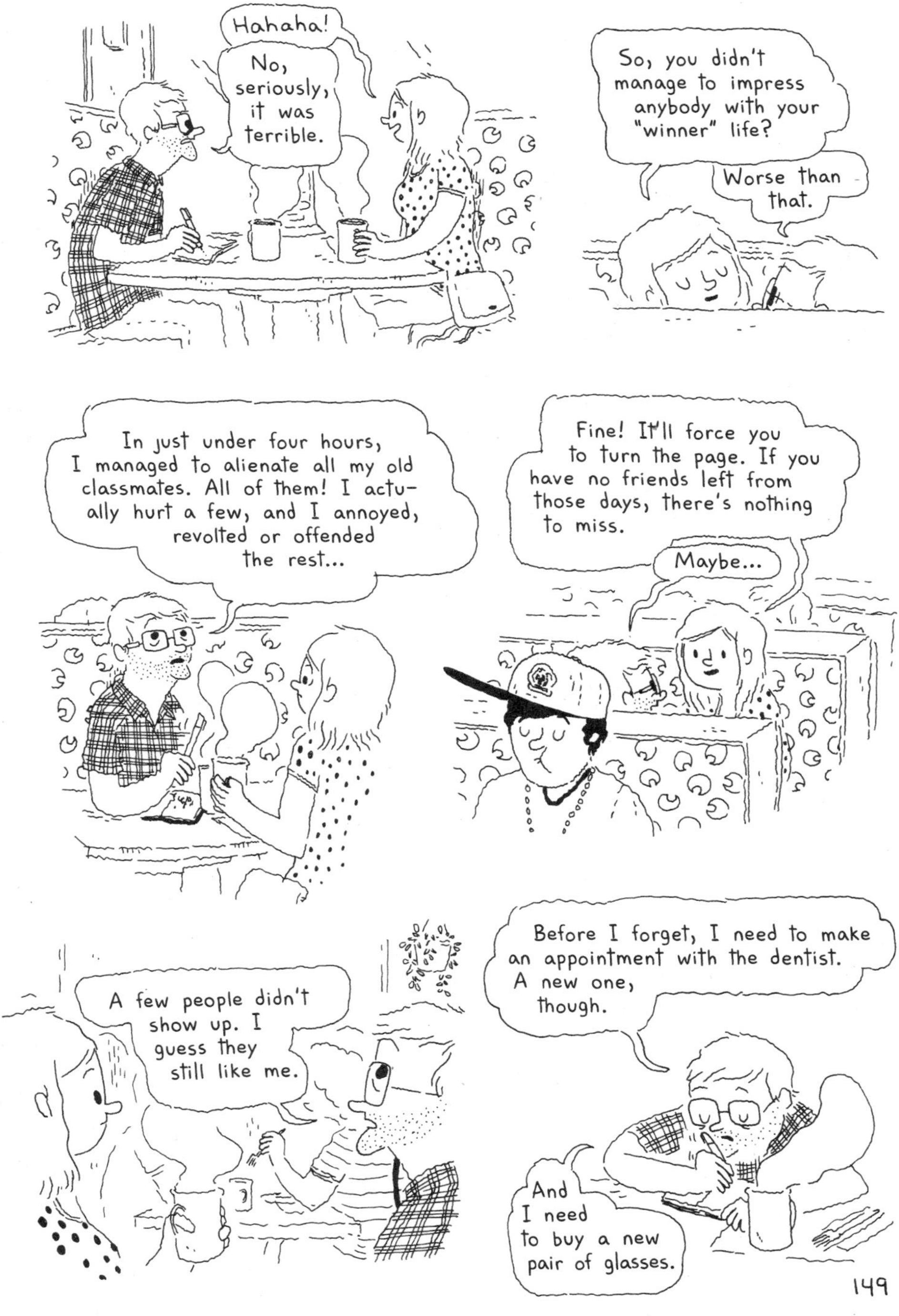

Hahaha!
No, seriously, it was terrible.
So, you didn't manage to impress anybody with your "winner" life?
Worse than that.
In just under four hours, I managed to alienate all my old classmates. All of them! I actually hurt a few, and I annoyed, revolted or offended the rest...
Fine! It'll force you to turn the page. If you have no friends left from those days, there's nothing to miss.
Maybe...
A few people didn't show up. I guess they still like me.
Before I forget, I need to make an appointment with the dentist. A new one, though.
And I need to buy a new pair of glasses.

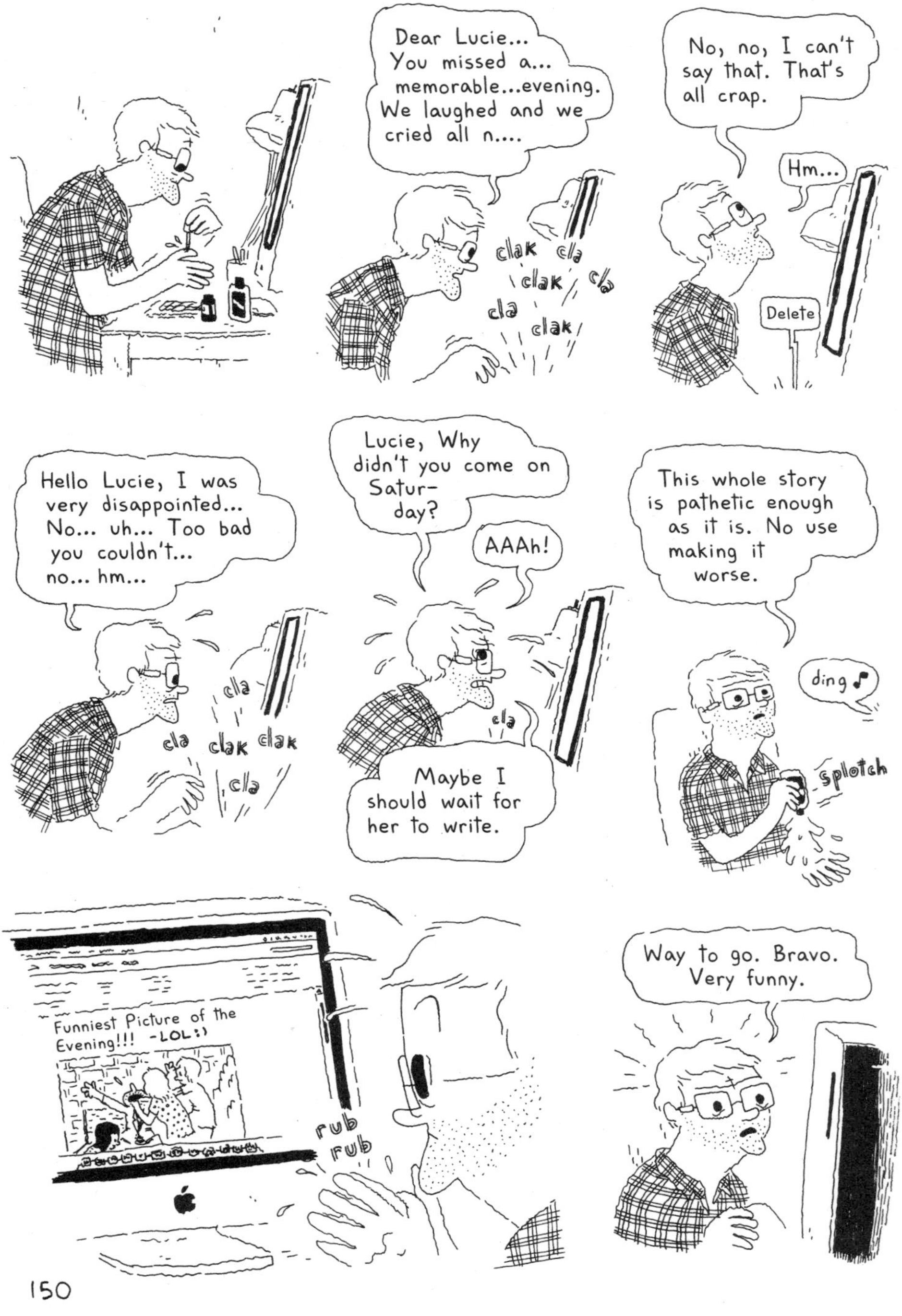
Dear Lucie... You missed a... memorable...evening. We laughed and we cried all n....
clak cla clak cla cla clak
No, no, I can't say that. That's all crap.
Hm...
Delete
Hello Lucie, I was very disappointed... No... uh... Too bad you couldn't... no... hm...
cla cla clak clak cla
Lucie, Why didn't you come on Satur-day?
AAAh!
cla
Maybe I should wait for her to write.
This whole story is pathetic enough as it is. No use making it worse.
ding
splotch
Funniest Picture of the Evening!!! -LOL:)
rub rub
Way to go. Bravo. Very funny.

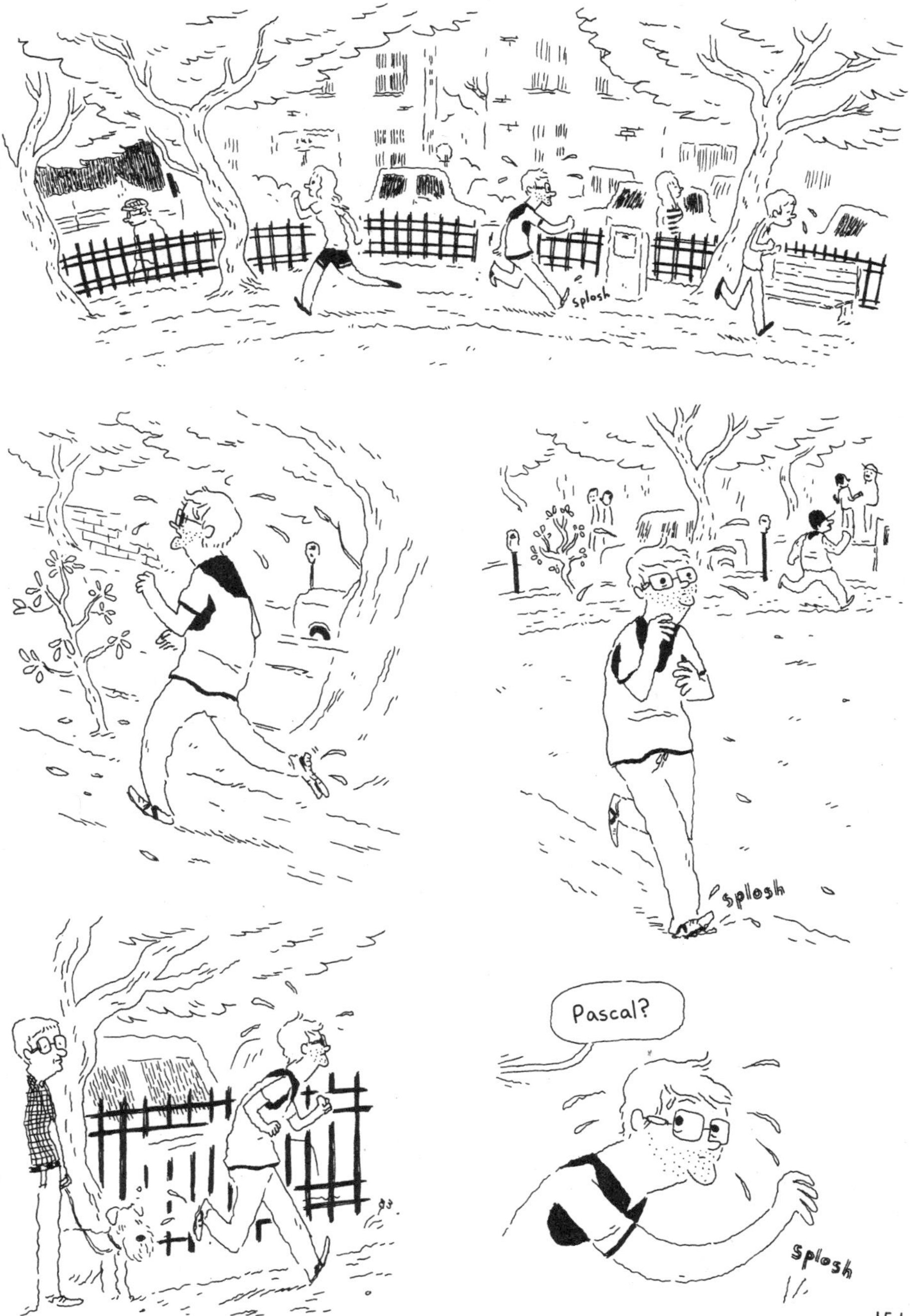
splosh
splosh
Pascal?
splosh

Pascal Girard! I've been looking for you for a month!
Aaaah... George... Hello...
You have?
I must have made a mistake when I took down your info. When I tried to call, an old lady answered, and there was a fish store at your address.
Ha ha...
Uh...
Y... Hm... You wear the shirt I gave you to run? It was new.
Ah... N... I cough Yes, it is... Yes...
That's not really what it's meant for.
It's not cheap, you know? And it's 100% cotton. Couldn't you have waited before sweating in it?
Who's this, George?
This is Pascal, a boy I went to school with. He's a metal worker like the guys who work for me.
Artist. I'm an artist. I draw.
My name's Carl.
Speaking of drawings, I found one of your sketches for sale on Ebay when I was looking for you.
O... Oh really?... Wh...What was it?

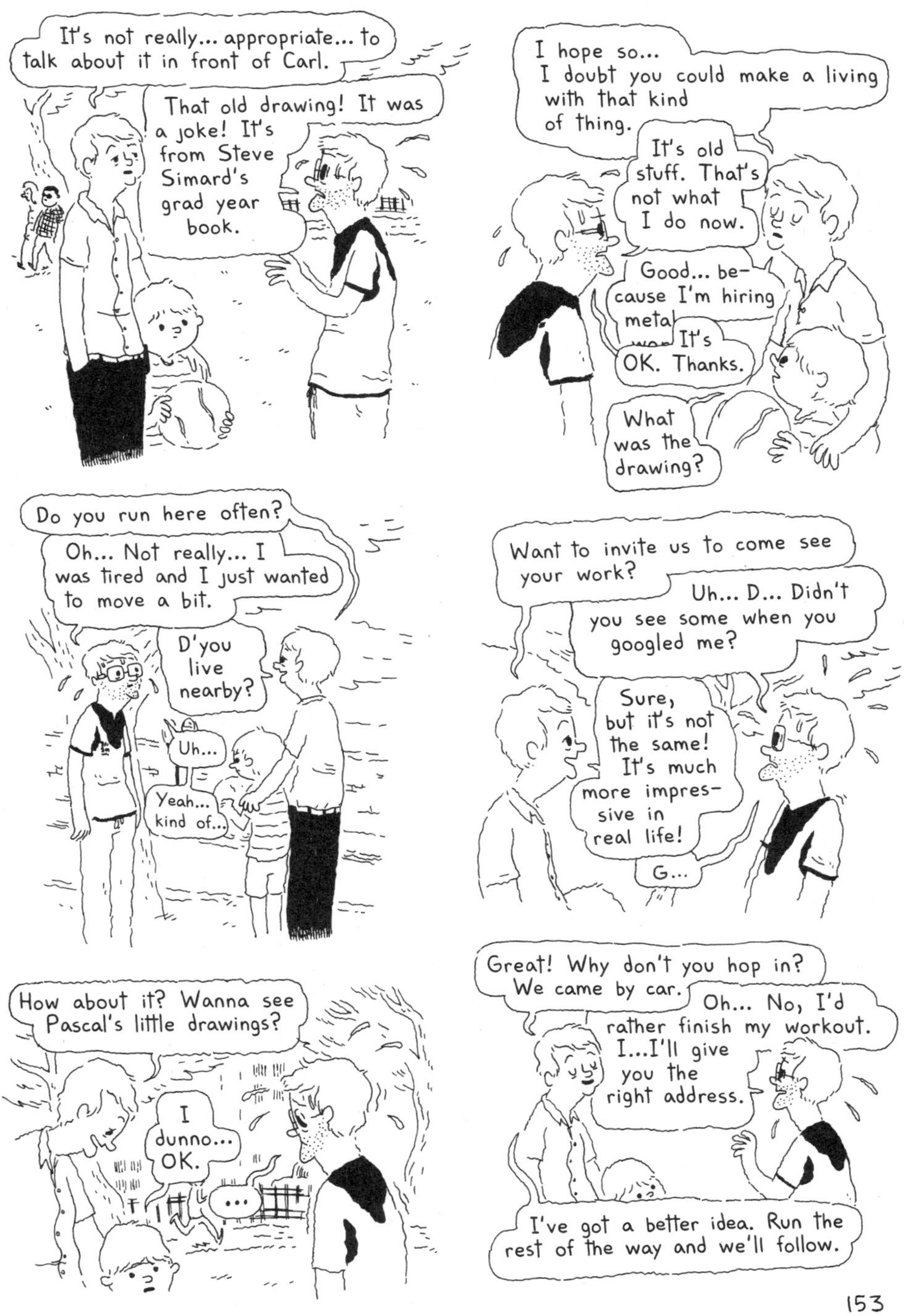
It's not really... appropriate... to talk about it in front of Carl.
That old drawing! It was a joke! It's from Steve Simard's grad year book.
I hope so... I doubt you could make a living with that kind of thing.
It's old stuff. That's not what I do now.
Good... be-cause I'm hiring metal
It's OK. Thanks.
What was the drawing?
Do you run here often?
Oh... Not really... I was tired and I just wanted to move a bit.
D'you live nearby?
Uh...
Yeah... kind of...
Want to invite us to come see your work?
Uh... D... Didn't you see some when you googled me?
Sure, but it's not the same! It's much more impres-sive in real life!
G...
How about it? Wanna see Pascal's little drawings?
I dunno... OK.
...
Great! Why don't you hop in? We came by car.
Oh... No, I'd rather finish my workout. I...I'll give you the right address.
I've got a better idea. Run the rest of the way and we'll follow.

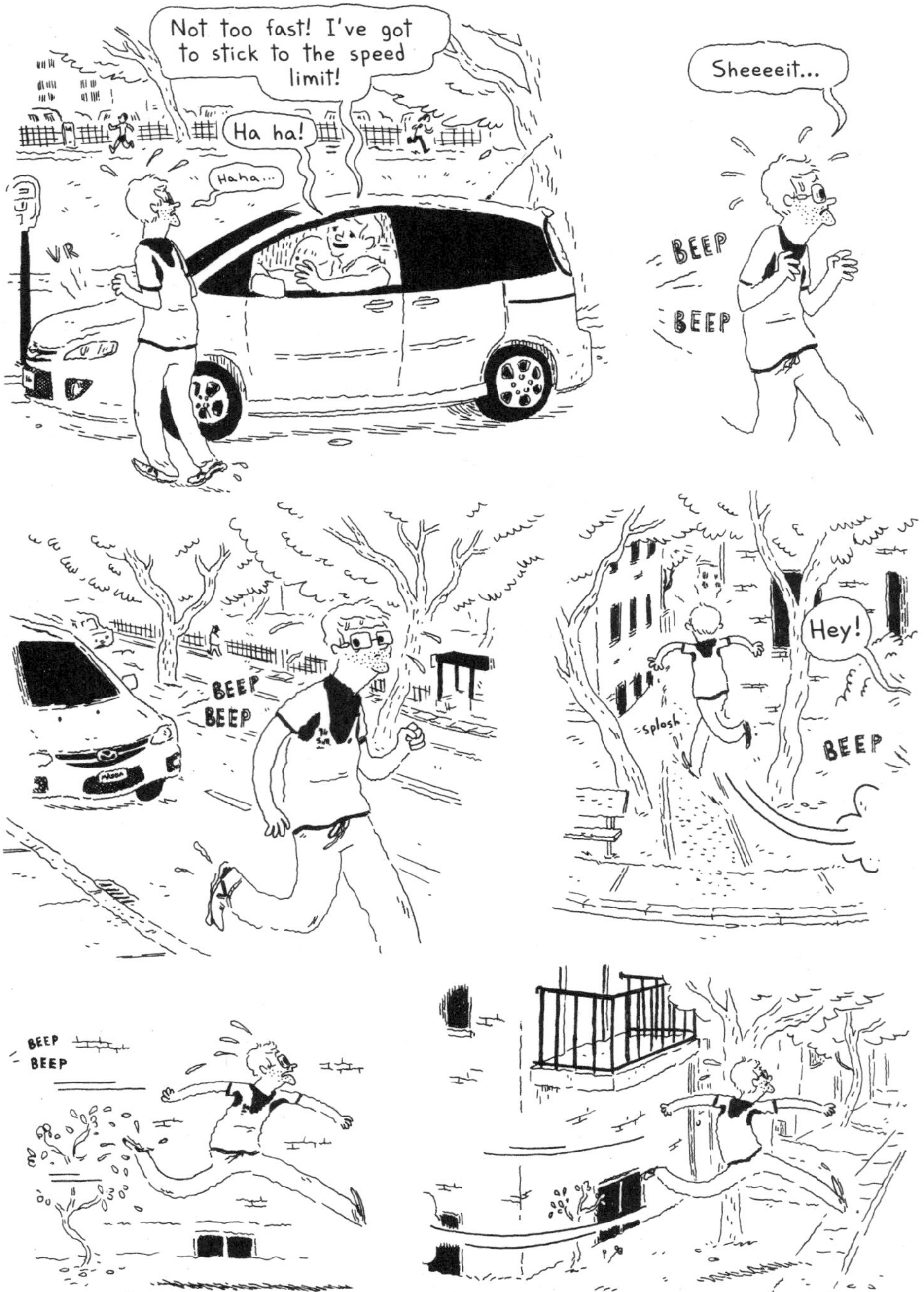
Not too fast! I've got to stick to the speed limit!
Ha ha!
Haha...
VR
Sheeeeit...
BEEP
BEEP
BEEP
BEEP
Hey!
splosh
BEEP
BEEP
BEEP

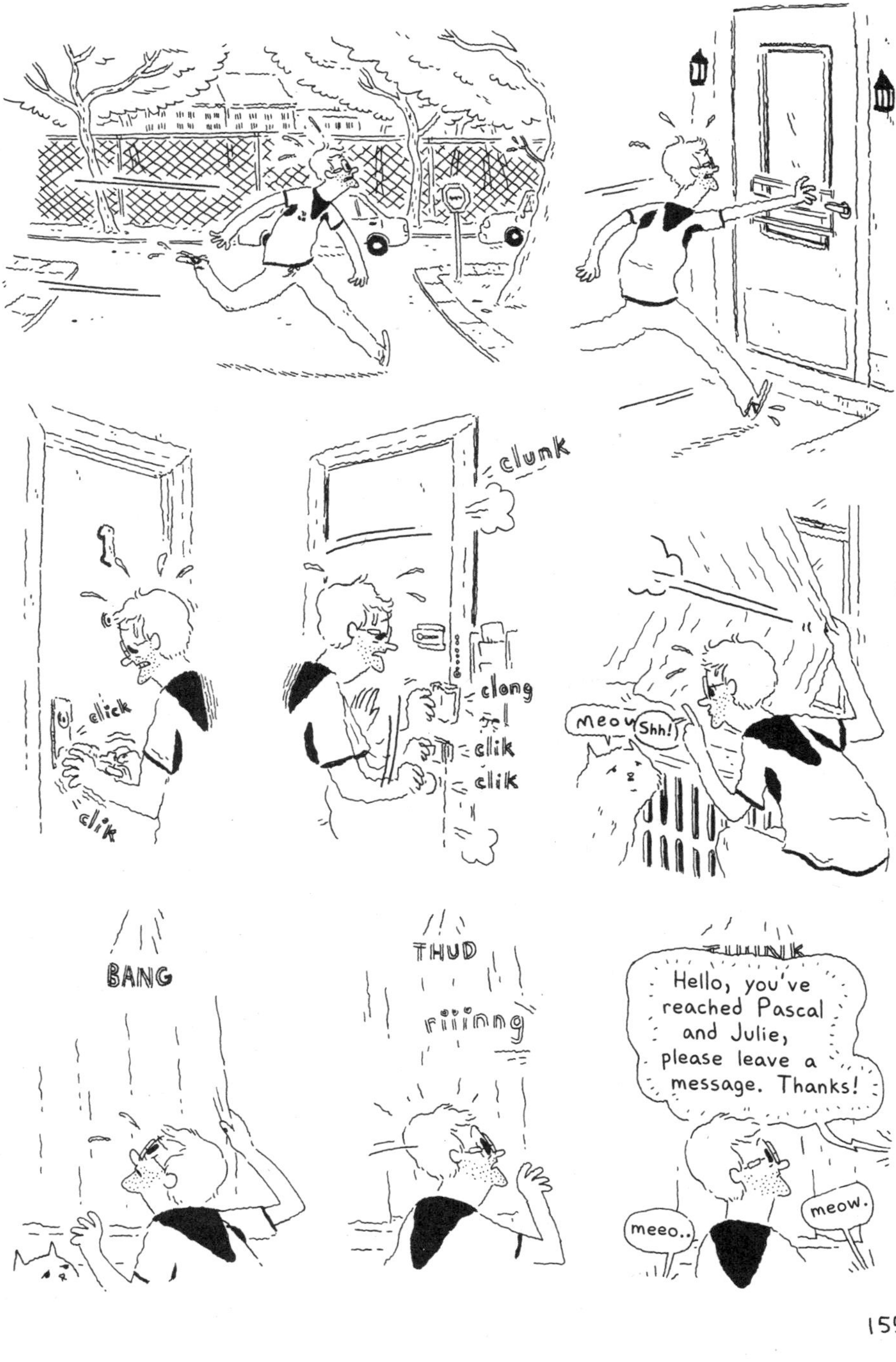

click
clik
clunk
clong
clik
clik
meow
Shh!
BANG
THUD
riiinng
Hello, you've reached Pascal and Julie, please leave a message. Thanks!
meeo..
meow.

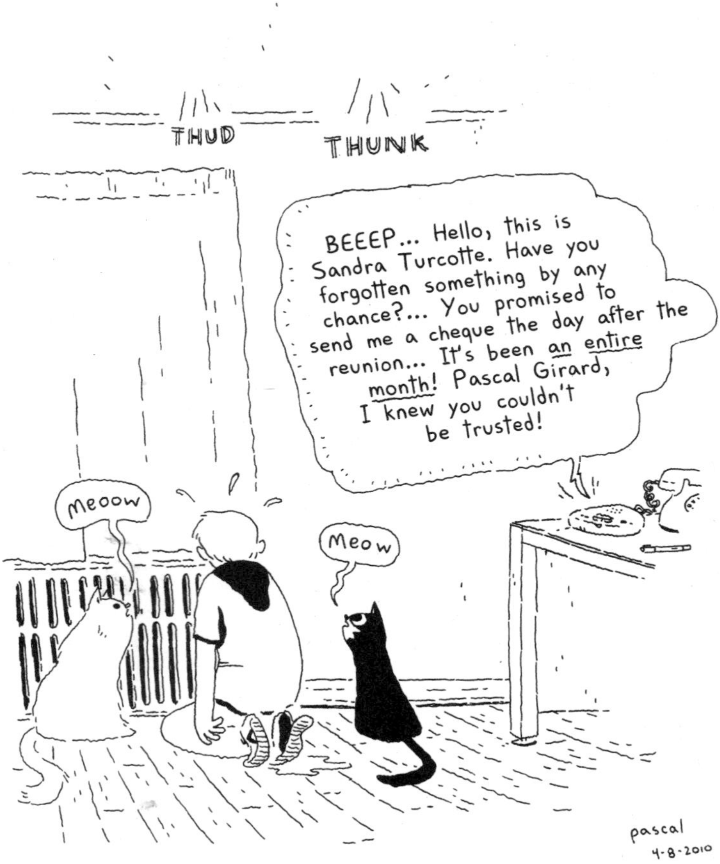
THUD
THUNK
BEEEP... Hello, this is Sandra Turcotte. Have you forgotten something by any chance?... You promised to send me a cheque the day after the reunion... It's been an entire month! Pascal Girard, I knew you couldn't be trusted!
Meoow
Meow
pascal
4-8-2010